GOD'S JUDGMENT IS COMING TO AMERICA UNLESS...

Our Nation's Only Hope

Rev. Jeff Niederstadt

www.repentance.us

ISBN-13:9780578727127

Cover design by: Unique Book Cover
Library of Congress
Printed in the United States of America

This book is dedicated to all those in America who have committed their lives to their Lord and Savior Jesus Christ and are fighting for the opportunity to freely serve Him in our country.

And it is further dedicated to all those in the military and government who are and have sworn to support and defend the Constitution of the United States against all enemies, even domestic ones.

All Gave Some and Some Gave All. It is to your honor and credit that this book is dedicated.

The Oath of Enlistment (for enlisted): "I, _____, do solemnly swear (or affirm) that I will support and defend the Constitution of the United States against all enemies, foreign and domestic; that I will bear true faith and allegiance to the same; and that I will obey the orders of the President of the United States and the orders of the officers appointed over me, according to regulations and the Uniform Code of Military Justice. So help me God."

After you read this book add your prayer of repentance at www.repentance.us

CONTENTS

GOD'S JUDGMENT IS COMING TO AMERICA.

Unless...

As I think about writing about judgment, it is a difficult subject to broach and not one that people will be drawn to by their human nature. We don't want to hear difficult words, we want to hear nice, fluffy words that make us feel better about ourselves. The problem is that if that is all that we hear, we will not have an accurate picture of or identification with our true nature. I remember my mom telling me once that when she heard the law preached to her that it offended her, because she was a "good" kid and thought that she didn't have any sin. When we omit the law, we become self-righteous instead of wearing the righteousness of Christ. In general, our society and the church have flipped from seeing God as a mean and just God where hell and brimstone were preached, into seeing God as a rich, loving, grandpa who should give us anything we want. Not that there wasn't some needed correction from preaching hell and brimstone every week, but it has flipped so drastically with prosperity and blessing being so primary that if any trouble comes our way, we begin to question the Almighty. The reality is, God doesn't owe us anything. In fact, we owe Him everything—our life, our breath, our possessions, our families, everything. In C.F.W. Walther's *The Proper Distinction Between Law and Gospel,* he states the necessity of both the law and the gospel: "The point of difference between the Law and the Gospel is not this, that the Gospel is a divine and the Law a human doctrine, resting on the reason of man...Nor is the difference, that only the Gospel is necessary, not the Law, as if the latter were a mere addition that could be dispensed with in a strait. No, both are equally necessary. Without the Law the Gospel is not understood; without the Gospel the Law benefits us nothing."[i] We need both the law *and* the gospel; without one or the other, we will chart off course. We have lived without the law for too long and there is a necessary course correction needed within our churches and within our nation, as evidenced by our changing laws, our behavior, and our current condition. In reality, preaching God's judgment is really the grace of God, because He is giving us time to repent and reminding us what's at stake. The message of repentance gives us hope that there is still time, but there will come a time when it will be too late if we don't respond.

God is merciful and God is just. These two forces must be reconciled in the time of eternity and within the age of man. Those who know the Bible know this to be true. The price of salvation had to be paid by the blood of God's Son, Jesus. The price of justice is still yet to be paid for all those who do not follow Christ in this life. God is slow to anger, abounding in love, and full of everlasting kindness. I wish this book was a message of mercy. I wish that I could declare the love of God and share the Father's heart for His people, for America, and for the world, but that is not this message. For God so loved the world that He gave His one and only Son. In fact, God *is* love, but God is also just. Both are true and both are undeniably reconcilable with the truth of God and His character. Just as the love of God led to the undeniable and inevitable sacrifice of Jesus for the possible salvation of the world, the justice of God will lead to the horse and rider, who will return with a sword protruding from His mouth and rendering vengeance upon His enemies.

The fact is, even Israel God's own chosen people, His beloved, experienced judgment when they turned away from God and refused to follow Him and His laws any longer. Will America fare any differently? Are we so arrogant to think that we have more to offer than Israel, or that because of our history as a Christian nation that we will be spared from the pain of judgment if we turn our backs on God? Lord, help us. I have no prophetic dream to report (although others have had them) about the coming judgment, but looking at the clear pattern of Scripture, there is a repeated pattern of those who turn their backs on God and His law afterward experience His judgment. Obviously, this is not a popular message, but it is necessary to proclaim the truth of our condition. If you go to the doctor and you have a serious condition, no matter how bad it is, you want the doctor to give it to you straight so that you know what you're dealing with. It would be unloving and unjust to hide or deny the condition of our nation and the coming consequences if there is no repentance. We don't wish judgment on anyone, and my fervent prayer is that America will hear the cry to repent and turn from her sins. I am so thankful for America, it is such a great place to live — prosperous and beautiful and free. But I don't worship America. I worship the God who founded America as an instrument for His glory. At this point, America is in danger of defaming the God who gloriously founded her, and I believe, based on the pattern laid out in Scripture and the history of Israel, that she is in grave danger.

I'm not saying that America is equivalent to Israel or essential to the church, for that matter. Israel is God's chosen people and His righteous branch, which He chose in the Old Testament to show His love, compassion, and justice. The church is God's bride, those who will overcome, and a picture of those to whom God can demonstrate His love, compassion, and justice. Not that God does not demonstrate His love, justice, and compassion for the world, but it is different, like a father who cares for his child versus a father who cares for another's child as a pastor or teacher. There are similarities, yet there are also distinct differences. I say all that to show that although America is not equivalent to Israel or even essential to the church, it is certainly a type of New Testament Israel in which God has divinely established and appointed a specific group of people to share His message, display His glory, and administer His justice. That is why the prophecies of the Old Testament are so applicable (and so damning) for the United States today. America is not Israel nor the future Israel, but yet just as Joseph and Joshua in the Old Testament were not *the* Christ; they were a type of Christ that foreshadowed Jesus and His mission. Similarly, we see that America in some ways has been treated and looked like Israel. If nothing else, we will certainly see that Americans believed this about themselves, as they saw God do miraculous things like take a ragtag bunch of farmers and defeat the greatest military force in the world at that time in the Revolutionary War. Or seeing it in the prevalent concept of manifest destiny and what that meant to early Americans. There was a belief that they had a special grace and calling by God as a nation.

When God picks you, establishes you, and makes you a light, there is a greater accountability to be the person or people that God has established you to be. God has certainly shed His grace on us, and we have corporately decided to spit in His face. It took Israel a while to fall away as well. They went through the pain and turmoil of being birthed as a nation and then experienced great success and prosperity as a kingdom and leaders in the world. But they became proud, and instead of continuing to depend on God, they leaned on their own understanding and broke His commandments and defiled His land. They were judged for it — severely. At first, only Israel faced judgment because Judah remained faithful, but eventually Judah succumbed as well and became subject to the same judgment after falling away. Prophets declared over and over again of the danger of the coming judgment and to turn back to God, but Israel wouldn't listen. Will America?

In his book *The Harbinger*, Jonathan Cahn states:

> Israel was unique among the nations in that it was conceived and dedicated at its foundation for the purposes of God. . . But there was one other-- a civilization also conceived and dedicated to the will of God from its conception. . . America. . . Long before the Founding Fathers[,]

> those who laid America's foundations saw it as a new Israel, an Israel of the New World. And as with ancient Israel, they saw it as in covenant with God...
>
> Not that [America] was ever without fault or sin, but it would aspire to fulfill its calling... To be a vessel of redemption, an instrument of God's purposes, a light to the world... No nation in the modern world has ever been given so much. None has been so blessed...
>
> [But] America began ruling God out of its life, turning, step by step, against His ways... In the middle of the twentieth century America began officially removing God from its national life. It abolished prayer and Scripture in the public schools... removing the Ten Commandments from public view, banning it from its public squares, and taking it down, by government decree, from its walls... God was progressively driven out of the nation's public life... The standards and values it had long upheld were now abandoned... [what we call "tolerance" is] a tolerance that mocked, marginalized and condemned those who remained faithful to the values now being discarded.[ii]

There are those who will refute the relationship between Israel and America and say that it's not helpful to have such an understanding because it will lead to pride and arrogance. Actually, we already have plenty of that, and if you make this argument, then you would also say it's not helpful to look at the similarities between Jesus and Joseph or Jesus and Joshua, because we might elevate those Old Testament personalities too much. The fact remains that there are similarities and we are going to look at them in order to try and learn from them and not distort them. Paul did the same thing when writing to the church in 1 Corinthians 10: "These things happened as a warning to us, so that we would not crave evil things as they did." You might be inclined to think, "Well, then this book is for the whole church and for every nation that is turning away from God." In some respects yes, but in others no. If you look at Old Testament patterns and history, there was judgment and discipline specifically sent by God to correct the nations that neighbored and opposed Israel, but the primary story is about what happened to Israel. Why is that? One of the reasons is because that's how you communicate information or tell a story; you share an example of the specific to explain the whole. Another reason is that throughout Scripture, God explains over and over that there is a greater accountability for those with whom He has taken the time and effort to establish a relationship. Whether it's Israel, the priests, the prophets, or God's people, there is a higher standard overall because, in effect, they should know better and because God has given them the necessary information and resources to be able to communicate in such a way that they are held to a standard of His requirements. My argument for you to see is that just as God communicated His laws to Israel and provided them with special favor and deliverance, He has similarly blessed America. As "America The Beautiful" states: "God shed his grace on thee." Fortunately, we have experienced that grace and blessing in the prosperity and success of America. Unfortunately, we have abused and neglected that blessing and have turned it into a reason for judgment and discipline because of our unfaithfulness.

People will also argue and make cases for the new covenant and for God's forgiveness and try and dismiss this message, but that will not change it or even delay it, only repentance can do that. Hebrews 12 makes it clear that there is a new covenant and forgiveness, but that does not negate God's moral law or His justice. Verse 24 says, "You have come to Jesus, the one who mediates the new covenant between God and people, and to the sprinkled blood, which speaks of forgiveness instead of crying out for vengeance like the blood of Abel."[iii] If that were the end of the chapter, or if the text took a different direction, the new covenant argument might be more valid. But the very next verse says, "Be careful that you do not refuse to listen to the one who is speaking. For if the people of Israel did not escape when they refused to listen to Moses, the earthly messenger, we will certainly not escape if we reject the one who speaks to us from heaven!"[iv] It's almost as if this verse intends to answer the question we are asking directly. But isn't it true that we have a greater grace and forgiveness under the new covenant so that we are not as responsible as the people of Israel? The writer to the Hebrews makes the point that not only are we accountable like the people of Israel, we are actually guilty to a greater degree because they didn't listen to an earthly messenger, but we are guilty of not listening to God Himself!

INTRODUCTION

There are several different groups of people who might be interested in reading a book like this. There are those that are part of the true remnant of the body of Christ and are already living in repentance and dependence on God for daily life, even now. These are the people that least need to read this book, but are those most likely to finish it. Then there are those who may go to church or believe in God, but He hasn't always been the most important thing in their lives. Then there are those who would call themselves "Christian" by name, but neither attend church nor live as such. Then there are those intellectually honest people who, by self-admittance, are not Christians and don't think of themselves as such. There are also those who are antagonistic to the Gospel and then there are still others. My prayer is that as you read this book, you will get what you need to out of it. For some, that may mean repentance and salvation, while for others it may simply mean an adjustment in a certain area of thinking. For still others, I pray that this will encourage your deeply held beliefs in Christ to be cemented and anchored for eternity as you recognize the depth of the riches and wisdom of God. There are some of you that need an encouraging hug and there are others that need a slap in the face to wake you out of your stupor. Only God knows your heart and I pray that He gives you exactly what you need.

While writing this, there were just more school shootings in Sante Fe, Texas, and the Atlanta area, and we haven't even recovered from the last one in Parkland Florida. In response to this swell of school shootings, some legislators have begun to lobby for gun control and better counseling for troubled students. I am so tired of hearing about things like gun control and counseling, even though they may be helpful in some cases. You'll never get anywhere trying to control or monitor sin, you need to deal with it. Why don't we see legislators fighting to get prayer back in school and start teaching about creation and the Ten Commandments again? That's the problem. You took God out of school and now you want to tell the devil what he can and can't do. Well, that's not how it works. Until you kick the devil out and let God back in, there will be more and more issues and problems. No gun control, counseling, or legislation will remedy it. It doesn't need a band aid, it needs an organ transplant. A band aid will not even delay death, but an organ transplant will provide new life. We need to take responsibility as the church, the voters, the parents, the judges, and the legislators that allowed this to happen on our watch. We must repent for allowing this to happen in our schools, for allowing evolution in our textbooks and schools, for prayer being removed from our cafeterias, and for allowing the Ten Commandments to be eradicated from school grounds. Those of us who have silently watched as God has been methodically removed from school are guilty, and we should all be on trial for the death of these students. These school shootings are the inevitable consequence of past actions and we think gun control is the answer. What foolishness. The song "God Against The Law" by The Carter-Robertson Band pretty much sums up this problem. The song was written back in 2003 when Judge Roy Moore of the Alabama Supreme Court was forced to remove the Ten Commandments from the judicial building.

They took his 10 commandments
and put them out of view

Said they might offend someone that would never do

Then they told him just to step aside
if they needed him they'd call

Then they went and made God against the law

They took him from our public
places took him out of school

Now drugs and violence have replaced the golden rule

And the nation he made strong
now stands against the One

Because of the few we made God against the law

They drew a line and told him He'd have to stay in church

He's not welcome on our streets or at our place of work

I wondered who we'll turn to when the next disaster falls

God can't come for he's against the law

When it becomes a criminal act to proclaim
to a lost and dying world

That Jesus is the only way of salvation
then let me be guilty

And when the lines are finally drawn

So that every man has to make a
choice on where he stands

Let me say emphatically and without reservation

As for me and my house we will serve the Lord[v]

After the shooting at a San Bernardino elementary school in 2017, a newspaper article came out with the headline "God Isn't Fixing This."[vi] This is the epitome of foolishness. To not only take God out of school and allow him to be methodically stripped from public education, but then have the gall to blame Him for not being there when something bad happens. If you want God to stop school shootings, then I would suggest you allow Him back into the school first. This is an example of judgment through the natural consequences of sin that are allowed to transpire because of the hardness of man's heart. God didn't cause those shootings to happen, but He allowed the sinful decisions that removed Him from those schools to bear the fruit from those rebellious actions.

In the book *The Trellis and the Vine*, published by Matthias

Media, the authors Marshall and Payne talk about the relationship between America and Israel and show the relevancy of Old Testament Scripture for America today:

> Modern churches (at least in the West) may not be under the direct attack and disaster that Israel was experiencing, but we certainly still wonder what God is doing in the world. Is he still listening? Is he going to act? I thought he was the Lord and Master of all –if so, what's the plan?!
>
> Many of the psalms plumb these depths. But Psalm 80 has the distinction of exploring these ideas via the image of Israel as God's vine:
>
> "Restore us, O God of hosts; let your face shine, that we may be saved! You brought a vine out of Egypt; you drove out the nations and planted it. You cleared the ground for it; it took deep root and filled the land. The mountains we covered with its shade, the mighty cedars with its branches. It sent out its branches to the sea and its shoots to the River. Why then have you broken down its walls, so that all who pass along the way pluck its fruit? The boar from the forest ravages it, and all that move in the field feed on it." (Ps 80:7-13)
>
> It is at this low point in the history of God's plans that the psalmist cries out for mercy and rescue. It is also at this point that the prophets cry out with God's answer—that there will be judgement in the first place for Israel's sin, but that there is also the promise of mercy, rescue and restoration, in God's own time and way.
>
> The prophets express the twin themes of judgement and mercy in many ways, but since we have started with the vine image, let us continue with it. Hosea condemned Israel as a luxuriant but ultimately false and doomed vine, but also prophesied that God would make the plant blossom once again:
>
> "Israel is a luxuriant vine that yields its fruit. The more his

> fruit increased, the more altars he built; as his country improved, he improved his pillars. Their heart is false; now they must bear their guilt. The Lord will break down their altars and destroy their pillars." (Hos 10:1-2)
>
> It seemed to all outward appearances that nothing was going on except sin, failure, and judgement. And yet the prophets promised that, like a phoenix from the ashes, Israel would rise again by the life-giving power of their God. The vine would blossom once more and grow to be a beautiful plant known throughout the world. But the path to these glories would be through suffering and judgement. There was no avoiding the consequences of sin. Somehow, at some future time, God would bring his people through judgement and out the other side into the sunshine of his salvation."[vii]

This passage shows us the pain of judgment and the hope of restoration. It is this judgment that we are attempting to avoid by calling America to repentance and by bringing change to our nation.

This change is desperately needed, as we see in the *Vox* article by Tara Burton written on June 25, 2018 entitled "Trump-Allied Pastor Tells Worshippers 'America is a Christian Nation.'"[viii] The article is about Pastor Robert Jeffress of the First Baptist Church in Dallas, who held a "Freedom Sunday" service in which he declared that America is a Christian nation and put billboards up in town declaring the same. That's all well and good. The problem is that there was such an outcry about the billboards that the church was forced to take them down. The point is not whether Donald Trump was God's choice or not, because there are plenty of people who could argue both ways about that. The problem is that people really believe and argue that America was not founded as a Christian nation. Whether or not America is *currently* a Christian nation is very debatable at this juncture in our history. The report that those billboards were forced to be taken down is certainly not a good sign, but it is indisputable that America was *founded* as a Christian nation. Whoever says otherwise just doesn't know the facts. There are plenty of atheists, agnostics, and antagonists who would like you to believe otherwise, but that's like trying to argue that someone is innocent when their prints are on the weapon, their likeness is captured on a recording of the assault, and multiple credible eyewitnesses put them at the scene of the crime. Unfortunately, that's how far we've fallen in this country — from indisputable evidence to protests and uprisings over the very statement that America is a Christian nation.

In Isaiah 30:8-17 it says:

Now go and write down these words.
  Write them in a book.
They will stand until the end of time
  as a witness
[9] that these people are stubborn rebels
  who refuse to pay attention to the Lord's instructions.
[10] They tell the seers,
  "Stop seeing visions!"
They tell the prophets,
  "Don't tell us what is right.
Tell us nice things.
  Tell us lies.
[11] Forget all this gloom.
  Get off your narrow path.
Stop telling us about your
  'Holy One of Israel.'"

[12] This is the reply of the Holy One of Israel:

"Because you despise what I tell you
  and trust instead in oppression and lies,
[13] calamity will come upon you suddenly—
  like a bulging wall that bursts and falls.
In an instant it will collapse

and come crashing down.
[14] You will be smashed like a piece of pottery—
shattered so completely that
there won't be a piece big enough
to carry coals from a fireplace
or a little water from the well."

[15] This is what the Sovereign Lord,
the Holy One of Israel, says:
"Only in returning to me
and resting in me will you be saved.
In quietness and confidence is your strength.
But you would have none of it.
[16] You said, 'No, we will get our help from Egypt.
They will give us swift horses for riding into battle.'
But the only swiftness you are going to see
is the swiftness of your enemies chasing you!
[17] One of them will chase a thousand of you.
Five of them will make all of you flee.
You will be left like a lonely flagpole on a hill
or a tattered banner on a distant mountaintop."[ix]

God's judgment will be swift and sudden. Notice the recurring theme in this section of Scripture for the opportunity to be saved through repentance. America was founded as a Christian nation, yet it has fallen so far that it no longer bears the marks of a Christian nation. There may technically be more people who call themselves Christians living in our country, but the voice of our nation, the example, the echo, and the fruit of our nation no longer bears the mark of Christ. We cannot expect God to sit idly by while His name is defamed and the nation which He established in His name and according to His precepts is destroyed spiritually. He did not sit idly by when Israel fell off the wagon and refused to listen to Him and His word. Sadly, America will be no different.

America is at odds with its Christian heritage. There will be judgment that follows, and part of that judgment will be the natural consequence of sin. The Bible says that in the last days, the love of many will grow cold. We see this now in America in all of our divisiveness. It's Democrats against Republicans, Christians against non-Christians, gay against straight, and minorities against Anglos. And it's not just opposition. In many cases, these differences have borne hatred and even violence and shootings. Blessed are the peacemakers, but there don't seem to be too many left. America has become a land for the "survival of the fittest," and whoever cries the loudest, fights the hardest, and digs their heels in the longest has the best chance of coming out on top. That doesn't sound very biblical. One of the realizations that Christians may have to come to is that to win the war, they may have to lose the battle. I am all for godly legislation, defending freedom, running for political office, and voting for people of character. At some point though, as this nation becomes less and less Christian, we, as people of faith, may have to let the government be the government and return to being the church — apart and separate from the ruling party. That is part of the difficulty, because America was founded as a Christian nation and has always been a Christian nation up to this point. The church is going to have to know when to let go of this nation and return it to God, who is the only one who can restore the foundation. The rallying cry of the repentant should be "the stone that the builders rejected has become the cornerstone" to hopefully see God once again rule and reign in America. Until that day, Christians may have to give up control and turn to God alone. There will be those, like in Jeremiah's day, who will argue that no judgment or harm will come to us in this country and that we must continue to fight and hold on to the very end. Those may be the ones who end up like Zedekiah, who are taken captive and have their sons slaughtered in front of them and their eyes gouged out. Judgment is coming, and unless there is widespread repentance, America will not stand because it is not united. The leaders of America will realize this as they did during the Babylonian captivity. "The captain of the guard called for Jeremiah and said, 'The Lord your God has brought this disaster on this land, just as he said he would. For these people have sinned against the Lord and disobeyed him. This is why it happened" (Jeremiah 40:2-3).[x] Nothing can change it beyond widespread repentance and turning from sin. God is the most loving, patient, and forgiving Father, but He is not mocked. No matter how much it pains Him for judgment to be brought against this nation, it *will* happen as the consequence of sin and disobedience. Do not judge the living God. Which of you, having a child that lived in your house who broke your rules, destroyed your home, despised your presence, hurt your other children, and mocked you to your face, would not inflict discipline? Even the most patient, loving parent has limits. Despite giving chance after chance, at some point the line must be drawn, the resources cut off, and access to the house denied.

In his article in *Time Magazine*, "My Generation was Supposed to Level America's Playing Field. Instead, We Rigged it for Ourselves," Steven Brill talks about the degradation of America over the past five decades and shows that the gap between the rich and the poor and the haves and the have-nots has continued to widen to a historic proportion, resulting in widespread dysfunction and inequality. These are some of his stinging comments about the state of our country and his argument that his generation broke America:

> Lately, most Americans, regardless of their political leanings, have been asking themselves some version of the same question: How did we get here? How did the world's greatest democracy and economy become a land of crumbling roads, galloping income inequality, bitter polarization and dysfunctional government?
>
> Key measures of the nation's public engagement, satisfaction and confidence—voter turnout, knowledge of public-policy issues, faith that the next generation will fare better than that current one, and respect for basic institutions, especially the government—are far below what they were

> years ago, and in many cases have reached near historic lows.
>
> For too many, the present is hard enough. Income inequality has soared: inflation-adjusted middle-class wages have been nearly frozen for the last four decades, while earnings of the top 1% have nearly tripled. The recovery from the crash of 2008—which saw banks and bankers bailed out while millions lost their homes, savings, and jobs—was reserved almost exclusively for the wealthiest. Their incomes in the three years following the crash went up by nearly a third, while the bottom 99% saw an uptick of less than half of 1%. Only a democracy and an economy that has discarded its basic mission of holding the community together, or failed at it, would produce those results.
>
> Although the US remains the world's richest country, it has the third-highest poverty rate among the 35 nations in the Organization for Economic Co-operation and Development (OECD), behind only Turkey and Israel. Nearly 1 in 5 American children lives in a household that the government classifies as 'food insecure,' meaning they are without 'access to enough food for active, healthy living.'[xi]

While Brill's comments are largely about the secular consequences of our actions, I would argue that it is because of our aversion to God and the things of God that we have landed in this position. So, what are we to do? What hope is there? What is the answer? At this point, there is no changing course, switching directions, or moving in a positive direction. There is only turning around or running aground. We must repent for allowing the stewardship of our freedom and country to be taken for granted and forgotten. We must repent that this Christian nation has become agnostic, indifferent, and even hostile under our watch. And we must repent that we have consumed the greatest benefits of ease and pleasure while the precepts of our faith have slowly eroded away from the foundation that they were founded upon. Then and only then can we have faith that God will have mercy on us as a nation and return us to our former glory. Brill also shares the following quote in his article:

> Daniel Markovits, who specializes in the intersection of law and behavioral economics, told the class of 2015 (Yale Law School) that their success getting accepted into, and getting a degree from, the country's most selective law school actually marked their entry into a newly entrenched aristocracy that had been snuffing out the American Dream for almost everyone else. Elites, he explained, can spend what they need to in order to send their children to the best schools, provide tutors for standardized testing and otherwise ensure that their kids can outcompete their peers to secure the same spots at the top that their parents achieved. 'American meritocracy has thus become precisely what it was invented to combat,' Markovits concluded, 'a mechanism for the dynastic transmission of wealth and privilege across generations. Meritocracy now constitutes a modern-day aristocracy.'[xii]

These are sobering conclusions made by secular authors who have seen the writing on the wall, so to speak: "God has numbered the days of your reign and brought it to an end, you have been measured and found lacking and your kingdom will be split." Secular and religious authors alike understand the disparity and tragedy of our times. Andy Stanley, who conducted the message series *God & Country*,[xiii] talks about our national conscience and makes a powerful argument that just as individuals have consciences, America has a collective conscience which has become increasingly dangerous. We have gone from a country with a national motto of "In God We Trust" to a country in which we cannot talk about God in school, society, or the media without backlash and consequence. Our national conscience, which used to fight against injustices like taxation without representation, civil rights in which all men are created equal, and fair labor laws for children, now taxes the poor, oppresses the alien, and kills children through legalized abortion. The nation which used to fight for God and country has now become "God or country," and we have not been defending God, who created and founded our country. Now, therefore, we are faced with the consequences of being a country without God, and such a country will not stand when the entire reason for its rise to prominence in the first place was because of God.

OVERVIEW

Micah 3:1-4

1-3 Then I said:

"Listen, leaders of Jacob, leaders of Israel:
  Don't you know anything of justice?
Haters of good, lovers of evil:
  Isn't justice in your job description?
But you skin my people alive.
  You rip the meat off their bones.
You break up the bones, chop the meat,
  and throw it in a pot for cannibal stew."

4 The time's coming, though, when these same leaders
  will cry out for help to God, but he won't listen.
He'll turn his face the other way
  because of their history of evil.[xiv]

The Bible says that judgment begins in the house of the Lord. It is not just the world that will receive the Lord's judgment, but the church as well. As part of the church, we need to understand that we also are held to a higher level of accountability, as this has happened in America on our watch. God knows each of our hearts and knows exactly what we need, but the church must recognize its ineffectiveness in society and in America. God is not mocked and the problems in our country grow by the minute. The accusations against the church are plenty and varied. The first is that the church is content with mediocrity and being lukewarm in its relationship with God. This is often disguised as wanting to be relational, welcoming, and loving, but it quickly morphs into compromise and lies. The people of the church are content with not being fully devoted followers of Christ. The people of the church are content with not taking up the cross. The people of the church are content playing country club instead of mission outpost. The church is content with accepting homosexuality, divorce, and adultery instead of calling people higher to the life that Christ calls us to. When Christ called His disciples, He beckoned them to forsake all — not just part of their life or part of their time. There was a distinct calling and recognition that followers were called to be set apart and different.

Churches used to be at the center of efforts of social justice and aid for the less fortunate. Churches used to build and found hospitals, schools, and aid centers, and now they primarily build buildings. The statistics are staggering if you look at the amount of money spent on buildings versus the amount of money spent on missions in recent years. The church has failed to market, proclaim, and share the good news of Jesus Christ as well as Coca-Cola and McDonalds have marketed themselves, especially in third world countries. The people in many third-world countries are familiar with and even have ready access to Coca-Cola, but have no one to share the love of Jesus Christ with them.

The church has become victim to participating in information overload. It has studied history, original languages, eschatological implications, hermeneutical principles and even turned God's word into song and created technological nuances. There is great value to these endeavors up to a point, but God's command was much simpler: "Teach them to obey all that I have commanded you." Imagine you asked your child to clean their room. After several days, you came back and saw that the room wasn't clean, so you asked them about it. Your child says that they decided to study cleaning your room instead and that they were writing a paper about their findings on the origins of cleaning and its usefulness. Next, they planned to examine the sociological effects of cleaning one's room. Finally, they planned to examine the most productive and effective way to clean one's room. At some point you would say, "I just want you to clean your room!" The church doesn't need more crowds of people capable of questioning God's methods, it needs more disciples committed to His teaching.

In the epitome of irony, some in the church have even dared to blame God and question His motives considering issues like starvation, school shootings and other terrible events. How prideful is it to blame God for letting you down? God hasn't let you down, the system that you put your trust in has. Korah blamed God when they were having troubles and tried to depose Moses and the earth swallowed him up and his whole family. Job questioned God about his troubles, and he was rebuked for three chapters. God is not to blame, He is the only one who can save us and who can set things right.

The church has not preached the whole counsel of God. The church used to preach fire and brimstone, but the pendulum has swung so far that now there is only grace — no hell, no sin, and no righteousness. The Bible has something to say about churches that preach what their itching ears want to hear:

Micah 3:5-8

[5] You lying prophets promise
security for anyone
who gives you food,
but disaster for anyone
who refuses to feed you.
Here is what the Lord says
to you prophets:
[6] "You will live in the dark,
far from the sight of the sun,
with no message from me.
[7] You prophets and fortunetellers
will all be disgraced,
with no message from me."

[8] But the Lord has filled me
with power and his Spirit.

I have been given the courage
  to speak about justice
and to tell you people of Israel
  that you have sinned.[xv]

The time has come to pay the piper. The Lord has been compassionate and gracious, slow to anger, abounding in love. He has beckoned to the church, to her leaders, to her teachers, to her pastors, to her prophets, and to her evangelists, "Come back to Me. Return to your first love. Repent and believe." But the church has thumbed its collective nose in God's face. The church has stolen its people's money only for pleasure and wealth and for establishing a bigger earthly kingdom. The church has not repented or turned away from apostasy. Instead, it has followed the ways of the world to become bigger and better by stepping on those in its way. It has discarded the widows and orphans and neglected the aliens to make room for the successful businessmen and women who give more money. The church is called to be a house of prayer, but instead it has become a den of thieves where people come to prey on the innocent and take advantage of the downtrodden. The Lord will not sit idly by any longer. When the Lord moves the business of church will be over. It will no longer be popular to be part of the church someday and then we will see who steals from who. The church has compromised the truth to allow an "anything goes" policy where anyone is welcome to defame the name of God. From now on, there will be a stark line between the true church and the false church and all will know the difference. God is not mocked and His name will not be blasphemed by His church any longer. The Lord's anger has been burning for generations toward Americans who receive God's blessings in one hand and slap Him with the other. Ever since the sexual revolution of the 60s, God has been calling, beckoning, and pleading with His people and His church to return to Him, to no avail. Instead of coming any closer, the church has pulled up anchor and set sail to a different destination. God has called, but the church has blocked His number. God has beckoned and the church has backstabbed. God has pleaded and the church was pleased to turn and run the other way.

Micah 1:2-9

[2] Listen, people—all of you.
Listen, earth, and everyone in it:
The Master, God, takes the witness stand against you,
the Master from his Holy Temple.

[3-5] Look, here he comes! God, from his place!
He comes down and strides across mountains and hills.
Mountains sink under his feet,
valleys split apart;
The rock mountains crumble into gravel,
the river valleys leak like sieves.
All this because of Jacob's sin,
because Israel's family did wrong.
You ask, "So what is Jacob's sin?"
Just look at Samaria—isn't it obvious?
And all the sex-and-religion shrines in Judah—
isn't Jerusalem responsible?

[6-7] "I'm turning Samaria into a heap of rubble,
a vacant lot littered with garbage.
I'll dump the stones from her buildings in the valley
and leave her abandoned foundations exposed.
All her carved and cast gods and goddesses
will be sold for stove wood and scrap metal,
All her sacred fertility groves
burned to the ground,
All the sticks and stones she worshiped as gods,
destroyed.
These were her earnings from her life as a whore.
This is what happens to the fees of a whore."

[8-9] This is why I lament and mourn.
This is why I go around in rags and barefoot.

This is why I howl like a pack of coyotes,
and moan like a mournful owl in the night.
God has inflicted punishing wounds;
Judah has been wounded with no healing in sight.
Judgment has marched through the city gates.
Jerusalem must face the charges.[xvi]

When the Puritans came to America, they came to found a new nation for the glory of God. As freedom was gained from the English, Americans established a firm foundation based on godly principles. Slowly, they began to seek the glory of their new nation instead of the glory of God. Now, after these many years of seeking the glory of our nation, the search for the glory of God has completely faded into the background and the glory of self has arisen to eclipse any former search for a beneficial glory. That glory of self now epitomizes what it means to be American, so much so that the unalienable rights of life, liberty and the pursuit of happiness have been cast asunder with regard to anyone but the self. The Bible talks about the end of days being the same as in the days of Noah when no one knew any better. Marriages, occupations, and recreation continued on, as they had since the beginning of time, but it all changed the day the rains fell and the floodgates opened. What was before became no more and what was going to be did not become, for the stench of wickedness had arisen to the nostrils of God. The hatred, the betrayal, and the contempt for God and for His creation could not be left unjudged, to do so would be unloving and unfair.

Isaiah 59:12-21

[12] For our offenses are many in your sight,
and our sins testify against us.
Our offenses are ever with us,
and we acknowledge our iniquities:
[13] rebellion and treachery against the Lord,

turning our backs on our God,
inciting revolt and oppression,
uttering lies our hearts have conceived.
[14] So justice is driven back,
and righteousness stands at a distance;
truth has stumbled in the streets,
honesty cannot enter.
[15] Truth is nowhere to be found,
and whoever shuns evil becomes a prey.

The Lord looked and was displeased
that there was no justice.
[16] He saw that there was no one,
he was appalled that there was no one to intervene;
so his own arm achieved salvation for him,
and his own righteousness sustained him.
[17] He put on righteousness as his breastplate,
and the helmet of salvation on his head;
he put on the garments of vengeance
and wrapped himself in zeal as in a cloak.
[18] According to what they have done,
so will he repay
wrath to his enemies
and retribution to his foes;
he will repay the islands their due.
[19] From the west, people will fear the name of the Lord,
and from the rising of the sun, they will revere his glory.
When enemies come in like a flood, the spirit of the Lord will put them to flight

[20] "The Redeemer will come to Zion,
to those in Jacob who repent of their sins,"
declares the Lord.

[21] "As for me, this is my covenant with them," says the Lord. "My Spirit, who is on you, will not depart from you, and my words

that I have put in your mouth will always be on your lips, on the lips of your children and on the lips of their descendants—from this time on and forever," says the Lord.[xvii]

God says to His enemies, "Vengeance is Mine. You have gone too far and done too much. You pervert justice and rob the poor, all the while thinking that you have gotten away with something. But your time is up. I have allowed your misdeeds to test My people, but the test is over, and you will pay for the lives you have ruined and the pain that you have inflicted. It will be an eye for an eye and a tooth for a tooth. What you have broken will be restored and what you have taken will be returned, but you will not see the light of day. You have been seen and found wanting and now you will see who is really in charge. There is no one who can save you now. You have relied on the wrong god and turned the wrong way, and now you will turn with nowhere to run. My people will run into My arms, but you will run as one who looks over their shoulder, continually wondering when you will fall. You thought you had the upper hand, but now I am releasing My fury to release My people and repay you for your sins. You thought that you made a wise choice to be on the winning team, but now you will lose and never win. No one can stand against Me or My word. There is no winning against Me and My plans. There is not even a second place. Take your measly plans and destroy them forever, because they will never work or come to fruition again. I am the Lord, and I'm taking charge now."

I would much rather write about mercy than judgment, it's easier, nicer, and more likable. But when is enough, enough? We aren't even Israel and God judged them – His own people. He handpicked Abraham, He took Joseph to the palace, He raised up Moses and delivered them from Egypt — and, oh, how He loved His son, David. God was completely invested in Israel and it still did not save them. God is merciful, but He is also just. His name cannot be defamed as outsiders look at His people and say, "That's what God is like." People in other countries look at America and base their opinion of God off our culture. How scary is that? God will not be mocked, nor will He share His glory with another.

In his sermon podcast "The Church In Babylon – When God Judges a Nation" Erwin Lutzer states, "When the cup of iniquity is full, God pours out His wrath. Judah felt that wrath as invading armies looted Jerusalem and took the people into captivity. America may soon feel that same wrath. In this message we discover lessons we must heed from the fall of a nation long ago."[xviii]

One of the reasons that we are in such danger is because of our guilt from how far we have fallen as a nation. By examining our founding and God's grace that He shed on our country, we will see how guilty we really are and how much we need repentance to sweep across our nation. There are so many instances where the providential and protective hand of God were present in the founding of America. We will explore more to show God's extraordinary goodness in the founding of our nation, but what follows are just a few examples.

In his most difficult times, General Washington constantly relied upon God and trusted in Him for success. God was faithful to answer Washington's prayers, and through Washington He eventually established our independence and secured the beginning of the most free and prosperous nation the world has ever seen. The following article from the Freedom Foundation called "Valley Forge: Crucible of Freedom" describes how prevalent God's providence was in the days of our founding.

> The winter of 1777-1778 was one of the most important in our nation's history, for that winter was the turning point of the American Revolution. During that winter the Ameri-

can Army faced as great an ordeal as any army in history. Before the American Army moved into Valley Forge in December of 1777, it consisted of undisciplined men who had obtained few victories in their war with Britain, but the next spring they marched out as a well-disciplined band, committed more than ever to their General and the cause of liberty. They were now prepared to see victory through their efforts. What was the ordeal this Army faced? How did such a change occur during the stay at Valley Forge? What was the cause behind this change?

As the American Army, under the command of George Washington, moved toward their wintering spot at Valley Forge, army troops had no clothes to cover their nakedness, nor blankets to lie on, nor tents to sleep under. Washington stated, "For the want of shoes their marches through frost and snow might be traced by the blood from their feet, and they were almost as often without provisions as with them." Hunger was even a greater danger. "The army frequently remained whole days without provisions," said Lafayette. "One soldier's meal on a Thanksgiving Day declared by Congress was a 'half a gill of rice and a tablespoonful of vinegar!' In mid-February there was more than a week when the men received no provisions at all."

It was said of Washington, in a sketch written by an American gentleman in London in 1779 that "he regularly attends divine service in his tent every morning and evening, and seems very fervent in his prayers." General Knox was one among many who gave testimony of Washington frequently visiting secluded groves to lay the cause of his bleeding country at the throne of grace. A number of people have recorded the story of how a Tory Quaker, Isaac Potts, came upon Washington while he was on his knees in prayer in the woods. Benson J. Lossing relates that Potts later made the following remarks to his wife: "If there is anyone on this earth whom the Lord will listen to, it is George Washington; and I feel a presentiment that under such a commander there can be no doubt of our eventually establishing our independence, and that God in his providence has willed it so."

How did God answer Washington's prayers? One miracle occurred that winter which helped eliminate their near-starving situation. Bruce Lancaster relates the event as follows:

One foggy morning the soldiers noticed the Schuylkill River seemed to be boiling. The disturbance was caused by thousands and thousands of shad (fish) which were making their way upstream in an unusually early migration. With pitchforks and shovels, the men plunged into the water, throwing the fish onto the banks. Lee's dragoons rode their horses into the stream to keep the shad from swimming on out of reach. Suddenly and wonderfully, there was plenty of food for the army. God's providence can again be seen as Baron Von Steuben, a veteran Prussian soldier, came to Valley Forge on February 23 and offered his services to the American Army. No one could have been more valuable at the time, for he trained the men to move together as a well-disciplined army. His rigorous drilling and training of the troops gave them confidence in themselves as soldiers, even as Washington had given them confidence as men. Not only had godly character and strength been forged and tempered within the army, but military skill had also been imparted to them at last. Another providential event occurred that winter when France became an ally to America. This meant much needed French money and troops would begin to pour into the new nation. The Continental Congress acknowledged this as the hand of God as they de-

> clared a National Day of Thanksgiving on May 7.
>
> In Washington's orders issued at Valley Forge, May 5, 1778, he proclaimed: "It having pleased the Almighty Ruler of the Universe propitiously to defend the cause of the United American States, and finally by raising up a powerful friend among the Princes of the earth, to establish our Liberty and Independence upon a lasting foundation; it becomes us to set apart a day for gratefully acknowledging the Divine Goodness, and celebrating the event, which we owe to His benign interposition."
>
> The troops' survival, the molding of a disciplined army, Washington's amazing leadership, and all the miraculous occurrences during the winter at Valley Forge can only be attributed to Almighty God. George Washington said following all this: "The hand of Providence has been so conspicuous in all this, that he must be worse than an infidel, and more than wicked, that has not gratitude enough to acknowledge his obligation."[xix]

As we're going to see, the fact that America was founded as a Christian nation is evident and documented. We have fallen so far that not only do we no longer resemble a Christian nation, we largely deny our Christian heritage that God so graciously gave us. The following is a summary of a presentation on America's history by David Barton where he talks about the evidence of our clear Christian heritage.[xx]

To think that the Bible and Christianity were so central to their education, importance, and world view is amazing. Those men thought Biblically, talked Biblically, and wrote Biblically. We can't even really imagine what it was like. There is a quote by John Adams where he says something to the effect that the person who knows the Bible shouldn't be seen as extraordinary, but that the person who doesn't know it should be ashamed. Biblical knowledge and understanding were part of early American culture and mind set. That doesn't mean that everyone was overtly Christian or that there weren't issues or flaws in these men, but their general understanding of the world was seen through the lens of the Bible. Barton talks about the first time that Congress met to talk about the Declaration of Independence; they had two hours of opening prayer and studied four chapters of the Bible. That was everyone as an official act of the group, not just part of the pre meeting. It sounds more like what you would do at church then at the first meeting of Congress. One of the chapters of the Bible that the group studied was Psalm 35, and John Adams wrote his wife and told her that the entire Congress was impressed that the Lord had spoken to them powerfully through the Psalm and that she should tell her father who was a pastor. Evidently, not only were they studying Scripture together, but they were discussing how God was speaking to them through it and how they would respond.

Another amazing fact is that Congress would, as an official act, declare days of fasting and prayer on regular occasions. In fact, there were so many declared by Congress for the entire nation that by 1815 they had instituted 1400 calls to fasting and prayer. That means in about a 40-year time span, the Federal Government of the United States of America as official proclamations for the people, had instituted prayer and fasting on an average of 35 days a year. I guess you're probably right they don't sound like Christians – they sound like disciples who lived and served the Lord Jesus.

My aim is to portray an accurate view of our founders while at the same time show that although some of the founders may have had faulty doctrinal understanding or moral shortcomings, they primarily had a Biblical and Christian worldview and to deny that is untrue and unjust. As Thomas Kidd shows in his recent *Yale Press* "Biography of Ben Franklin" even those founders with unorthodox beliefs held world views that were largely shaped by the Bible:

> Some of the leading Founders, such as Franklin and Washington, did not go to college, but virtually all of them had a level of Bible literacy that far surpasses that of the average American today. The self-described "Deist" Franklin grew up in a Boston Puritan family, and from a young age knew the whole text of Scripture quite intimately and could quote it at will. Even a skeptic like Thomas Jefferson was virtually obsessed with the Bible, which accounts for his two compilations of the Gospels, which we call the "Jefferson Bible." Jefferson avidly read the Bible and even the Septuagint in Greek, but his multiple-language editions of the Gospels removed most of the miracles, including the resurrection.[xxi]

I include this information because I am trying to be fair and show that these men may not have all been orthodox in their faith, but even the least religious founders like Jefferson and Franklin knew the Bible and its contents better than any other piece of literature and believed and counted on God and His mercies. For instance, in the resource *God's New Israel* by Conrad Cherry he indicates:

> On July 4, 1776, Congress directed Franklin, Jefferson, and Adams to design a seal for the United States. Franklin proposed a portrayal of 'Moses lifting his hand and the Red Sea dividing, with Pharaoh in his chariot being overwhelmed by the waters, and with a motto in great popular favor at the time, 'Rebellion to tyrants is obedience to God.' Jefferson suggested 'a representation of the children of Israel in the wilderness, led by a cloud by day and pillar of fire by night.'[xxii]

These are the men that are supposed to be the "least" religious of all our founding fathers and their work is Biblical and honoring to God and His sovereignty over the founding of our nation. That is not to mention the other 95% of the founders who had an orthodox Christian faith that can be seen and documented through their letters and writings.

One of the more convincing speeches that showed America's acceptance and understanding of its Christian founding is from the very first inaugural address given in this great nation. In George Washington's inaugural address, he states very plainly the relationship that he saw between the prosperity of America and the morality of its people. If he was right, then the adverse would also be true and America is in for a rude awakening unless she repents. His comments are encouraging as we consider our founding and disparaging considering our current state.

> "I behold the surest pledges, that as on one side no local prejudices, or attachments—no separate views, no party animosities, will misdirect the comprehensive and equal eye which ought to watch over this great assemblage of communities and interests; so, on the other, that the foundations of our national policy will be laid in the pure and immutable principles of private morality; and the preeminence of free government, be exemplified by all the attributes which can win the affections of its citizens, and command the respect of the world—I dwell on this prospect with every satisfaction which an ardent love of my country can inspire. Since there is no truth more thoroughly established, than that there exists in the economy and course of nature, an indissoluble union between virtue and happiness; between duty and advantage, between genuine maxims of an honest and magnanimous policy, and the solid rewards of public prosperity and felicity.

> Since we ought to be no less persuaded that the propitious smiles of heaven, can never be expected on a nation that disregards the eternal rules of order and right, which heaven itself has ordained. And since the preservation of the sacred fire of liberty, and the destiny of the republican model of government, are justly considered as deeply, perhaps as finally staked on the experiment entrusted to the hands of the American people."[xxiii]

It is this sense of morality which has sharply declined and left us picking up the pieces and asking ourselves what happened. We must recognize what Washington and the founders knew and declared was that morality and prosperity are closely connected for our country. Because morality is now in drastic decline, we can assume that prosperity will not be far behind and the experiment entrusted to the hands of the American people (which Washington mentions) is about to be over...unless... Consider the following chart, which shows the number of school shootings per decade.[xxiv] It is alarming to see the trend and understand when the stark increases started. With the advent of teaching evolution in schools and the removal of prayer, the Ten Commandments, and the Bible, it was just a matter of time before the disasters started.

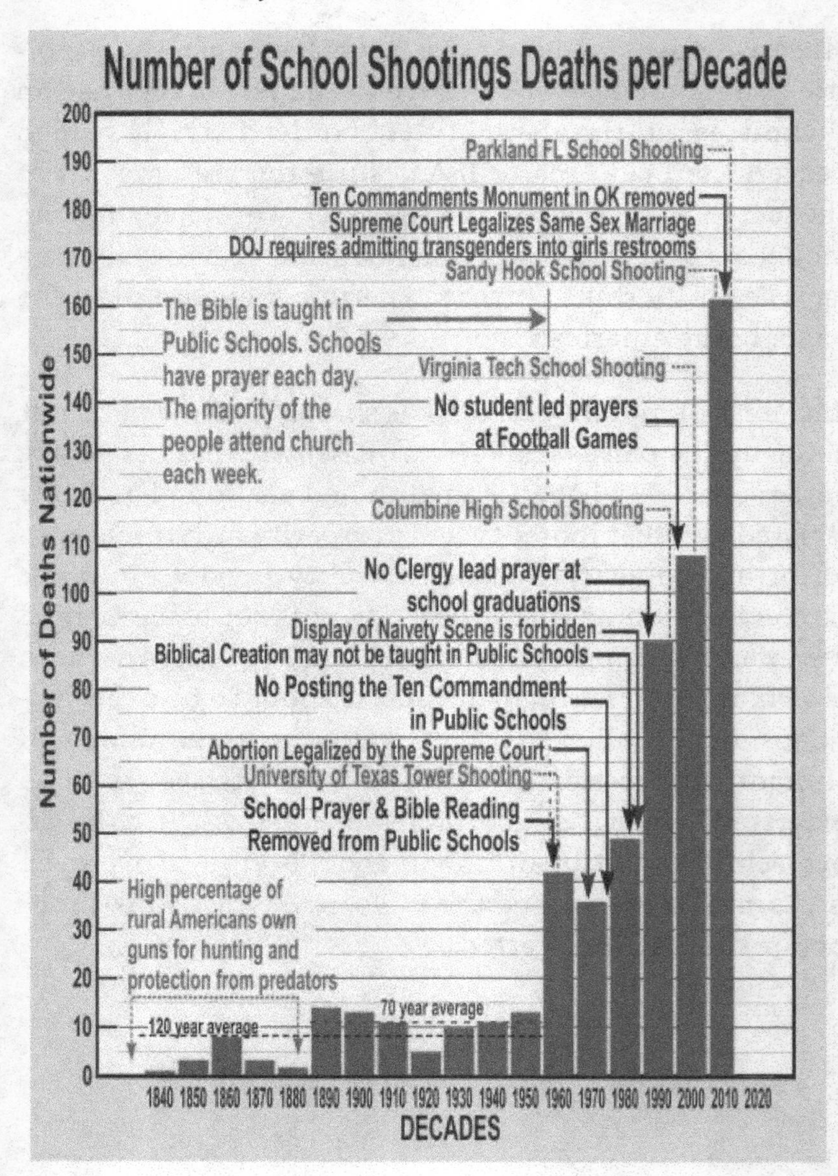
Number of School Shootings Deaths per Decade
Number of Deaths Nationwide
200
190
180
170
160
150
140
130
120
110
100
90
80
70
60
50
40
30
20
10
0
Parkland FL School Shooting
Ten Commandments Monument in OK removed
Supreme Court Legalizes Same Sex Marriage
DOJ requires admitting transgenders into girls restrooms
Sandy Hook School Shooting
The Bible is taught in Public Schools. Schools have prayer each day. The majority of the people attend church each week.
Virginia Tech School Shooting
No student led prayers at Football Games
Columbine High School Shooting
No Clergy lead prayer at school graduations
Display of Naivety Scene is forbidden
Biblical Creation may not be taught in Public Schools
No Posting the Ten Commandment in Public Schools
Abortion Legalized by the Supreme Court
University of Texas Tower Shooting
School Prayer & Bible Reading Removed from Public Schools
High percentage of rural Americans own guns for hunting and protection from predators
120 year average
70 year average
1840 1850 1860 1870 1880 1890 1900 1910 1920 1930 1940 1950 1960 1970 1980 1990 2000 2010 2020
DECADES

After the Columbine High School shooting there was a congressional hearing conducted in which the father of one of the murdered students testified:

> On Thursday, May 27, 1999, Darrell Scott, the father of Rachel Scott, a victim of the Columbine High School shootings in Littleton, Colorado, was invited to address the House Judiciary Committee's sub-committee. What he said to our national leaders during this special session of Congress was painfully truthful. They were not prepared for what he was to say, nor was it received well. It needs to be heard by every parent, every teacher, every politician, every sociologist, every psychologist, and every so-called expert! These courageous words spoken by Darrell Scott are powerful, penetrating, and deeply personal. There is no doubt that God sent this man as a voice crying in the wilderness. The following is a portion of the transcript:
>
> Since the dawn of creation there has been both good and evil in the hearts of men and women. We all contain the seeds of kindness or the seeds of violence.
>
> The death of my wonderful daughter, Rachel Joy Scott, and the deaths of that heroic teacher and the other eleven children who died must not be in vain. Their blood cries out for answers. The first recorded act of violence was when Cain slew his brother Abel out in the field. The villain was not the club he used. Neither was it the NCA, the National Club Association. The true killer was Cain, and the reason for the murder could only be found in Cain's heart.
>
> In the days that followed the Columbine tragedy, I was amazed at how quickly fingers began to be pointed at groups such as the NRA. I am not a member of the NRA. I am not a hunter. I do not even own a gun. I am not here to

represent or defend the NRA — because I don't believe that they are responsible for my daughter's death. Therefore, I do not believe they need to be defended. If I believed they had anything to do with Rachel's murder I would be their strongest opponent. I am here today to declare that Columbine was not just a tragedy — it was a spiritual event that should be forcing us to look at where the real blame lies! Much of the blame lies here in this room. Much of the blame lies behind the pointing fingers of the accusers themselves.

I wrote a poem just four nights ago that expresses my feelings best. This was written way before I knew I would be speaking here today:

Your laws ignore our deepest needs
Your words are empty air
You've stripped away our heritage
You've outlawed simple prayer

Now gunshots fill our classrooms
And precious children die
You seek for answers everywhere
And ask the question "Why"?

You regulate restrictive laws
Through legislative creed
And yet you fail to understand
That God is what we need

Men and women are three-part beings. We all consist of body, soul, and spirit. When we refuse to acknowledge a third part of our make-up, we create a void that allows evil, prejudice, and hatred to rush in and wreak havoc. Spiritual influences were present within our educational systems for most of our nation's history. Many of our major colleges began as theological seminaries. This is a historical fact.

What has happened to us as a nation? We have refused to honor God, and in so doing, we open the doors to hatred and violence.

And when something as terrible as Columbine's tragedy occurs — politicians immediately look for a scapegoat such as the NRA. They immediately seek to pass more restrictive laws that contribute to erode away our personal and private liberties. We do not need more restrictive laws. Eric and Dylan would not have been stopped by metal detectors. No amount of gun laws can stop someone who spends months planning this type of massacre. The real villain lies within our own hearts. Political posturing and restrictive legislation are not the answers.

The young people of our nation hold the key. There is a spiritual awakening taking place that will not be squelched! We do not need more religion. We do not need more gaudy television evangelists spewing out verbal religious garbage. We do not need more million dollar church buildings built while people with basic needs are being ignored. We do need a change of heart and a humble acknowledgment that this nation was founded on the principle of simple trust in God! As my son Craig lay under that table in the school library and saw his two friends murdered before his very eyes — He did not hesitate to pray in school. I defy any law or politician to deny him that right! I challenge every young person in America, and around the world, to realize that on April 20, 1999, at Columbine High School prayer was brought back to our schools. Do not let the many prayers offered by those students be in vain. Dare to move into the new millennium with a sacred disregard for legislation that violates your God-given right to communicate with Him.

To those of you who would point your finger at the NRA I

> give to you a sincere challenge. Dare to examine your own heart before casting the first stone!
>
> My daughter's death will not be in vain! The young people of this country will not allow that to happen![xxv]

There are consequences to our actions as individuals, as the church, and as a nation. We saw this with the people of Israel, and we will see it in America, unless something changes. America is beautiful physically, but spiritually we are falling apart at the seams. This will affect us physically unless something changes.

Before we turn to the sub sections and chapters of the book where we examine these concepts more fully, let me address a basic understanding about judgment that is being demonstrated throughout this book. Looking at Paul's first letter to the Corinthians, he talked about the difference between types of judgment. In 1 Corinthians 4, he talked about a man inside the church engaged in sexual sin and recommended removing him from the fellowship. When the Bible talks about not judging, it is talking about those outside of the church. We need to remember that as we talk about judgment, we are not saying that God's judgment is coming only because of those outside of the church. There are some instances in Scripture where God judges those outside of His family — like Sodom and Gomorrah and the surrounding nations that opposed God's will toward His nation Israel. But as we compare America to God's people, Israel, the realization is that judgment will begin in the house of God. This book is not intended to only be a warning to those outside the church. We do see judgment enacted upon non-covenantal people, but when you examine the history of Israel, God did not bring judgment upon them because of the foreigners. It was because of His people who were influenced by the foreigners. We see and know the sin of our culture. At times, we see its travesty and perversion and we are called to preach repentance and share the love of God with those people in the culture. But when judgment comes to America, it won't primarily be because of those outside the church, it will be because we in the church allowed and stood by as our spiritual walls crumbled around us and we did not do enough to stop it. We have to be careful not to point fingers at "those" people and ignore the plank that is in our own life.

We also discover the theology of the cross when we examine suffering, discipline, and judgment with regard to history and America. We cannot appreciate the glory of the gospel until we understand the severity of the cross. Hebrews chapter 12, verses 7 through 9 describe discipline as God's love and suffering as discipline given by God. This is hard to comprehend and even harder to experience. It also tells us in verse 11 that no suffering feels good at the time, but in the end, if we submit to God and the process, it will yield the peaceful fruit of righteousness. We must understand that not all suffering is discipline or judgment from God in the narrow sense because He did not cause it. But in the broad sense, we understand it as suffering that is not prevented by God and so in some way can be perceived as discipline since God deems us fit to be able to endure it. We also know that He will not allow us to endure anything that He does not give us a way out of or the capability to endure. Of course, in the narrow sense of the causation of discipline, suffering and pain, we should be very careful not to assign things to the hand of God of which we are unsure, as this has caused much pain, uncertainty and bitterness toward God and the church. We must understand the difference between allowing the consequences of sin versus causing the judgment itself. As far as consequences go, we could speak of them as judgments that are a result of the natural sinful state of man running its course. Sexually transmitted disease, marital issues because of adultery, and even global warming issues are examples of judgments that did not happen because of God, but because of man's sinful nature and the consequences of sinful actions. There are, of course, times when we see clearly in Scripture where God does severely judge and discipline people or nations, as well as times when even His greatest prophets are allowed to suffer or experience the consequences of sin. Some would be seen as judgment in the narrow sense as being caused by God and others would be in the broad sense as they were allowed by God. Just to note a few examples, David's child dies as a result of his behaviors (i.e., murder and adultery), the families of Korah are swallowed up by the earth for their rebellion against Moses, and Saul is removed from his throne for his disobedience. There are also instances where judgments were given and then taken back for both individuals and the people of Israel. Jonah was swallowed by a whale and repented, Moses' sister rebelled, and she was struck with leprosy, which was later removed upon her repentance. There were further disciplines in the broad sense that God's prophets were allowed to experience even though they were not directly caused by God, like the emotional anguish of Elijah and his great despair, or the imprisonment of John the Baptist and his eventual death.

Suffering, discipline, and judgment are some of the most difficult and challenging subjects in the Scripture. There are those who study this topic their entire lives and still cannot explain all of the facets of God's will, just as it is equally difficult to comprehend His great grace. For God will have mercy on whom He will have mercy and He will judge whom He will judge. He's God, He can do that. In fact, He can do whatever He wants. One of the most important concepts to remember is that God is 100% loving as well as 100% just. So, as we think about judgment and discipline, it is important that we avoid the extremes. One extreme is that God is responsible for all suffering, because if He is capable of stopping it then He must be held accountable for its occurrence. This line of thinking is prideful, naïve, and mistaken. The other extreme is that God does not judge at all. The thought is that because God is all-loving, He does not cause any discipline or exercise any judgment. This line of thinking is equally naïve, altruistic, and mistaken. Instead, there are many examples in Scripture where both are simultaneously true, and others where God cannot possibly be responsible, and others still where He makes it abundantly clear that His own hand has made it happen. So how do we know the difference? The easy answer is: we don't. We must operate with the grace of God which assumes that others are not guilty and that we *are* guilty so that we do not judge others and we do not become prideful. The Israelites were God's chosen people, described as His own children. The premise of this book is that if God's own children did not escape judgment and discipline, how can we expect anything different in America? Are we so prideful that we believe we have some sort of special exemption that promotes us above even the Israelites?

We must accept that we reap what we sow. We are not under the old covenant because of the sacrificial death of Christ and His resurrection. We now live in the covenant of grace, but there are limits to that grace that can be rejected. This new covenant is based on relationships with individuals, cities, and nations. We see throughout Scripture that God establishes and deposes leaders and nations. We should not be deceived to think that contemporary history is any different. Much of the reason that we do not see cities and nations rise and fall in the New Testament is simply a matter of the length of time that transpired during its inception. The Old Testament was written over thousands of years, but the New Testament writings spanned simply around a hundred. The realization that we are accountable as a nation is not just tit for tat, like a married couple going through divorce when one has been unfaithful, because God has infinitely more patience than your spouse, but there are limits. When God says, "You just crossed a line," then you shall receive the just payment coming to you. God gives grace to the humble but opposes the proud. In this relationship, there is an understanding of the new covenant that is founded on faith in Jesus Christ, and when it is broken continually and habitually eventually there are consequences, because of the nature of the relationship.

When we talk about judgment, we need to remember that it is a very broad term which is understood by different people to mean different things. Technically, we would say that a judgment is a neutral event. To judge in a court of law really means "to evaluate." The judgment regarding the facts of a case could render positive or negative results in your direction. This would be the understanding of judgment that we have in the church when we talk about standing before the judgment seat of God and that we confess in the judgment of the living and the dead. Then we also know that the Bible speaks of judgment with regard to peoples' actions and motives. We are told specifically not to judge others in their actions without evaluating ourselves first and without understanding others' circumstances. This type of judgment refers to a negative attitude of criticism and fault-finding. Then there is judgment which is understood to be a negative action taken upon someone for their inappropriate action or behavior.

As we evaluate suffering, discipline, and judgment, it is vital for us not to assume or accuse others as they walk through pain, like Job's friends did. Without direct communication from God, it is impossible for us to know if a circumstance is discipline or judgment from God, because of the consequences of personal sin or of the fallen world, or even if it is an attack of the enemy. The apostle Paul himself, described the thorn of the flesh as a messenger of Satan sent to torment him. He asks three times for it to be removed, and God's response is, "My grace is sufficient for you." And that was the apostle Paul. There is another instance in Luke chapter 13 where people shared with Jesus the adverse circumstances of others with the implication of asking Him why this was allowed to happen. Jesus refers to a tower which fell and killed 18 people in a nearby area. He says, "Or those eighteen on whom the tower in Siloam fell and killed them, do you think that they were worse sinners than all other men who dwelt in Jerusalem?"[xxvi] He was basically suggesting that it wasn't their sin or their fault that they died, yet He concluded with an interesting reminder for all (and the message of this book): "I tell you, no; but unless you repent you will all likewise perish."[xxvii] This reminder shows us that the cause of death or suffering that people go through is not nearly as important as the lesson to be learned from it – repent. The realization of suffering and pain is a message to us all.

As Christians, we view suffering as "discipline," but for those who do not follow Christ we view it as receiving "punishment." Discipline is for the benefit of the receiver, but punishment is to satisfy the penalty of an offense. The benefit of following Christ is that Jesus already took the full and eternal punishment of sin and we are left to deal with the side effects. That means we can interpret our trials and hardships through the loving hand of a Father who allows difficulty in our lives to bring good out of it. That is hard to grasp (and even harder to embrace), but eventually we will see as God's people that even the worst of what the devil or the world may throw at us must come through the filter of God's love, and that His intention is for our good and our benefit, even if that doesn't come until eternity. Listen to how Psalm 66 in verses 10-12 describes our suffering and the following interpretation from the commentary:

> You have purified us with fire, O Lord, like silver in a crucible. You captured us in your net and laid great burdens on our backs. You sent troops to ride across our broken bodies. We went through fire and flood. But in the end, you brought us into wealth and great abundance.[xxviii] From one point of view, times of distress constitute a testing of God's people as to their trust in and loyalty to God. The metaphor is borrowed from the technology of refining precious metals, which included heating the metals in a crucible to see if all impurities had been removed.[xxix]

As God's people and followers of Christ, we have to believe that God is working to bring good out of every situation, even when we can't see it or understand it. It is never fun to endure discipline, but it is helpful when we see it through the eyes of the giver instead of the through the experience of the pain. We then have the opportunity to see purpose, good, and hope, even in the midst of trial. No discipline seems pleasant when it is experienced, but in the end, discipline always yields the peaceful fruit of righteousness.

We are all broken. The wheels have fallen off in America and we are faced with the reality of fixing it. As we talk about judgment, we have to be careful not to think in terms of individuals judging others. We are talking about God and His ability to judge because He is holy, righteous, and perfect. If you are reading this and hoping to gain fodder for judging others, the church, or even the government, I hope you are disappointed. As we view other individuals, we must remember that mercy triumphs over judgment. It really gets back to the proper distinction between applying the law or the gospel. If someone is proud about their sin and unrepentant, then they need to hear the law to point to their fallen nature. But if they are struggling and trying and attempting to live for Christ, then they need the comfort of the gospel. Blessed are the merciful, for they shall obtain mercy. When we talk about a need for repentance and the potential judgment without it, we need to realize that in most cases we are referring to systemic issues that have to be resolved across the board. It is not going to be helpful for you to confront someone else unlovingly about their sin or their lifestyle without a relationship with them. If it is a friend, family member, acquaintance, or someone in your sphere of influence, you most likely have a responsibility to have a tough conversation with them about these issues. The problem is that we are much more likely to talk to or judge the people that we don't know and take issues out on them while we ignore and disregard the people that are right in front of us because confronting them is so much harder and more uncomfortable. The main point of this resource is to lead us in repentance, which comes from examining our own shortcomings rather than listing the faults of others. Please, as you read this, let it drive you to repentance and action to make a difference instead of toward judgment for others.

When we don't listen or respond to the Lord's warnings, there comes a time where He moves in judgment. Finally, after patience, loving, and kindness come warnings and more warnings—like the Egyptians, like Israel, like Judah, and like all the nations that oppressed Israel. America will be no different. Heed the warning, take up the cause, respond in repentance, because the Lion of the tribe of Judah has readied His chariot and is preparing to come. Please listen, please respond, do not ignore this plea.

As I was preparing, studying, and writing this book, the Lord put it in my heart to establish a website with regard to the call of repentance for future use. So one day, near the beginning of 2020, I registered the domain www.repentance.us As we started experiencing the COVID-19 virus in America, I happened across a timeline of the onset of the virus across the world in a *New York Times* article by Derrick Bryson Taylor entitled "A Timeline of the Coronavirus," which stated that the virus started in November and that the first death attributed to the virus was on January 11, 2020. I thought to myself, "Hmm...That sounds pretty close to when I signed up for the website." I looked it up and sure enough, it was the exact same day I registered the domain name. Please do not disregard God's warning and pray that further judgment is halted through repentance.

God is in control and He will manifest His presence to provide for His people. That's why in the next section we will examine the concept of the remnant because we need to see that no matter how bad it gets or how severe the judgment, that God always protects a remnant. He is able to protect and deliver His followers while judging the wicked. None of us should desire judgment because it affects us all, but that does not mean that we shouldn't share the inevitability of judgment without repentance. I pray that the Lord will give you wisdom to know the difference and grace to hear what the Spirit is saying.

All is not lost — there will always be a remnant. The concept of the remnant is where we pick up with hope and encouragement. We see throughout the Old Testament that no matter how bad it got or how severe the judgment, God was always faithful to preserve His remnant. As followers of Christ, we can rest in the concept of the remnant. We don't have to panic or worry about judgment because we can't make other people repent. We can repent ourselves and proclaim the truth of God's word and share His love, hoping that others will repent, but at the end of the day, as followers of Christ, we must rest in God's sovereignty and His plan for the remnant. We know as disciples that we are not intended to endure wrath or judgment. That doesn't mean that we won't experience it as the byproduct consuming others in this life, but our lot is eternal bliss and salvation, not judgment and wrath. "For God hath not appointed us to wrath, but to obtain salvation by our Lord Jesus Christ" (1 Thessalonians 5:9).[xxx] With that in mind, as we see and experience judgment around us, we continue to serve the living and true God, "And to wait for his Son from heaven, whom he raised from the dead, even Jesus, which delivered us from the wrath to come" (1 Thessalonians 1:10).[xxxi]

THE REMNANT

This book is challenging on several levels. To realistically think about the possibility of America experiencing judgment is painful and frightening. To take a deep, realistic, and introspective evaluation of ourselves and our churches is downright intimidating. To think about how we could have done more or how we have contributed to the problem can be discouraging and eye-opening. So I wanted to make sure that we highlighted the concept of the remnant. It's kind of like starting with the dessert first when you know that you are having liver for dinner (or something else you don't like). The point being that the concept of the remnant is infinitely encouraging and uplifting, no matter what other circumstances are presented for us, because we can be sure that everything is going to turn out alright. It's like watching a thrilling, plot-twisting, tragedy when you know the ending of the movie is going to be good. You watch it with a different attitude and perspective if you know the ending. When you know you are part of the remnant, while the thought of experiencing judgment still doesn't feel good or sound exciting, you can take solace in the fact that everything is going to be ok eventually, because you already know the ending. Over and over and over again, we see God faithfully provide for His people - even in the midst of judgment and trial. When you are a devoted follower of Christ, there is nothing in this life that can be taken away from you because there is nothing in this life that you possess, not your father, mother, kids, home, goods, or wife — even your own life is not your own. Therefore, you are not afraid to lose it or have it taken away, because it wasn't yours to start with. It is the difference between seeing with physical eyes and spiritual eyes, and the difference between focusing on what is seen versus what is unseen. When we have the right perspective and understanding, the pain and suffering of judgment becomes much easier to bear because you know the end of the story. Of course, the hope is that we won't experience judgment, but that will be based on our response of repentance and change. You can't control the effects of judgment or what other people do, but you can control your own point of view, your focus, and your perspective of the end of the story.

What is the remnant? Here is a great definition from the *Holman Bible Dictionary*:

> Something left over, especially the righteous people of God after divine judgment. Several Hebrew words express the remnant idea: *yether*, "that which is left over"; *she' ar*, "that which remains"; *she' rith*, "residue"; *pelitah*, "one who escapes"; sa*r* id, "a survivor"; and, *sheruth*, "one loosed from bonds." In the New Testament, remnant or leftover is the equivalent of the Greek words: *kataleimma*, *leimma*, and *loipos*.
>
> Several activities of everyday life are associated with these words. Objects or people may be separated from a larger group by selection, assignment, consumption (eating food), or destruction. What is left over is the residue, or, in the case of people, those who remain after an epidemic, famine, drought, or war.
>
> Noah and his family may be understood as survivors, or a remnant of a divine judgment in the flood (Genesis 6:5-8; Genesis 7:1-23). The same could be said of Lot when Sodom was destroyed (Genesis 18:17-33; Genesis 19:1-29); Jacob's family in Egypt (Genesis 45:7); Elijah and the 7,000 faithful followers of the Lord (1 Kings 19:17-18); and Israelites going into captivity (Ezekiel 12:1-16). They were survivors because the Lord chose to show mercy to those who had believed steadfastly in Him and had been righteous in their lives.
>
> About 750 B.C. Amos found that many people in Israel

believed that God would protect all of them and their institutions. With strong language, he tore down their mistaken ideas (Amos 3:12-15; Amos 5:2-3; Amos 5:2-3; Amos 5:18-20; Amos 6:1-7; Amos 9:1-6). Divine judgment would be poured out on all Israel. He corrected the tenet that everyone would live happily and prosper (Amos 9:10) with the doctrine that only a few would survive and rebuild the nation (Amos 9:8-9; Amos 9:8-9; Amos 9:11-15). This new life could be realized if one and all would repent, turn to the Lord, and be saved (Amos 5:4-6; Amos 5:4-6; Amos 5:14-15).[xxxii]

The Seventh-day Adventist fundamental Belief #13 states about the remnant - The universal church is composed of all who truly believe in Christ, but in the last days, a time of widespread apostasy, a remnant has been called out to keep the commandments of God and the faith of Jesus. This remnant announces the arrival of the judgment hour, proclaims salvation through Christ, and heralds the approach of His second advent. This proclamation is symbolized by the three angels of Revelation 14; it coincides with the work of judgment in heaven and results in a work of repentance and reform on earth. Every believer is called to have a personal part in this worldwide witness (Rev. 12:17; Rev. 14:6–12; Rev. 18:1–4; 2 Cor. 5:10; Jude 3; Jude 14; 1 Peter 1:16–19; 2 Peter 3:10–14; Rev. 21:1–14).[xxxiii]

As the remnant of God's people, we are not to be afraid of coming judgment, as it says in Isaiah chapter 8, verses 11 through 17:

11

"For in this way the Lord spoke to me with His strong hand [upon me] and instructed me not to walk in the way of this people [behaving as they do], saying,

12

"You are not to say, 'It is a conspiracy!'
In regard to all that this people call a conspiracy,
And you are not to fear what they fear nor be in dread of it.
13
"It is the Lord of hosts whom you are to regard as holy *and* awesome.
He shall be your [source of] fear,
He shall be your [source of] dread [not man].
14
"Then He shall be a sanctuary [a sacred, indestructible shelter for those who fear and trust Him];
But to both the houses of Israel [both the northern and southern kingdoms—Israel and Judah, He will be] a stone on which to stumble and a rock on which to trip,
A trap and a snare for the inhabitants of Jerusalem.
15
"Many [among them] will stumble over them;
Then they will fall and be broken,
They will even be snared and trapped."

16 Bind up the testimony, seal the law *and* the teaching among my (Isaiah's) disciples. 17 And I will wait for the Lord who is hiding His face from the house of Jacob; and I will look eagerly for Him.[xxxiv]

The perspective of judgment for the remnant is different than the perspective of judgment in the rest of culture. Instead of being afraid of judgment, we are afraid of the living God who can bring it. What a great encouragement of what we are supposed to be about and doing as the remnant from Isaiah. In summary of these verses we see that Isaiah is encouraging us to — preserve the teaching of God, instruct them to His followers, and wait for the Lord as we put our hope in Him. That will preach – sounds like a good end time theology for His remnant.

The remnant is whoever truly loves God, no matter what their standing in this life. It is the invisible church because only God knows people's hearts. That means that those in the persecuted church are also included in this group. There are those in the United States who are persecuted spiritually, emotionally, and socially. This is much different than the persecuted church in foreign countries where it is illegal to be a Christian and to worship Jesus. The persecuted church in other countries is a physical persecution, where it is clearly evident that it is unwanted and illegal to believe, preach, and speak about Christ. The result of that persecution may be imprisonment, physical restraints, fines, or other interventions. Persecutions for those in the United States and other places where Christianity is legal can be characterized as non-physical. Persecution for Christians in America may look like isolation, bewilderment, confusion, health issues, and accusation. How comparable is that persecution? It depends on your perspective. Despite living in a persecuted nation, you may be in a remote area with very loose standards and oversight, which allows you to function in a regularly "normal" fashion. Alternatively, you may be in America or another nation that allows the preaching of the Gospel but feel like you are on an island, cut off from every avenue of help, making your persecution feel very tangible. The opposite is also true. You could be in prison in a persecuted country and your suffering would obviously be very real, or you could be in a nation like the United States and have no idea what I'm talking about in terms of spiritual and emotional difficulty. The point is, no matter where you are at on the spectrum and no matter what your circumstances are, God is in control. He knows what you are going through. Even if no one else understands or supports you, God does. He is the defender of the oppressed and the releaser of the captives and He will never let you down. He will never leave you or forsake you. Circumstances and surroundings may seem hopeless and desperate, but nothing can separate you from God's love. Whether it is a physical prison or an invisible prison that you fight against, God is for you (and don't ever forget it). In the end, He will say, "You did it. You did it. You're perfect." Nothing is secret that will not be made known, and nothing is hidden that will not be revealed. God is working on your behalf as the remnant, so don't ever give up and don't ever give in.

The Day of the Lord brings horrible judgment upon the wicked and those who oppress God's people, but it also brings safety and assurance for His people. Listen to these verses from the perspective of the remnant.

Joel 2:32
And it shall come to pass
That whoever calls on the name of the Lord
Shall be [a]saved.
For in Mount Zion and in Jerusalem there shall be [b]deliverance,
As the Lord has said,
Among the remnant whom the Lord calls.[xxxv]

Joel 3:16
The Lord roars from Mount Zion;
his voice thunders from Jerusalem;
earth and sky tremble.
But he will defend his people.[xxxvi]

1 Thessalonians 5:2-5
2 For you yourselves know perfectly well that the day of the [return of the] Lord is coming just as a thief [comes unexpectedly and suddenly] in the night. 3 While they are saying, "Peace and safety [all is well and secure!]" then [in a moment unforeseen] destruction will come upon them suddenly like labor pains on a woman with child, and they will absolutely not escape [for there will be no way to escape the judgment of the Lord]. 4 But you, [a]believers, [all you who believe in Christ as Savior and acknowledge Him as God's Son] are not in *spiritual* darkness [nor held by its power], that the day [of judgment] would overtake you [by surprise] like a thief; 5 for you are all sons of light and

sons of day. We do not belong to the night nor to darkness.[xxxvii]

1 THE REMNANT HELPS YOU HAVE THE RIGHT PERSPECTIVE

In a recent sermon series at our church, we talked about our need for repentance as individuals, churches, and even as a nation. We looked at the people of Israel and saw what happened to them as they abandoned and ignored the God of heaven. God, in His mercy, sent prophet after prophet to warn the people that they needed to repent or face judgment. That is a difficult message for us to hear, especially when we see the condition of our country and how it is trending spiritually. At the same time, it should not frighten us or cause us to despair as followers of Christ who stand up for the truth and live our lives for God. The reason for that assurance and hope is because of the remnant that God has always preserved in the midst of a perverse generation. No matter how vile or corrupt a family, city, or nation became, God always found a way to save His remnant. Even in godless Sodom and Gomorrah, God spared Lot and his family. Noah and his family were a remnant that were saved in the flood and the Israelites always had a remnant that God spared, even when the rest of the nation fell into captivity.

The concept of the remnant runs throughout the entire Bible. It gives us faith that no matter what the future of America may hold corporately, God is able to preserve His remnant. When the people of Egypt fell under judgment for their treatment of God's people, there was a territory where the Israelites lived just outside of Egypt called Goshen. The Bible tells us that God spared the Israelites from the judgments visited upon the Egyptian people. For many of the plagues, the only place spared was the region of Goshen, where the people of Israel lived (Exodus 9:26).

There is a realization that a special blessing comes from serving the Lord. Psalm chapter 91 verse 7 says, "If a thousand fall at my side or ten thousand at my right hand it will not harm me." If you are a man or woman after God's own heart, you have nothing to fear because you are a part of the remnant. There was a remnant of people that had not bowed their knee to Baal that Elijah was not aware of. Sometimes we despair over the condition of our nation, churches, or families, but God's plan is always to preserve and protect a portion of His people for His divine purposes. That should give us hope as we follow Christ, that no matter what happens or how things go, we can have assurance and faith because of God's remnant. Sometimes we don't understand God's purposes or actions, but in the end it all makes sense, just as in the case of Joseph. In Genesis, Joseph explained to his brothers that God sent him to Egypt to preserve a remnant of God's people in the midst of a great famine: "[7] And God sent me before you to preserve for you a remnant on earth, and to keep alive for you many survivors. [8] So it was not you who sent me here, but God. He has made me a father to Pharaoh, and lord of all his house and ruler over all the land of Egypt" (Genesis 45:7-8).[xxxviii]

That doesn't mean that if you follow Christ you will never have any problems. In fact, the opposite may be true, but you can take solace in the fact that God is in complete control. We don't have to fear because God will always spare a remnant. And the alternative to being saved as part of the remnant isn't half bad either — eternity in the bliss of heaven. In either case, there is nothing to fear because God is with you. He is by your side and He will see you through, all the way to the end of the line.

In his daily devotional from "Upwords," Max Lucado shares an illustration about perspective with our problems. When you're a middle school kid, you have a different perspective about problems — a zit on your nose, a pop quiz, a bad social media post, or maybe you bought the wrong skin on Fortnite — but if you talk to your dad about those things, he might say something like, "I'm sorry, but it will be ok," because he brings perspective. He knows that in the grand scheme of things, those issues probably aren't going to matter very much, even though it may feel very important and painful at the moment. When you look at the big picture in the scope of eternity, it gives us a different perspective and reality of our problems. It is very similar to when things happen to us that are serious and seem to be devastating, but God reassures us that it will be ok.

There is no doubt that being part of the remnant brings great challenge. Whenever there is pain, suffering, or judgment on a national level, everyone usually experiences it to some degree. I am not saying that as part of the remnant you will necessarily be spared from the consequences of sin, but it will be better because of your perspective. You know that you have a hope and future and that anything in this life is temporary. There may be setbacks and there may be difficulties or challenges, but they will all be tempered through your understanding of your circumstances.

Part of the hope of the remnant is that God is in control. When you know who's at the helm or who's flying the plane, you feel a lot better. You might have been uncomfortable or anxious the first time you flew in a plane, but if you went to the cockpit before you took off and saw Jesus in the pilot's seat, you wouldn't be scared anymore. God is in complete control. He is orchestrating a symphony with hundreds, thousands, even millions of parts all playing together to create the sound of the redeemed. God is at work bringing it all together, conducting churches, ministries, and leaders to accomplish His will and bring about His eternal plan. When we are in the midst of the pain and difficulty, it can sometimes be hard to see, but that is the perspective necessary for us to focus on the hope that we have as the remnant.

There is a song called "Symphony" by Switch that artfully explains the fact that even when we are in the midst of darkness and pain, we know that God is up to something good as the Master Conductor.

Sometimes it's hard to breathe
All the thoughts are shouting at me
Trying to bring me to my knees
And its overwhelming
Darkness echoes all around
Feels like everything is crashing down
Still I know when my hope is found

And it's only you
You say you're working everything for my good and
I believe every word

'Cause even in the madness, there is peace
Drowning out the voices all around me
Through all of this chaos
You were writing a symphony, a symphony
And even in the madness, there is peace
Drowning out the voices all around me
Through all of this chaos
You were writing a symphony, a symphony[xxxix]

God is writing a beautiful story for eternity. It may not feel or look beautiful if you look at it right now through eyes of discontent, but if you will look through God's perspective, you will see it is beautiful and it will be for eternity. A symphony is typically not a short, one-song event. In addition to the multiple parts, there are multiple songs or parts with breaks and intermissions and crescendos, all compiling the entire story of the symphony. That is the perspective that we need for our lives and our circumstances. The meaning of our life is not confined to one part, one song, or even one note, it is all part of the eternal sound of glory that is calling to His chosen ones.

In the Battle of Waterloo in 1815, the Duke of Wellington attempted to take on Napoleon, who had conquered most of the known world up until that point. The battle was in Belgium, which was quite far from England, where Wellington was from. In those days before cell phones, news from the battlefront was sent the quickest way possible; in this case, it was by ship. Those on board used flags to notify those on land awaiting the message from the ship so that they could relay the message as quickly as possible. As the story goes, when the message ship came into port in England after the battle, they began to flag the message "W-E-L-L-I-N-G-T-O-N D-E-F-E-A-T-E-D" to those on land. At this point, the ship was still quite far out, and a thick fog interrupted the transmission. Those on land didn't know there was more to the message and immediately began to tell everyone the bad news that Wellington had been defeated. By the time that the ship docked at port, the entire city had heard the dreadful news, but what they didn't know is that the rest of the message was "T-H-E E-N-E-M-Y," which provides a much different picture and conclusion. Instead of being defeated, Wellington had done the unthinkable and beaten Napoleon.

How often do we accept incomplete or incorrect information and assume the worst instead of having the perspective that God is in control, in charge, and working for our eternal good? When we have the right perspective, we will have the right attitude, and when we have the right attitude, we will have hope for our future as the remnant.

2 THE REMNANT OF BELIEVERS WILL BE BLESSED

Some of you might think that the concept of the remnant sounds like works righteousness in which those that follow Christ or who are good enough will be spared. But that could not be further from the truth, as it is God that gives the grace for that righteousness. Without Him, we have no ability to follow Him or become one of the remnant. The concept of the remnant is by God's design and election. It is not if you're good enough to get on the bus. There is a participation in our walk with God that He looks for (2 Chronicles 16:9), but it is more of a, "Are you still holding on?" rather than a, "Have you climbed high enough?" In the concept of the remnant, as we near Christ's return, it will be the grace of God that preserves us until the end and allows us to stand. Being one of the remnant and one of God's chosen people is a great honor and a blessing that He alone can bestow on us. Being one of the remnant may raise similar questions as to those that are saved and those that are not. Why some and not others? Ours is not to question why, but to trust the God on high. Our part is to stand, hold on, and keep the faith no matter the circumstances; we can leave the rest in the hands of a loving and powerful God. The remnant is a protected class of people because of God's sovereign will. There is great solace and comfort in the concept of the remnant because we don't have to live in fear of the circumstances around us. We can't control all our external circumstances. We can do our part and we can be in faith about our churches and about America, but at the end of the day, we can only do so much. We have to leave the rest in God's hands. That is comforting, because then we don't have to be frightened or concerned if we see the wall crumbling around us. We can know that God is in complete control and that He will always preserve His remnant. We simply seek to continue to live our lives following Christ to the best of our ability and know that we can leave the rest up to Him. Part of me would love to be part of the remnant that God preserves while the other part of me doesn't want to see it get that bad, but I know that no matter what happens, God is in control. Wherever you find yourself on the remnant spectrum, you can trust that if you follow Christ, He will be with you and care for your soul until the very end. No matter how much we talk about or see judgment in our lives or in America, it should never cause us to fear because God is in control. As followers of Christ, we don't fear death or judgment. In some ways, we look forward to it, because we know it will be our salvation. We don't *want* death, but we don't fear it either. We long for the restoration of all things, just as the saints of old in Revelation: "They cried out with a loud voice, 'O Sovereign Lord, holy and true, how long before you will judge and avenge our blood on those who dwell on the earth?'" (Revelation 6:10).[xl] So whether we are part of the remnant or not, we trust that God is in control and that we should not fear, because we will be delivered.

The blessing of the remnant is declared over and over throughout Scripture by God. We see it in Joel 2:18-3:21, that the promises for the remnant who repent include the promise of restoration, the promise of the Lord's Spirit, and the promise of judgment against the enemy. We also see the blessing in the book of Zechariah. Over and over in this section of Scripture, God repeats Himself emphatically, saying, "Thus says the Lord of hosts." The following passage is a bit lengthy, but it is important to see God's great intentions for the remnant, as He tells them that He will save them and not to fear, but to be strong. God also tells them that He is determined to do good to them and to all who follow Him.

> Zechariah 8:4-15
>
> [4] The Lord Almighty declares that Jerusalem will have peace and prosperity so long that there will once again be aged men and women hobbling through her streets on canes, [5] and the streets will be filled with boys and girls at play.
>
> [6] The Lord says, "This seems unbelievable to you—a remnant, small, discouraged as you are—but it is no great thing for me. [7] You can be sure that I will rescue my people from east and west, wherever they are scattered. [8] I will bring them home again to live safely in Jerusalem, and they will be my people, and I will be their God, just and true and yet forgiving them their sins!"
>
> [9] The Lord Almighty says, "Get on with the job and finish it! You have been listening long enough! For since you began laying the foundation of the Temple, the prophets have been telling you about the blessings that await you when it's finished. [10] Before the work began there were no jobs, no wages, no security; if you left the city, there was no assurance you would ever return, for crime was rampant.

> [11] "But it is all so different now!" says the Lord Almighty. [12] "For I am sowing peace and prosperity among you. Your crops will prosper; the grapevines will be weighted down with fruit; the ground will be fertile, with plenty of rain; all these blessings will be given to the people left in the land. [13] 'May you be as poor as Judah,' the heathen used to say to those they cursed! But no longer! For now *Judah* is a word of blessing, not a curse. 'May you be as prosperous and happy as Judah is,' they'll say. So don't be afraid or discouraged! Get on with rebuilding the Temple! [14-15] If you do, I will certainly bless you. And don't think that I might change my mind. I did what I said I would when your fathers angered me and I promised to punish them, and I won't change this decision of mine to bless you.[xli]

After Hurricane Katrina in New Orleans — when everything was devastated and there were thousands and thousands of people that had been evacuated and were moving away — the Lord brought this Scripture in front of me, talking about the restoration of New Orleans. When you are going through the most difficult parts of suffering or difficulty it is hard to see the blessing through the other side. That is why it is so important to hold on to God's word and His promise to bless the remnant. Then when the problems come, when the storms rage, or when the pandemics rise, we don't have to fear because of God's promise to His remnant.

The concept of the remnant gives us hope and encouragement to be able to face whatever life throws at us because we know that God is ultimately in control and no matter how bad it gets (or seems to get), God will never stop being in charge. Everything goes through Him and by Him. That may make it hard for us to understand sometimes, but ultimately it gives us security and hope knowing that the world revolves on His axis. In Joel chapter 2 verse 11, there is evidence that even in instances of great trouble and judgment God is at the helm, achieving His purposes and plans. "The Lord is at the head of the column. He leads them with a shout. This is his mighty army, and they follow his orders. The day of the Lord is an awesome, terrible thing. Who can possibly survive?" So whether the direct result is an action of God, a result of the fallen world, or the result of an attack of the enemy, we can be assured that God knows about it and that He is working good in the midst of it. We are taught by this to ask God "How are you at work in this situation?" rather than "Where are you at work?" as the first has a positive connotation of faith that sees God working spiritual good out of every situation and the latter has a negative connotation of "Are you even there God?" When we ask the right questions, we are much more likely to end up at the right conclusion.

These promises give us hope. Our ultimate hope is not anything in this world, because it will all disappoint. Even the promises of restoration, the Lord's Spirit, and judgment against the enemy are only partial and incomplete, because they are in this world. Only what is beyond this world can give us hope that supersedes the disappointments in this life. The only true source of ultimate hope comes from God and the promise of eternal life through His Son, Jesus Christ. That is the only hope that will never fail. That is the only hope that will never fade away. That is the only hope that is full and complete. And that is the only hope that will be eternal. That is why it is so important not to worry about the negativity of this world and the coming judgment, because that is not where our hope lies. We can say like Joshua, "As for me and my house, we will serve the Lord and be faithful to the end," but we cannot control the actions or decisions of others. If they do not repent and follow Christ, then there will be judgment. But just as we don't put our hope in this life, we also don't allow the difficulties of this life cause us to despair. Because this is not the end, this is only the beginning. This is only the intro and prologue for the great play of eternity. When we truly understand our eternal destinies and nature, it gives us the proper perspective for this life.

> [3] All honor to God, the God and Father of our Lord Jesus Christ; for it is his boundless mercy that has given us the privilege of being born again so that we are now members of God's own family. Now we live in the hope of eternal life because Christ rose again from the dead. [4] And God has reserved for his children the priceless gift of eternal life; it is kept in heaven for you, pure and undefiled, beyond the reach of change and decay. [5] And God, in his mighty power, will make sure that you get there safely to receive it because you are trusting him. It will be yours in that coming last day for all to see. [6] So be truly glad! There is wonderful joy ahead, even though the going is rough for a while down here (1 Peter 1:3-6).[xlii]

Imperishable, undefiled, and unfading — that is something to get excited about that you will have for all of eternity. That is hope. Do not let the circumstances of this world or the condition of your life, or even America, put you in despair or fear, because your hope does not come from how America is doing. Your hope doesn't come from how you're doing materially. Your hope comes from God! God's promise for the remnant is always for abundance and provision for all of eternity. We can be confident that God's plan is to preserve a remnant and to provide great things for that remnant. We don't know when or how it will come, but we can be sure that being part of the remnant involves tremendous blessing and provision from the Lord.

3 THE REMNANT HELPS YOU REMEMBER WHO GOD IS AND WHAT HE IS CAPABLE OF

As you read this book there is a very serious message of repentance to avoid the potential judgment that Israel underwent, but we should never be afraid or in despair over that prospect. It should drive us to repentance and to communicate repentance, not to fear and trepidation. Fear of God is the goal, not fear of man or consequences. It is vital that the right spirit is taken from this book and that it is not to cause fear of circumstances or people. When the people of Nineveh heard from Jonah that the city would be destroyed in 40 days, people turned toward God in repentance, not away from God in fear of their circumstances. There is a huge difference there, and in a world that promotes fear and trauma, we need to understand the difference. Fear does not come from God. Perfect love casts out fear, therefore the only fear that we should have as followers of Christ is the fear of God. What can man do to me? No matter what happens to you in this world it is not worth submitting to fear, because God is the only one who can determine the status of your soul for eternity.

The message of the prophet Haggai came at a time when there was just a remnant of Jews that had returned after the Babylonian captivity. The people of Israel had been captured and taken to Babylon for 70 years and then they were sent back to rebuild their city and the temple. They had returned to Israel and had lost focus and direction about building the temple — God's house.

Haggai 1:2-11

[2] A Message from God-of-the-Angel-Armies: "The people procrastinate. They say this isn't the right time to rebuild my Temple, the Temple of God."

[3-4] Shortly after that, God said more and Haggai spoke it: "How is it that it's the 'right time' for you to live in your fine new homes while the Home, God's Temple, is in ruins?"

[5-6] And then a little later, God-of-the-Angel-Armies spoke out again:

"Take a good, hard look at your life.
  Think it over.
You have spent a lot of money,
  but you haven't much to show for it.
You keep filling your plates,
  but you never get filled up.
You keep drinking and drinking and drinking,
  but you're always thirsty.
You put on layer after layer of clothes,
  but you can't get warm.
And the people who work for you,
  what are they getting out of it?
Not much—
  a leaky, rusted-out bucket, that's what.

[7] That's why God-of-the-Angel-Armies said:

"Take a good, hard look at your life.
  Think it over."

[8-9] Then God said:

"Here's what I want you to do:
  Climb into the hills and cut some timber.
Bring it down and rebuild the Temple.

Do it just for me. Honor me.
You've had great ambitions for yourselves,
but nothing has come of it.
The little you have brought to my Temple
I've blown away—there was nothing to it.

9-11 "And why?" (This is a Message from God-of-the-Angel-Armies, remember.) "Because while you've run around, caught up with taking care of your own houses, my Home is in ruins. That's why. Because of your stinginess. And so I've given you a dry summer and a skimpy crop. I've matched your tight-fisted stinginess by decreeing a season of drought, drying up fields and hills, withering gardens and orchards, stunting vegetables and fruit. Nothing—not man or woman, not animal or crop—is going to thrive."[xliii]

The good news is that the people of Israel immediately repented. In verse 12, it says "...the whole remnant of God's people began to obey the message from the Lord their God. When they heard the word of the prophet Haggai, whom the Lord their God had sent, the people feared the Lord." The bad news is that we must respond in the same way (on a large scale) or something even worse may come upon us. We have built our luxurious houses to the detriment of God's house, which lies in ruins. We have taken our time and resources and talents and poured them into our own portfolios at the expense of the church and our spiritual heritage in America. If we want God to stay His hand and release the blessing of the land upon us again, we need to drop everything to rebuild His house. We need to be invested with all that we have to lead, give, and support the church if we hope to avoid calamity and fulfill our destinies. We need to correct the wrongs, we need to proclaim the truths, and we need to build His house and His name instead of our own agendas.

When God saw the response of the remnant of the people of Israel, He immediately sent another message: "I am with you!" This sparked great enthusiasm and the work on the Lord's house began in earnest. Even though there was only a small remnant and they received opposition – because the Lord was with them, they were able to complete the work anyway. God repeatedly encouraged them and aided them to complete the work beyond all likelihood. God will help the remnant of the church today in a similar fashion if we will stop building our fine houses and return to build the house of the Lord. The house of the Lord is not forsaken — it is broken, neglected, and even corrupted, all of which the Lord can and will fix if His remnant will return to Him and drop everything to restore the foundations of His house.

God took a considerably small number of people that returned from Babylon to complete the monumental task of rebuilding the temple, and He can do the same with His church in America today if His people will obey the message from the Lord and once again fear the Lord. That is the encouragement of being part of the remnant; you may be one of a smaller number of people, but any number with God is always a majority. In fact, God specializes and sometimes even provokes smaller numbers of people to complete large tasks so that He gets the glory and man does not take the credit. Just think, for example, about Jericho, Gideon, and even the disciples. The number of people doesn't matter near as much to God as the heart of the people. There is no limit to what God can do with people that are surrendered to Him and Him alone. Once the people committed in their hearts and lives to pursue God and to rebuild His church, God promised them that all of His power and resources would be at their disposal for accomplishing the task.

There is no limit to His power. There is no limit to His resources. There is only a limit in what we can be trusted with. There is no task too big, there is no undertaking too hard, and there is no mission too impossible. God has never failed and He never will. God promised to raise up a people who were more numerous than the sands of the seashore and He did. God promised that David would always have a descendant to sit on the throne and he does. God promised Moses that He would deliver

His people into the Promised Land and they went. God has also promised to raise up an end-time church that will shine in the glory of their purity to usher in the coming of the king and He will. No matter how small the number, He will bless and preserve all those who obey the words of prophecy written in His book. Come Lord Jesus! The Spirit and the bride say, Come.

4 THE REMNANT GIVES YOU HOPE FOR THE FUTURE GLORY

As we talked about in the last chapter, the message of Haggai was to the remnant of Israel who returned to the land of Israel after the Babylonian captivity. Most people are familiar with Ezra and Nehemiah's efforts, but Haggai encouraged two other individuals as well. The first is Zerubbabel the governor, and the second is Joshua, the high priest and son of Jehozadak. Haggai told the people about their misdirected efforts and then responded by telling them to get to work on what they were really supposed to be doing. Then, after the people responded, he delivered a very interesting message for them about the coming glory. To understand the significance of what he said, we have to remember the glory of the first temple. The former glory of the first temple included the Ark of the Covenant, and when they dedicated it and Solomon prayed, the Shekinah glory filled the temple. Fire came from heaven and consumed the offering. It was so glorious the priests couldn't even enter the area and all the people bowed to the ground. That is the former glory, so for Haggai to talk and prophesy about the future glory being greater is amazing, to say the least.

> "On the twenty-first of the seventh month, the word of the Lord came by Haggai the prophet saying, [2] "Speak now to Zerubbabel the son of Shealtiel, governor of Judah, and to Joshua the son of Jehozadak, the high priest, and to the remnant of the people saying, [3] 'Who is left among you who saw this [a]temple in its former glory? And how do you see it now? Does it not [b]seem to you like nothing [c]in com-

> parison? 4 But now [d]take courage, Zerubbabel,' declares the Lord, 'take courage also, Joshua son of Jehozadak, the high priest, and all you people of the land take courage,' declares the Lord, 'and work; for I am with you,' declares the Lord of hosts. 5 'As for the [e]promise which I [f]made you when you came out of Egypt, [g]My Spirit is abiding in your midst; do not fear!' 6 For thus says the Lord of hosts, 'Once more [h]in a little while, I am going to shake the heavens and the earth, the sea also and the dry land. 7 I will shake all the nations; and [i]they will come with the wealth of all nations, and I will fill this house with glory,' says the Lord of hosts. 8 'The silver is Mine and the gold is Mine,' declares the Lord of hosts. 9 'The latter glory of this house will be greater than the former,' says the Lord of hosts, 'and in this place I will give peace,' declares the Lord of hosts."[xliv] (Haggai 2:1-9)

Can you imagine the response? They must have thought Haggai was crazy or that he was way off base or something. "You mean to tell me that God isn't going to just do the same thing, but it's going to be even better? There's going to be more glory? How is that even possible?" Haggai gives us some great reminders that if we want to see God work in our lives, there are some things that God tells us we should remember and keep at the forefront of our lives, just as the Israelites had to do.

The first characteristic that we need to employ is faith. The same faith that we need in our lives is the faith that the Israelites needed to rebuild the second temple. In their natural minds they couldn't see how this temple would ever have a greater glory, but that is often how we must work as followers of God. We must set aside the things that are seen and press forward to what is unseen. There were no physical signs or evidence that this temple would have a greater glory then the first temple. In fact, up until this point they had trouble even completing the work, much less seeing God's glory. That is how faith works though; we don't know the details or the when, but we must trust God and His word that He is going to accomplish what He said He would. If God said that He would bring a greater glory to America, would we believe it? How could God do that? Is that even possible? If all things are possible with God, then how could you demonstrate your faith to restore God's glory to America?

In Haggai 2:18-19 we see that we have to have faith that God's plans are good for us and that He will accomplish that which we are not able to. Up to this point, the people of Israel hadn't seen much success after their Babylonian captivity, but once they repented the Lord says, **18** 'Do [a]consider from this day [b]onward, from the twenty-fourth day of the ninth *month*; from the day when the temple of the Lord was founded, [c]consider: **19** Is the seed still in the barn? Even including the vine, the fig tree, the pomegranate and the olive tree, it has not borne *fruit*. Yet from this day on I will bless *you*.'"[xlv] They hadn't seen the fruit or the blessing from the work of their hands, but God said that now they would. There had to be faith to continue to believe and move in that direction. It is this same faith that we must continue to look toward to restore the foundations of America.

The second notable characteristic from Haggai is focus for the work that God calls us to. His intention is that our faith leads to getting to work, because if we have faith and get excited but don't do anything about it, nothing will get done. Focus provides us the ability to actually put into practice that which will make a difference in our lives. Once we hear the word of the Lord then we must determine if we are going to respond to it in faith with focus on God's direction or if we will ignore it in unbelief. The Israelites faced the same reality when Haggai spoke to them.**12** Then Zerubbabel the son of Shealtiel and Joshua the son of Jehozadak, the high priest, with all the remnant of the people [who had returned from exile], listened carefully *and* obeyed the voice of the Lord their God and the words of Haggai the prophet, since the Lord their God had sent him. And the people [reverently] feared the Lord. **13** Then Haggai, the Lord's messenger, spoke the Lord's message to the people saying, "'I am with you,' declares the Lord." [14] So the Lord stirred up the spirit of Zerubbabel the son of Shealtiel, governor of Judah, and the spirit of Joshua the son of Jehozadak, the high priest, and the spirit of all the remnant of the people; and they came and worked on the house of the Lord of hosts, their God (Haggai 1:12-14).[xlvi] It was their focus on the work that enabled them to begin what God had commanded them to do, and through it we see God blessing the work of their hands.

The next characteristic we notice that we need to accomplish God's plans is the fear of God. I'm sure that there were plenty of naysayers that didn't like what God had to say or how Zerubbabel and Joshua were leading. That is why the fear of the Lord is so important as we try to accomplish God's will on the earth. We must continually remind ourselves that we are not slaves to fear, but that we are children of God. Our actions cannot be dictated by other's opinions and fears if we want to focus on God's work for us. Haggai reminds us that we serve the God who owns all the silver and the gold. What can man do to us and what can they withhold from us when the Lord is on our side? Haggai also reminds us of the magnitude of the Lord's power and His work on behalf of His people.

Haggai 2:20-23

20-21 God's Message came a second time to Haggai on that most memorable day, the twenty-fourth day of the ninth month: "Speak to Zerubbabel, the governor of Judah:

21-23 "'I am about to shake up everything, to turn everything upside down and start over from top to bottom—overthrow governments, destroy foreign powers, dismantle the world of weapons and armaments, throw armies into confusion, so that they end up killing one another. And on that day'"—this is God's Message—"'I will take you, O Zerubbabel son of Shealtiel, as my personal servant and I will set you as a signet ring, the sign of my sovereign presence and authority. I've looked over the field and chosen you for this work.'" The Message of God-of-the-Angel-Armies.[xlvii]

Why would we fear man when God's power is so clear and evident? Let the name of the Lord be praised and let everyone in the temple cry glory.

The final characteristic that Haggai reminds us of is the faithfulness of God. When we see and remember the faithfulness of God in the past, it gives us strength and power to believe Him for the future. It is through that faithfulness that God establishes Himself as trustworthy and that we gain perspective and hope for the future. In the book of Haggai, we see the call to repentance and to work on the temple, we see the encouragement to the leaders to be strong and to put their hands to work, we see the people's response to follow the Lord's direction, and we see the Lord's promise to bless their future. In evaluating God's faithfulness, a few Scripture passages can help us interpret how things will turn out. The first is from Ezra, as he relays what happened with the temple.

Ezra 6:13-22

13 Then Tattenai, the governor of *the province* beyond the River, Shethar-bozenai and their colleagues carried out *the decree* with all diligence, just as King Darius had sent. **14** And the elders of the Jews [a]were successful in building through the prophesying of Haggai the prophet and Zechariah the son of Iddo. And [b]they finished building according to the command of the God of Israel and the decree of Cyrus, Darius, and Artaxerxes king of Persia. **15** This [c]temple was completed [d]on the third day of the month Adar; it was the sixth year of the reign of King Darius.

16 And the sons of Israel, the priests, the Levites and the rest of the [e]exiles, celebrated the dedication of this house of God with joy. **17** They offered for the dedication of this temple of God 100 bulls, 200 rams, 400 lambs, and as a sin offering for all Israel 12 male goats, corresponding to the number of the tribes of Israel. **18** Then they appointed the priests to their divisions and the Levites in their orders for the service of God [f]in Jerusalem, as it is written in the book of Moses.

[19] The exiles observed the Passover on the fourteenth of the first month. [20] For the priests and the Levites had purified themselves together; all of them were pure. Then they slaughtered the Passover *lamb* for all the exiles, both for their brothers the priests and for themselves. [21] The sons of Israel who returned from exile and all those who had separated themselves from the impurity of the nations of the land to *join* them, to seek the Lord God of Israel, ate *the Passover*. [22] And they observed the Feast of Unleavened Bread seven days with joy, for the Lord had caused them to rejoice, and had turned the heart of the king of Assyria toward them to [g]encourage them in the work of the house of God, the God of Israel.

How amazing to see the specifics of the completion of the work of the temple and the celebration that followed. What started out as a pretty pathetic effort of working on the temple became a glorious celebration because of the people's faith, focus, and fear of God and the faithfulness of the Lord. But still you may be wondering about the glory of the second temple. It is amazing that they finished it and were celebrating its completion, but where was the Shekinah glory and the greater glory that was still to come which Haggai had predicted? Well it didn't come when they thought it would, but it certainly came. Here is a passage of Scripture explaining the glory of the second temple.

Matthew 12:1-8

At that time Jesus went through the grainfields on the Sabbath. His disciples were hungry and began to pick some heads of grain and eat them. [2] When the Pharisees saw this, they said to him, "Look! Your disciples are doing what is unlawful on the Sabbath."

[3] He answered, "Haven't you read what David did when he and his companions were hungry? [4] He entered the house of God, and he and his companions ate the consecrated bread—which was not lawful for them to do, but only for the priests. [5] Or haven't you read in the Law that the priests on Sabbath duty in the temple desecrate the Sabbath and yet are innocent? [6] I tell you that something greater than the temple is here. [7] If you had known what these words mean, 'I desire mercy, not sacrifice,'[a] you would not have condemned the innocent. [8] For the Son of Man is Lord of the Sabbath."[xlviii]

Not just the glory came, but God Himself in the person of His Son Jesus. What an amazing answer to God's promise for a greater glory that was yet to come. Not only does Jesus say that He is greater than the temple but that He is over the Sabbath as well. Talk about the glory of God – the manifest presence of God was living, breathing, and walking around the temple. The glory of God revealed in real flesh and blood who not just filled the temple, but through His death and resurrection filled the whole earth with God's glory. We may not know the how or the when of God's faithfulness, but we can trust in it and in the future hope of the remnant.

We don't always know how the future glory will be greater than the former glory, but we can have faith that it will be. For Zerubbabel and Joshua, it was 500 years later in the form of Jesus Christ. I don't know if it will be in this lifetime or in this world, but the future glory *will be* greater than the former glory. We don't know exactly what it will look like, but we know it will be glorious. We know that the wolf and lamb will lie down, signifying the peace that will be present, and we know that there will be no more tears of pain or sorrow. We know that there will be an amazing dominion that we will be entrusted with - to rule over the new heavens and the new earth. We don't know the details or the when, but we can trust the hope of the future. Let's have faith to believe, have focus to do the work, the fear of God to believe He is able, and the faithfulness to see the work completed.

5 THE REMNANT WILL REMAIN — PRESERVATION IS GOD'S SPECIALTY

A remnant must remain in the Lord and following His ways. In order to remain that remnant, one must not give up and must not quit; then, no matter what, you will win. Be thou faithful unto death and you will receive the crown of life. The remnant is part of God's design. That is how He has performed in the past and that is how He will continue to operate.

Being part of the remnant is the grace of God. Remaining part of the remnant is also the grace of God, but God calls us to use that grace in a way that honors Him. As the remnant becomes more and more apparent and the visible church begins to shrink under the pressure of culture, there is a realization that God calls us to be participants in His grand story. He gives us commands like, "Do not give up gathering together in the household of God," and, "If you remain in Me and My words remain in you, then you can ask Me for whatever you want." But there is also a sober reminder in John 15 that without God we can do nothing. If we want to accomplish anything in life spiritually, it will only happen as a result of being connected to the vine. That is the ultimate and essential factor of bearing fruit — staying connected to the vine. That means two things: one is that we have to protect ourselves from being cut off unless God is pruning us, and the other is that we must be intentional about staying close to the vine.

If I eat too much pumpkin pie during the holiday season and I want to lose some weight, I might join a gym. But honestly, just joining a gym will not help me get in shape or lose weight. It's a good thing for me to join a gym, to make preparations to work out, and to be intentional about my plan, but if all I ever do is join, I will not get in shape and I will not lose weight. The same is true for us in the church. It is a great thing to go to church and to join and become a member of a local Bible-believing church, but if all I ever do is join, I will never get in shape spiritually and I will not be able to remain in the vine. Being part of the remnant is an honor, not a right. Just because you are part of the remnant, part of the church, or part of whatever, doesn't mean that you're good. It means that God has chosen you for a special purpose: to honor and serve Him. It's not a "sit back and relax, I'm done."

That's what Ezra communicated to the Israelites in chapter 9. He told them that they were part of the remnant but that if they didn't change some things and do things differently, there would be problems. They were breaking God's commands and had intermarried with the people of the land. Ezra was trying to get their attention and tell them that they needed to start following God's commands. As it says in Psalm 119:136, "I cry rivers of tears because nobody is living by your book."

When you are the remnant, it makes you more aware and willing to change. Hurricane Dorian just finished its devastation of the northern Bahamas, but if you live in the northern Bahamas and your property didn't flood while everyone else around you has lost everything, it would make you question why and make you more thankful. That needs to be our attitude as the remnant in the church. We need to be thankful that we are still around and take it as an opportunity to serve the Lord faithfully, and not squander it. That does not mean that nothing bad will happen to God's remnant, but it does mean that everything that happens to God's remnant will be filtered through God's sovereign will. Think about how the church began in Jerusalem and then suddenly there was persecution. There was a purpose to that persecution — to scatter the believers into every area of the earth. God will preserve, protect, and ultimately have a purpose for His remnant, and the gates of hell will not prevail against it.

The Israelites that survived Babylonian captivity knew that they were the remnant, but they weren't acting like it, and Ezra called them on it. They needed to turn toward God, repent of their sin, and start living according to His commandments. Ezra's sober words warned them of their impending destruction if they didn't change. As the remnant of the church, we need to understand similarly that just because we are the chosen, it does not relinquish us from all responsibility in our walk with Christ.

Revelation 12 makes it clear that we are at war with the enemy and that if we want to be part of the remnant that remains and overcome, we must hold fast to the testimony of Jesus and take our faith so seriously that we are not afraid to die because of it. "They overcame him by the blood of the Lamb and by the word of their testimony; they did not love their lives so much as to shrink from death (Revelation 12:11)."

Because we are part of the remnant, we can have the assurance of eternal life in heaven and overcome the fear of death. But in order to remain a part of that remnant, we must overcome every other fear as well. The fear of insignificance, the fear of loss, the fear of sickness, the fear of being left alone, the fear of poverty, the fear of failure, and every other fear that may try to rear its ugly head. We know that it takes Jesus to overcome the world (John 16:33) and that we overcome through faith in Jesus (1 John 5:5), but we will not maintain our faith in Jesus without knowing our true identity. The film *Overcomer* by the Kendrick Brothers addresses this truth, that at the core of our ability to overcome lies the truth of our identity. If we have the wrong identity, it will lead us to fall to our fears or temptations, but when we know who we are in Christ, there is nothing that can be taken from us because our faith in Christ cannot be stripped away from us. The good news is that God knows how to rescue the godly, as seen with people like Noah and Lot who were in much worse scenarios than we might find ourselves. The question is, are we tormented in our souls by the lawless deeds of those around us like they were?

2 Peter 2:4-9

[4] For if God did not spare angels when they sinned, but sent them to hell,[a] putting them in chains of darkness[b] to be held for judgment; [5] if he did not spare the ancient world when he brought the flood on its ungodly people, but protected Noah, a preacher of righteousness, and seven others; [6] if he condemned the cities of Sodom and Gomorrah by burning them to ashes, and made them an example of what is going to happen to the ungodly; [7] and if he rescued Lot, a righteous man, who was distressed by the depraved conduct of the lawless [8] (for that righteous man, living among them day after day, was tormented in his righteous soul by the lawless deeds he saw and heard)— [9] if this is so, then the Lord knows how to rescue the godly from trials and to hold the unrighteous for punishment on the day of judgment.[xlix]

God can simultaneously judge the wicked and save the righteous. You don't have to worry about what's going to happen to you if you serve the living God. You may be subject to some of the consequences of judgment through association, but in the end, you will be saved if you will simply remain.

What is your identity? Are you a parent, a husband or wife, an employee, a friend, a sports fan, an author? Whatever you think you are, those are roles that can be lost or stripped away, while your identity as a child of God, as a servant of the king, and as a follower of the Lord Jesus Christ cannot be taken from you. If you are leaning on any other identity than that of your standing in Christ, then you are standing on shaky ground. In order to overcome and in order to remain, Jesus makes some pretty serious statements to His followers. He's not waiting until it's convenient and Andrew and Peter are on vacation or it's the slow time of the season. He says, "Come and follow Me now. Leave your father. Leave your business. Come and follow Me." To a rich, young ruler He says, "Sell everything you have and give it to the poor." To another follower He says, "Let the dead bury their own dead. You come and follow Me." We also know that once we surrender our lives to Christ, He takes that very seriously and we are never to give up on that inheritance. Not that we have to work to keep it, but that we are never to willingly surrender it so that, as Peter says, "for it would have been better for them not to have known the way of righteousness, than having known it, to turn from the holy commandment delivered to them" (2 Peter 2:21). The point being that if we want to be part of the remnant that is going to remain until the end and overcome, we are going to have to at some point make a life-changing commitment and then continue to keep that faith that connects us to the vine. Jesus doesn't sugarcoat it; He tells it like it is. He says, "If you want to follow Me, you may have to give up house or home or brother or sister or mother or father for My sake." I hope you can say with me "my identity will forever be as a lover – loved by you."

That comes from this idea of identity, that your deepest and truest identity is what drives you. So what is it? We all have lots of identities, but who are you? Everything else can be stripped away, but who you are in Christ, the fact that you are a child of God, can never be taken from you. You can give it up or reject it, but it can't be taken. That's why identity is so important, because when you know who you are then everything else in life can line up. Once we make that life-changing commitment to receive Jesus, it is a daily realization that we are to take up our cross and follow Him. No matter what the cost. No matter what the circumstances. No matter what anybody else thinks or says. No matter what. Being part of the remnant that remains is a realization that if you don't quit you win. You can't be beat, it's impossible; you are undefeatable that is, unless you quit. If you don't quit, you win. End of story.

We have a large family with five kids, so one of the rules that we made in our family early on was that once you started an activity, a game, or a sports season, you couldn't quit. It was inconvenient and painful at times, but it taught the kids a good lesson. I understand that things happen sometimes, and changes are necessary, but it is way too easy to quit anything in our society —jobs, relationships, families, churches. It is a good reminder to us that we have to teach the character of patience and long-suffering better in the church. It is a fruit of the spirit that our society does not appreciate or esteem, but if we want to remain as part of the remnant, we will need to be long-suffering. Only then will you remain — not just for this life, but for all of eternity. God can preserve you from any attack, any plan, any enemy — even an entire army — but you have to commit not to surrender. As David said, "Though an army may encamp against me, my heart shall not fear; though war may rise against me; in this I will be confident" (Psalm 27:3). Or where he says, "For by You I can run through a troop, by my God I can leap over a wall" (Psalm 18:29).

THE CHURCH

This article by "Got Questions" is a great place to start our section about the church:

> **Question: "What does it mean that judgment begins at the house of God?"**
>
> **Answer:** Judgment is a recurring theme throughout the Bible (see Psalm 82:8). God's plan includes a final judgment on the wicked and all who reject the sacrifice of Jesus Christ as payment for their sins (Matthew 10:15; Romans 2:2; Hebrews 9:27; 10:26–27). A cursory reading of 1 Peter 4:17 seems to suggest that Christians may face God's judgment too: "For it is time for judgment to begin at the household of God; and if it begins with us, what will be the outcome for those who do not obey the gospel of God?" Is the "judgment" that begins at the house of God the same as the judgment of the wicked?
>
> The context of 1 Peter 4:17 explains more about the judgment that begins at the household of God. In this chapter, Peter is exhorting the church — the house of God — which was facing persecution, to persevere. The believers were also struggling to separate from the former worldly sins that had once enslaved them (verses 1–4). Peter reminds them that the wicked will face God's judgment (verse 5) but that believers in Christ must hold themselves to a higher standard than they once did. The "fiery trials" that they were facing were to help refine them like gold (verse 12).
>
> God allows difficulties and suffering in the lives of His people to purify them. When we are persecuted for the cause of Christ, we share in His sufferings (1 Peter 4:13–

14). And when we share His suffering, we know Him a little better (Philippians 3:10). Paul echoes this theme in Romans 8:17: "Now if we are children, then we are heirs — heirs of God and co-heirs with Christ, if indeed we share in his sufferings in order that we may also share in his glory." Part of God's judgment upon sin is physical suffering. When His own children experience such suffering, it is not for our harm but to make us more like Jesus. "Judgment" for the children of God can be considered discipline (Hebrews 12:4–11). It is designed to purge the sin from our lives and teach us obedience.

A loving father does not discipline the kids down the street, because they are not his. A father disciplines his own children. Likewise, the discipline of our heavenly Father begins at His own household, with His own children, the church. He is reserving for the wicked an ultimate, final judgment that His children will never experience (Romans 8:1). Scripture makes a distinction between God's purifying discipline of the church and His ultimate condemnation of the wicked: "When we are judged . . . by the Lord, we are being disciplined so that we will not be finally condemned with the world" (1 Corinthians 11:32).

In this present age, God allows painful circumstances in the lives of His own household, not to condemn but to mature, convict, and bring repentance (2 Corinthians 7:10). Through suffering we learn patience (James 1:2–4). This kind of judgment is to encourage us to abandon selfishness and draw nearer to Him (James 4:8). The ultimate, final judgment for unbelievers will be eternal separation from God, from life, and from all that is good and beautiful (Matthew 8:11–12; Revelation 21:8).

The judgment that begins at the household of God also includes church discipline. Church discipline is not for unbelievers but for believers. "What business is it of mine to judge those outside the church? Are you not to judge those inside?" (1 Corinthians 5:12). Believers are commanded to take responsibility for other followers of Christ who may be slipping or headed toward sin (James 5:20). First Corinthians 5:11–13 commands us to avoid fellowship with anyone claiming to be a brother or sister in Christ but who insists on maintaining a sinful lifestyle. Jesus lays out the process for church discipline in Matthew 18:15–17. Someone who has been confronted multiple times and warned that the choices he is making are in opposition to God needs to repent. If he refuses to listen to the church, we are to turn away from him in the hope that this drastic action will bring about repentance (see 2 Corinthians 2:7 and Galatians 6:1). As believers, we are to pursue holiness and encourage each other to pursue it, too (1 Peter 1:15–16). We are to judge ourselves as God's household (1 Corinthians 11:31). In this way, judgment begins in the house of God.

God's desire is that His people learn to walk in holiness and fellowship with Him (Romans 8:29). As any loving parent would do, God will bring unpleasant consequences upon His children for rebellion. He expects the ones He has redeemed by the blood of His son to set the example for the rest of the world. If the church is not in pursuit of holiness, the world sees no need to change its allegiance. So judgment begins in the household of God, with His own children, as He teaches us to live like Jesus.[1]

As we write about judgment coming to the church, there is an understanding that those inside or outside the church could become critical of the existing systems and hierarchy that are in place at their own churches. Some of that would be good if it resulted in repentance and reform, but some would use it as an excuse to attack well-meaning pastors and leaders who are doing the best they can in incredibly difficult situations, not to mention the pressure from the surrounding culture. Those of us inside the church must take responsibility for our own action or inaction and lead in the model of repentance. It is not going to be helpful for someone who casually attends church to take this material and run with it, so to speak, and either confront leadership as a bunch of hypocrites or abandon the church altogether. Neither of those options is going to accomplish godly reconciliation and change in the thinking and structure of the church. This has to be owned from within and it must be the pastors, staff, elders, deacons, council members, and leaders who come forward in their area of leadership to acknowledge that they have dropped the proverbial ball and need help. In a short period of time, the church is either going to rise up and be the church (and its membership will thin, as it will be perceived to be judgmental and unloving) or it will cease to lead and simply become an insignificant part of the whole. Neither option is appealing, but only one honors Christ and His death for His bride. The only other option is revival and awakening, and we all pray that God brings this. To prostitute the church as something where anything goes and there are no moral absolutes defames the name of Christ and cheapens His sacrificial death. As the church, we must rise up to speak the truth in love. We cannot speak the truth without love, and we cannot love without the truth. To pretend to love without truth is not love at all, it is the fear of man masqueraded as a church which fails to call out sin. Without widespread repentance, I am afraid that the entire system will have to fall in order to wake those who slumber beneath its surface. People have already begun to leave the local church in favor of loving Jesus from a distance — via TV, computer, radio, and the internet. That is not the church that Jesus established, but it is a convicting prescription of the real problem — that people see no value in being a part of the local church. Those of us inside the church are quick to point out that God commands us to be a part of a local fellowship of believers, yet we are slow to love, quick to judge, and constant in our refusal to change. American Christians are persecuted to the extent that they find it more fulfilling to love God from a distance rather than fight the battle in the church. Christians in hostile territories at least know who their accusers are, but in America it is the illusive reality of ingenuine people casting doubt and shame. That is one of the primary reasons why the church has been in steep decline and unable to reach millennials, because they sense something is amiss even if they can't put their finger on what it is. This must change, or the consequences will be dire. Moses said, "Let my people go!" and when Pharaoh did not comply, there were serious consequences. God will build His church, even if He has to burn it to the ground in order to get back to a proper foundation.

> The de-Christianizing of American public life and the open rejection of our historic Biblical foundations has resulted in a nation exploding in crime, sexual anarchy, wrecked homes and lives, now leaving massive human pain and carnage in its wake. Who is to blame for the dramatic downturn of American culture?...There are many other groups and movements where it is tempting to place the blame for the coarsening of American culture. But truth be told, the fault cannot be laid solely at the feet of the secularists —or the Progressives, or liberal academia, activist judges, hostile media, tone-deaf politicians, or any of the other groups openly attacking our foundations. No doubt each of these has contributed much to the damage done to the nation, but America is in deep trouble primarily because the Church in America today has become largely impotent and irrelevant—it no longer functions collectively as salt and light and is neither a preservative in the culture nor a guiding beacon for the nation to follow.[li]

In a study conducted by Barna, it was reported that only 10% of pastors are willing to address controversial topics that are referenced in the Bible like abortion, same-sex marriage, gambling, immigration and others. Barna reports, "They are concerned about being seen as political, not wanting to risk the loss of numbers of people or donations, and concern about the status of the church's non-

> profit designation...Conservative churches have a Biblical mandate to teach these things but are choosing to ignore the opportunity in favor of remaining safe...When Millennials and others describe Christian churches as 'irrelevant,' they are not talking about styles of music and dress codes as much as they are attacking the focal point of church services: the teaching. These days, people value their time too highly to invest it in hearing lectures on topics that do not intersect with their life questions and daily struggles.[lii]

In session 1 of his study "Radical," David Platt shares an illustration of the church and the difference between the peace time and war time attitudes that the church exemplifies:

> In the Christian church today, we don't have a war time faith. We have a peace time faith. In war time you are always asking what can I sacrifice to advance the cause? How can I spend every resource I have? How can I best contribute to accomplishing the mission? Making sacrifices not indulging in pleasantries. In peace time, pleasantries are the name of the game – asking questions like how can we be more comfortable? How can we have more fun and how can we try new pleasures that we never have experienced before. There is a war time and a peace time way to approach life and Christianity. You can see the difference between the two in a ship now docked in a harbor of Long Beach, California called the Queen Mary. It was built earlier in the 20th century as a luxury liner for the whole array of indulgences designed to entice wealthy patrons. It could fit up to 3,000 wealthy patrons on it at one time. Larger more massive then even the Titanic. What's interesting is that for six years during World War II while the country was in a state of national emergency, they took this same ship and called upon it to help with transporting troops. And all of a sudden, this ship was transformed from a luxury liner into a source of transport for troops.

> Whereas before 3,000 people could get on the ship, now it could transport 15,000 soldiers at a time. The whole ship was completely turned upside down to accommodate accomplishing a mission instead of accommodating pleasures for wealthy patrons. You go today to this ship that is a museum because of its history and what you can see is that some places they have it designed for troop transport and you can see 8 bunks high where people would sleep and everything and every detail was used to accomplish mission. And then you can look at another room and you can see it designed as a luxury liner for people to enjoy the pleasures of the ship. I would ask you which image better describes Christianity in our context today? In our lives, our families, and our church – I would put before us to consider the cost, ladies and gentlemen.[liii]

The church is not a building. The church is not a country club. The church is not a place to simply gather socially or to find friends or spouses who espouse similar values. The church is the body of our Lord Jesus Christ, who is the head of the church. We are the bride of Christ, prepared in holiness to be joined and wed to our Lord and Savior. We have failed to recognize the necessity that Jesus clearly understood, that it was dangerous to gather crowds who were not committed to the cross for the purpose of growth and momentum. Whenever Jesus began to draw crowds, He would disappear. When they would try and make Him king by force, He would walk the other way. As soon as He started to gain momentum, He would say something controversial that would drive people away like, "Whoever wants to be one of My disciples must eat My flesh and drink My blood." What? The disciples must have been dumbfounded, thinking, "Finally we're gaining traction and gathering supporters and then Jesus always has to go and do something to drive them away!" Like when he said, "Let the dead bury their own dead you come and follow Me." Jesus cared greatly for the crowds and for the poor and sick and He helped them continually and sacrificially. But as far as those who were committed followers, He would continually challenge and drive them away rather than beg them to stay. He loved and ministered to all, but His disciples were few in number and completely committed. We have tried to gather all to save some, but it appears that Jesus did just the opposite: to challenge all in order to keep the few.

We know that the church looked much different after His death and resurrection because of the power of the Holy Spirit. Thousands were added to the number of the church in a matter of days. Jesus' pattern of ministry does not need to become a law to us for small ministries or churches, but it certainly should give us pause about how we think about our approach to ministry. Jesus never watered down expectations, created loopholes, or made it easier to become one of His followers. If anything, we see that Jesus raised the bar so high to be one of the members of His community that only a very few elected to give up all to follow Him. Does that sound like the church in America today?

6 THE CHURCH IN AMERICA IS GUILTY OF SYNCRETISM – WITH POLITICS

2 Kings 17:30-33

30 The people from Babylon made Sukkoth Benoth, those from Kuthah made Nergal, and those from Hamath made Ashima; 31 the Avvites made Nibhaz and Tartak, and the Sepharvites burned their children in the fire as sacrifices to Adrammelek and Anammelek, the gods of Sepharvaim. 32 They worshiped the Lord, but they also appointed all sorts of their own people to officiate for them as priests in the shrines at the high places. 33 They worshiped the Lord, but they also served their own gods in accordance with the customs of the nations from which they had been brought.[liv]

Syncretism is the combination of two different cultural identities. This is not always a bad thing, but when it leads to sin and the lowering of standards that the Lord has given us, it becomes a serious problem. The nation of Israel did not abandon God completely at first. They began by intermarrying with unbelievers and adopting their customs, adding them to their own. Sometimes they would go to mass and sometimes they would go to temple. That is why God set such clear boundaries with the Israelites about intermarriage and why He so stringently demanded the complete destruction of the opposing nations, because He saw this day coming. As the people of Israel began to get more and more comfortable with opposing cultures and practices, they began distancing themselves further and further from God.

This same phenomenon has happened in America today. Christians unequally yoke themselves to unbelievers on a regular basis and the result has been tragic. Now our country is filled with those who once called themselves Christians but now, through marriage, apathy, distraction, or choice, have left their first love. The church has tolerated this negative influence to such an extent that it has become something other than the church. One of the areas where this has become the most noticeable is in the area of politics. No matter what your political view, both Republicans and Democrats in the last 20 years have sacrificed tenets of their faith to try and win elections. There is a better way. The church was called by God to be separate and above the influence of government so that it can be free to speak the truth. Not that it is wrong to be politically active or involved in government as a Christian, but anyone can see that the government has influenced the church far more than the church has influenced the government in recent years. That is not how it used to be. When this nation started, the church was an authoritative voice that directed the government and gave advice and discernment. If there is to be lasting and revolutionary change in this country it will not come through a political party, it will come through the Gospel of Jesus Christ. The next Great Awakening isn't going to happen because we narrowly vote in a "Christian" candidate. It will come through the prayer and repentance of the church. I am all for voting for Christian candidates, and I pray for just laws and godly servants who serve in the government, but ultimately that is not the answer. The answer does not lie in having the right Supreme Court justices or even in legislating morality. These things may help, they may be nice, and they might make our lives easier or make us feel good, but ultimately, they won't be the answer. The answer lies in Christ alone and in the release of His sovereign grace to uncover blind eyes and to turn hearts toward Him and away from sin. If we spoke up for and defended the name of Christ even half as much as we did our favorite political candidate, there would be revival in this nation again.

God has called the church to carry the keys of His kingdom, but instead we have been so busy trying to carry the keys to the kingdom of this world that we have dropped the keys that God called upon us to carry. God has called His church to be the spiritual caretakers and overseers, and instead we have tried to become the physical stewards and rulers. The church is supposed to be proclaiming and building the kingdom of God, but in America this line has become blurred so that it is no longer clear which is which. God has called us in the church to be a voice of reason, declaring the wisdom of God for our nation. Instead, we are begging political candidates to see our point of view. To use a baseball analogy, it's as if God has called us to be the scouts to give counsel, advice, and input and instead we have decided that is not good enough and we want to be one of the coaches instead. When that doesn't work, instead of returning to the place God has called us, we say, "Well, if being an assistant coach isn't working, I should be the head coach. And if that doesn't work, I'll be the general manager..." Soon we will be vying for God's job as owner. The church in America must give up its syncretistic allegiance to political candidates and proclaim the word of God with boldness in a way that transforms our nation spiritually, not politically. We must be the scouts and watchmen that God has called us to be so that when the time comes to speak the Word of God with boldness we can, because we are not tied to a political agenda.

Regardless of political persuasion, the church must once again take up the mantle of being the influencer of culture, rather than being influenced by culture and government. If culture and government reject the church, then so be it. At least then the church will be that which God has called her to be – holy even as He is holy. God is bigger than our nation. He is the King of Kings and the Lord of Lords. He is not just King of our nation He is King of the Universe. I love our nation. I pray for our nation. I hope that nothing tragic happens to our nation. But our hope in the church cannot be in our government. Our hope is in the one who has the government upon His shoulders and there is no end to the extent of His peace. He shall be called the Wonderful Counselor, Mighty God, Everlasting Father, and Prince of Peace. Are you putting your trust and allegiance in the government or the leaders of the government, or are you worshipping the creator of government?

This does not mean that we should abandon the political realm as the church. It means that we must influence the political realm and not let it influence us. When Jesus come back again, He's not just coming back to be head of the church. He will rule over every sphere of society including the government. Some of the greatest justices that have ever been accomplished have been within the political system. In England, William Wilberforce's fight against slavery took long, arduous years that were painful and costly, but the abolition of slavery is one of mankind's greatest victories over human injustice. This came about through his involvement in politics. Although he was a deeply spiritual man who considered abandoning politics to become a pastor, Wilberforce's friends encouraged him to take his faith to fight against slavery in the political realm. As the church, we cannot be deterred, we cannot acquiesce, and we cannot compromise any longer with the culture of politics. The church has a higher accountability than the government, and when Christ returns, He will evaluate the church based on the purity of its message and the love of its people, not on the amount of influence it has in the government. If culture, government, and people reject the church, then that is their detrimental prerogative, but the church can no longer reject the message of God for the sake of culture, government, people, or an election.

God has given His authority to the church and the church has relinquished that authority in the name of understanding and compassion. God has called us to be like John the Baptist who said to the king, "You should not commit adultery," and like Jesus, who embraced humility by being in very nature God, but did not consider equality with God as something to be grasped. We are called as Christians and the church to exercise authority and love. God has given us the keys to His church, and we have laid them down and said, "We don't want them." Jesus said, "Whatever you bind on earth will be bound in heaven and whatever is loosed on earth will be loosed in heaven." Instead of exercising authority, we have taken the weak and easy road where we do not wrestle with sin and corruption, choosing to sweep it under the rug instead or dismiss it as love because, after all, we must love. The problem is that the most loving thing to do in the face of rebellion and sin and debauchery is to call it out and to call people away from it. As individuals and as the church, we have failed to call out sin and we have broken the tipping point with abortion, definition of marriage, and even the battle for sexual identity. God calls us to lovingly exercise our authority, but instead we have turned the other cheek. There is a time to turn the other cheek and there is a time to exercise authority. We have to return to being the voice in the wilderness crying out to prepare the way of the Lord, calling people to holiness, and carrying the message of repentance because without that, America is in big trouble.

There are just as many white Americans guilty of disrespecting, dishonoring, and defaming President Obama and his leadership as there are African Americans guilty of the same thing toward President Trump. That is not an easy truth to deal with, but in reality, we have loved our political party or our political candidate more than our brothers and sisters in Christ and more than Jesus Himself. We have not stood up for the truth and we have inappropriately kept silent for the sake of our cause and what we have desired. We have been duplicitous by not standing up to those in authority and calling out sin. When President Obama stated that we were not a Christian nation, where was the correction? And when President Trump made racially divisive comments and actions, who stood for the truth? Our answer in the church cannot and should not be political candidates of any party. We have loved our way more than The Way. We have loved our truth more than The Truth. And we have lived for our lives instead of for The Life.

7 THE CHURCH IN AMERICA IS GUILTY OF IDOLATRY

Looking at the book of Isaiah, we see in the first five chapters that God is talking to His people. This is not a message to outsiders, but to those who are His own. If we look at these verses, we will recognize and hear problems that are very similar to those we are faced with today in America. God is angry because His chosen people have rejected Him and turned their back on Him. America has plenty of people who do not know or serve God, but that is not our primary problem. No, America will be disciplined because those who *do* know or have known God have forsaken Him and His will. Those who have been raised in the church and who know the truth, those who are in the church and do not live according to the Gospel, and those who were a part of the church and have rejected or walked away from Christ are the people that Isaiah was talking to then and who these words are applicable for now:

Isaiah 1:2-3

[2] Listen, O heavens! Pay attention, earth!
This is what the Lord says:
"The children I raised and cared for
have rebelled against me.
[3] Even an ox knows its owner,
and a donkey recognizes its master's care—

but Israel doesn't know its master.[lv]

Isaiah 1:21-23

21 See how Jerusalem, once so faithful,
has become a prostitute.
Once the home of justice and righteousness,
she is now filled with murderers.
22 Once like pure silver,
you have become like worthless slag.
Once so pure,
you are now like watered-down wine.
23 Your leaders are rebels,
the companions of thieves.
All of them love bribes
and demand payoffs,
but they refuse to defend the cause of orphans
or fight for the rights of widows.[lvi]

Isaiah 2:6-8

6 For the Lord has rejected his people,
the descendants of Jacob,
because they have filled their land with practices from the East
and with sorcerers, as the Philistines do.
They have made alliances with pagans.
7 Israel is full of silver and gold;
there is no end to its treasures.
Their land is full of warhorses;
there is no end to its chariots.
8 Their land is full of idols;
the people worship things they have made
with their own hands.[lvii]

Isaiah 5:4-6

[4] What more could I have done for my vineyard
that I have not already done?
When I expected sweet grapes,
why did my vineyard give me bitter grapes?

[5] Now let me tell you
what I will do to my vineyard:
I will tear down its hedges
and let it be destroyed.
I will break down its walls
and let the animals trample it.
[6] I will make it a wild place
where the vines are not pruned and the ground is not hoed,
a place overgrown with briers and thorns.
I will command the clouds
to drop no rain on it.[lviii]

None of that sounds very good — and that's not even the worst of it. It doesn't take much to see that if we replaced "they" or "Israel" with "America," the statements would still be true, thus indicating that America is on the same path of destruction as ancient Israel.

Looking at these verses in Isaiah, we see that the people of Israel had great excess and that it corrupted them. They were vain and jealous and chased after money, just like us in America today. They were selfish and only thought of themselves. They treated money as their god. Are we so different today, with our mega churches, Sistine chapels, bookstores, and espressos? I am no different. I wonder which temples Jesus would clear and which ones He would pray in. Which churches are taking advantage of people and taking their money for personal gain and which churches are giving to the poor, taking care of the orphans and widows, and pouring money into spreading the Gospel? We may never know on this side of heaven, but I know that there are both and that the church in general needs to repent for not being better with their finances and for not being better stewards of what God has entrusted to them. In this way, the church has modeled the world instead of setting itself apart. Just like in corporate America, it is the biggest and best, the fastest growing, the most innovative, and the most successful that receive all of the attention and accolades. These are all good things and blessings, but how is it different from the world? Is this what John meant by "being in the world, but not of the world"? We need to ask these difficult questions because some churches may be growing, but culture is crumbling all around us. When Jesus comes back, He's not going to go to the government and say, "What did you do? Look at this mess!" He's going straight to the church to ask, "What have you done with My bride? Where are My people? How have you taken care of My little ones, My neglected, My forgotten, and My despised?" We in the church can't control how culture, government, or industry responds, but we can be faithful with the message and the resources that God has given to us.

In his book *Something Needs To Change*, David Platt says, "In Luke 5 Jesus touched a man whom society deemed untouchable and unclean. Jesus didn't turn from need; He ran to need. The Gospels are filled with accounts when Jesus alleviated suffering, healed sickness, and treated people with mercy. However, if we're not careful, it's dangerously possible to live our Christian lives insulated and isolated from urgent need around us. A Christians' impulse should be to run to need and proclaim the goodness, grace, and favor of our God to those in need."[lix]

Like Jesus, we need to run to the need that is all around us. We need to stop adulterating our churches and idolizing religious figures. God said that He would not share His glory with another. Instead, He calls us to take up our cross and follow Him on the narrow road that He has called us to. We must be free to carry that cross and God will bring judgment upon the church and upon those who do not allow His people to serve Him in righteousness and justice. "Let my people go!" God declares to those who hold His people captive. "It is because of you that this judgment is released on the earth." Something has to change indeed, and God does not delight in bringing it to bear, but His hand has been forced for the sake of His people and for the ones yet to come. Look and you shall see the salvation of the Lord, for there will be no permanent oppression of His people that will be permitted. For those who make themselves bond servants of the Lord Jesus Christ, they will be made free. For if the son of God sets you free, you shall be free indeed.

Is the church more and more like the world, or is the world looking more and more like the church? Whether it's pastors, speakers, or musicians, we all have our favorites who we follow, subscribe to, or buy products from. In the world, we call them "idols," but in church we call them "leaders." The fact that we have leaders is not the problem, it's how we treat and esteem them. Respect and honor for God's anointed is an appropriate behavior, but we need to recognize the thin line between a respected believer and an idol. By looking at the percentage of leaders, pastors, and musicians that have fallen into sin, I think we can see that we have created an unhealthy and destructive pattern for which we need to repent. The biggest problem is that it is not producing fruit that will last. That is God's claim in Isaiah 5. We have become enamored with Christian personalities, preachers, leaders, and musicians and statistics show that the percentage of committed Christians is actually less now.

We have lulled ourselves to sleep, patting ourselves on the back because we can fill a stadium or are part of a mega church. All the while, Christians grow less committed and culture is suffering all around us. We have been duped into believing that we are making a significant difference, when in reality we have been content to enjoy the temperate climate on our island while the mainland burns to the ground. It is like we have created our own little islands of Christian bliss in the middle of chaos, depravity, and poverty, all the while patting ourselves on the back for a job well done. "For example, although the number of megachurches has increased at a brisk rate (from 600 in 2000 to 1,642 today), at the same time, national church attendance is steadily falling from (41 percent down to 36 percent), and the median size of all churches is only seventy congregants. So the impressive growth of megachurches is a false positive."[lx]

That does not mean that the church has not done great things or that it has not made a significant difference. Everyone's experience and church is different, and we know the tremendous value of lost people being saved as the angels in heaven rejoice when even one sinner repents. But every church must face the reality of the statistics and culture, which demonstrate that we are losing ground with the percentage of Christians, the younger generation, the understanding of what it means to follow Christ, and the very reality of being a disciple. We should not be celebrating that we have been able to maintain the status quo in our own little bubble while everything crumbles around it. That sounds to me like the one who hid his talent in the ground and had a really good excuse for it. This is not a time to celebrate what the church has done, it is a time to repent, recalibrate, and ask God to be the Lord of the church again because we have made a mess of it in America. The proof is in how far we have fallen, the current culture, the legislation, and the court rulings which have been detrimental to the future of the church.

8 THE CHURCH IN AMERICA IS GUILTY OF FAVORITISM — NEGLECTING THE POOR

In the church, we judge ourselves according to the Old Testament with regard to our accumulation of wealth and according to the New Testament with regard to our giving. The truth of the matter is that Jesus actually verifies the concept of the tithe in the New Testament and challenges the accumulation of wealth. Jesus commends the distribution of wealth, not the accumulation of it. That does not mean that He commands all to sell all that they have like He asked of the rich, young ruler, but it should be a potential option. That is, after all, how Jesus lived. We as Americans need to wrestle with the fact that we live in luxury while countless others live in abject poverty. Does it even bother us? How much is too much? What have our churches done to alleviate this concept of entitlement? The church is guilty of taking from the poor and giving to the rich instead of taking from the rich and giving to the poor. We have had it backwards and the "name it and claim it" theology has destroyed an entire generation of the church. The idea that you can have anything you want if you have enough faith scoffs in the face of God and all of His teachings. To believe that God wants to bless you more than He wants you to be obedient or follow His teachings has permeated our churches to the point that people cannot even hear the difference between needs and wants anymore. It is tantamount to the parent who fails to discipline their child and gives them whatever they want. We all know where that leads: to a spoiled child. That is what the church has taught for decades in terms of matters of finance and possessions.

I bet you can think of 10 other financial tenants of the faith that Jesus and the Bible teach about without even looking them up. Yet, if there was one primary financial message that the church has taught over the past decades, it is resoundingly that God desires to bless you and how you can be blessed. God *does* desire to bless you, but that is like the number 10 priority not number 1 with regard to finances. In fact, in Jesus' teachings, the blessing that He taught about was always related to the rewards of giving. "Give and it will be given unto you a good measure pressed down, shaken together, running over..." "Give in secret to your Father in heaven and your Father who sees you in secret will reward you openly." God desires that you give. God desires that you are a good steward. God desires that you help the poor. God desires that you stay out of debt. God desires that you do not serve money. God desires that you do not worry about money. God desires that you do not cheat people and you are fair with money. There are a lot of other areas that the church could legitimately be teaching about money that God cares about, but it has overwhelmingly taught that God desires to bless you. Why do you think that is? Where has that led us? How has that worked out for us? How are we different than the world?

In the church, we have not taught people to live below their means. We look exactly like the world with regard to our finances. We have put the same value on finances that the world does. If we looked at the finances of the church, what percentage of the church's annual income goes toward missions? How about to help the poor? What about for a building fund? I think we would be sadly disappointed to see that in our churches we have set up the same standards as most American people have in their personal finances.

This focus on the blessing of the Lord and on the accumulation of wealth has led to a weak and misguided church. There must be repentance in the area of finances and how the church has taught for its own benefit that those who are rich are the blessed of God. The truth is that Jesus didn't have this focus. He pointed out the old widow who gave everything and praised her above all others. Jesus didn't teach His disciples how they could get a new boat. He taught them how to forget about their boat and fish for men. Jesus didn't teach people how to avoid suffering, he taught them how to endure it. Jesus didn't teach a preference for the rich and successful, he taught us to judge by the heart. In your church today, which person would have greater honor: the "poor" restaurant worker trying to make ends meet who is a faithful servant, husband, and father, or the rich and successful businessman who cheated on his wife, divorced, and is now remarried? Who would be chosen as the next leader, elder, or even pastor? Be honest. Why is that? It is because the church is off-center with regard to teaching about finances and the perspective of success being equal to blessing. Something has to change indeed.

In his book, *The Purpose Driven Life*, Rick Warren teaches that God is much more concerned about your character than He is about your comfort. This has not been the focus or the teaching of the church at large and that needs to change. Repent, for the kingdom of God is at hand. That is not to say that the opposite is true either — that it is more spiritual or beneficial to be poor — but we have unknowingly become an unbiblical church in our teaching about finances. We are meant to evaluate people in God's house based on character and Christlikeness, not based on finances or success in the eyes of the world. This is a gross injustice and the temple must be cleansed.

In the book *Radical*, David Platt tells a story about a newspaper article that he saw when he was getting ready to go on a mission trip:

"I remember when I was preparing to take my first trip to

Sudan in 2004. The country was still at war, and the Darfur region in western Sudan had just begun to make headlines. A couple of months before we left, I received a Christian news publication in the mail. The front cover had two headlines side by side. I'm not sure if the editor planned for these particular headlines to be next to each other or if he just missed it in a really bad way. On the left one headline read, 'First Baptist Church Celebrates New $23 Million Building.' A lengthy article followed, celebrating the church's expensive new sanctuary. The exquisite marble, intricate design, and beautiful stained glass were all described in vivid detail. On the right was a much smaller article. The headline for it read, 'Baptist Relief Helps Sudanese Refugees.' Knowing I was about to go to Sudan, my attention was drawn. The article described how 350,000 refugees in western Sudan were dying of malnutrition and might not live to the end of the year. It briefly explained their plight and sufferings. The last sentence said that Baptists had sent money to help relieve the suffering of the Sudanese. I was excited until I got to the amount. Now, remember what was on the left: 'First Baptist Church Celebrates New $23 Million Building.' On the right the articles said, 'Baptists have raised $5,000 to send to refugees in western Sudan.' Five thousand dollars. That is not enough to get a plane into Sudan, much less one drop of water to people who need it. Twenty-three million dollars for an elaborate sanctuary and five thousand dollars for hundreds of thousands of starving men, women, and children, most of whom were dying apart from faith in Christ. Where have we gone wrong? How did we get to the place where this is actually tolerable? Indeed, the cost of nondiscipleship is great. The cost of believers not taking Jesus seriously is vast for those who don't know Christ and devastating for those who are starving and suffering around the world. But the cost of nondiscipleship is not paid solely by them. It is paid by us as well."[lxi]

I don't think I need to spend time listing the many Bible verses which extoll helping the poor. I think we already know them. The issue is that we are not living like we do.

9 THE CHURCH IN AMERICA IS GUILTY OF IGNORING GOD'S WORD

Mother Angelica, who was the founder of the Eternal Word Television Network, knew what the result of ignoring God's Word would become. Listen to what she had to say about a World Youth Day in Denver and subsequent newspaper article in 1993.

> At one point during the festivities at World Youth Day, there was a drama of the Stations of the Cross that featured a woman playing the part of Jesus. Mother Angelica read an article from *The Denver Post* that called it "ironic... since the Catholic Church won't ordain women as priests."
>
> "No, it's not ironic," Mother Angelica responded, "it's blasphemous."
>
> She spent the next 20 minutes or so calling out the "Liberal Church in America" for its dissent from orthodoxy destroying good things about the Church and its failure to attract new converts to the faith.
>
> "I'm tired of your tricks," she said. "I'm tired of your deceits. I'm tired of you constantly making a crack, and the first thing you know there's a hole, and all of us fall into it.
>
> "I'm so tired of you Liberal Church in America. And everything you've ever done is done in silence. Nothing, nothing

you've done, from your witchcraft, to your anagrams, to your centering prayer, to all this Earth spirituality, to replacing holy water with sand. To destroying our churches and closing churches that are viable and ready to go.

"No, this is not an accident. We've swallowed this now for 30 years, and I'm tired of it. We've swallowed enough of your idea of God. You have really no God, you have no dogma, no doctrine, and no authority...You don't believe in the Eucharist, you don't believe in the Immaculate Conception, you don't believe in the Virgin Birth... you don't believe in religious life, you don't believe in being a spouse of Christ.

"You *do* believe in teaching to little children of the 3rd grade sex education. You do believe in forcing centering prayer and forcing inclusive language upon us. And now you depict Jesus as a woman. You are sick.

"But I admit you have a right to your ways. You have a right to think your own thoughts. You have a right before God and this nation to do what you do. But I resent you trying to destroy the Catholicity of the simple and the poor and the elderly by your ways. I'm not going to accept that.

"I'm a Roman Catholic. I'm a Latin rite. I believe in God as Father, creator of heaven and earth. I believe that Jesus is his Son, his only Son. I believe that the Spirit proceeds from Father and Son, that there is a Trinity. I believe that Baptism puts into my heart and soul that wondrous Trinity. It is not an initiation into a club.

"I believe that he died and he suffered and he rose. He rose. It wasn't the rising of the resurrection of Jesus in the thoughts of men. It wasn't something we have to remem-

> ber. It was a physical resurrection. I believe in that, you don't.
>
> "But you spread your errors to children. And our children don't even know the Eucharist anymore. They don't understand that that is the Blessed Sacrament, that that is the body and blood, soul, and divinity of Jesus. Your catechisms are so watered down, they say nothing but love your neighbor. No, you've got to love God first. [...]
>
> "We're not going to go for all those crazy things that you're pushing out as new, and cultural, and American. They're not American. America was built on God. America was built to trust in God. And you've made it pagan. You've helped to make this nation pagan.
>
> "Because you have no spirituality that attracts. Your religious orders are going down. You don't have vocations, and you don't even care. Your whole purpose is to destroy.
>
> "You're not builders, you're destroyers. I'm not going to take that anymore. I am proud to be Roman Catholic."[lxii]

Whether you refer to yourself as catholic, protestant, evangelical, or simply Christian there is a realization that the authority of Scripture is and has been under attack. This attack has resulted in the weakening of the church, the defaming of God's name, and the misunderstanding of the Gospel in America. According to Ralph Drollinger who wrote the article "Theological Liberalism in America," we have seen the progressive degradation of the authority of Scripture in America since the early 1800s.

He notes that in 1805, a man by the name of Henry Ware

> was elected President at Harvard, which was a conservative theological institution at the time. Shortly after his election, Ware denied the biblical doctrine of the Trinity and became a Unitarian. Around that same time, a nationally known pastor in Boston by the name of William Ellery Channing did the same thing, and reason and rationalism were born in America. Around that same time, Universalism, which teaches that all will be saved based on God's desire, began to gain traction as well, and Nathaniel Taylor introduced his New Haven Theology, which denied the sinful nature of man and his need for repentance. Horace Bushnell took this a step further and taught that Christ's death wasn't substitutionary, but only an example of sacrificial love, thus creating the historical Jesus who was not needed for salvation, only to perceive from a distance for his admirable qualities.

In his description of neo-orthodoxy, Drollinger notes the next theological missteps:

> Kant and Schleiermacher add yet another aberrant confluence of sweeping theological error: Neo-Orthodoxy. This "new" orthodoxy in essence represents full-blown subjectivism — truth is "what it means to me." Gone was the propositional authority of the revealed truth of Scripture. Neo-Orthodoxy promoted (and today promotes) pietistic awe: true religion is based on one's inner, subjective experience. Perhaps a good illustration of the prevalence of present-day Neo-Orthodoxy is this: "Bible studies" where individuals state, "This is what this passage means to me" in the place of an objective study of authorial intent. Accordingly, the Bible gets its authority from my faith, versus the other way around. The applicable takeaway point? Truth is derived from how I feel about things: my feelings are my authority, not God's Word.

Drollinger notes that what eventually came forth was a higher criticism of Scripture that questioned and cast doubt on the validity of Scripture itself:

> The last major aberrant theological wave to encroach upon the American church prior to the Social Gospellers coming on the scene was a theologically intellectual movement that cast doubt on the authenticity of the source documents which comprise the Scriptures themselves. Baur, Strauss, and Wellhausen were the major proponents of this assault. Baur, in his intellectual pride, asserted that neither Paul, Peter, nor John wrote the NT books attributed to their names. Strauss proposed that the Gospel accounts were a myth. Wellhausen chose to discount the miracles of the Bible. All three popularized a critical approach to Scripture, casting doubt in the minds of believers. The result: Man became the overt judge of Scripture, versus Scripture being the judge of man.[lxiii]

I would like to point out that these teachings and beliefs were conceived and birthed in the church. In many of the previously respected churches and theological institutions — not just in America, but in the world — it is the church (Jesus' bride) that failed to successfully refute these teachings. The church which is to bind and loose. The church which holds the keys. The church which Jesus said He would build. The church which Jesus cared, loved, and died for has prostituted itself and she must repent. To much of the church today, the word that became flesh has become the flesh without words. Jesus is simply seen as a historical figure with little or no authority, whose kind acts show us how to love. When in all reality, He is the Alpha and the Omega, the beginning and the end. And when He returns again, it will not be in the humility of a child but in the exaltation of a mighty warrior coming to judge the world of sin.

When Jesus stood up to read the Isaiah scroll in the temple, He didn't argue that it wasn't really Isaiah, it was actually such and such. Why do we think it would be good to question what Jesus didn't question? Jesus didn't question the authenticity of the Scriptures; He questioned the leaders who interpreted them for their own benefit. If your primary job description is getting people to question the Bible and you are trying to do that with your work, you might want to consider another line of work. I don't think that's going to look very good on your "resume" when you get to heaven and stand before Jesus – just sayin. In reality, what has happened is that we have embraced the Marcion heresy which rejects the Old Testament and diminishes the role of the Father. This is done by emphasizing the role of Christ at the exclusion and expense of the Father and the Holy Spirit. No one is suggesting that we diminish the work of Christ, but when you diminish any of the Trinity, you end up in error. The idea that Jesus' example to love trumps all has removed authority to rebuke sin or the power to overcome it. When in reality, God is love and that love contains both justice and mercy. We cannot portray God as justice without mercy and we cannot portray God as mercy without justice. Love is both justice and mercy, and without that understanding, any definition of God or love is destined to fail and come short of God's intended wholeness.

10 THE CHURCH IN AMERICA IS GUILTY OF SIN — EXAMPLES OF MORAL FAILURES

I don't think it's really necessary to name names here. There are countless examples of prominent Christian leaders that have been accused of or confessed to everything from embezzlement, to substance abuse, to physical abuse, to homosexuality, to outright atheism. There is no shortage of examples of moral failures in church leadership. On one hand, that should not surprise us, but on the other hand, it should scare us to death because we need to take seriously the care of Christ's bride. The call of overseer is a noble work and it is not to be taken lightly. Not all of it is true either. We know that part of the enemy's work is to discredit God's stewards and His church. We must remember that ultimately, we do not find our identity in a ministry, leader, or even a church. Each of us is a part of Christ's own body and Jesus will never let us down or turn us away.

While the number of moral failures on the part of pastors, priests, or Christian leaders is significantly troubling, almost as disturbing is the pedestal on which we put these leaders. We should all keep in mind "but for the grace of God, there go I," but when pastors and leaders are given such ultimate power and success, in the past it has only been a matter of time before they fell. We see nothing different in the Old Testament. The saddest instances are when we hear of abuse and neglect toward those who are young or weak. There is no excuse for this, as the very people that the leaders of the church are called to support, protect, and empower are the ones being preyed on. [6] "But if you cause one of these little ones who trusts in me to fall into sin, it would be better for you to have a large millstone tied around your neck and be drowned in the depths of the sea. [7] What sorrow awaits the world, because it tempts people to sin. Temptations are inevitable, but what sorrow awaits the person who does the tempting" (Matthew 18:6-7).[lxiv]

That is why God says that judgment must begin in the house of God, because that is where the greatest responsibility lies. We are not talking about unnecessary guilt for those who serve in the church, but judgment for those who intentionally and willfully corrupt and malign Christ's bride. There will be no pause, no error, and no recourse, only the strong hand of the living God manifested in power. God cares too much about His bride for His Son to see it go on without intervention. It is not embarrassing to God to see it exposed, He already knew about it. It is wicked and evil to see it hidden; it grieves God's heart. All that is secret will be exposed and all that is hidden will be made known. God demands the purification of His bride. He is not coming back for a backslidden, abusive, neglectful church and it will be purged. This purge has only begun, but it will continue until He is taken seriously and there is great reform. It is part of the judgment that must take place because of what the church has become and what the church has allowed. The name of Christ must be cleansed from association with those who abuse, neglect, and despise His bride. He is a jealous God, and zeal for His house will consume Him. If you thought the clearing of the temple was bad when Jesus lived, then prepare yourselves to see true cleansing in the New Testament church, which knows better and has the tools to prevent it.

In Amos chapter 5 verse 6 it says, "Seek the Lord and live, lest He break out like fire in the house of Joseph, and devour it, with no one to quench it in Bethel." There is so much at stake at this time because God is clear: seek Him and live. But if the church seeks herself, or seeks her leaders or their own blessings, then it is in danger of facing the Lord's fury. The Lord says, "Vengeance is Mine. I will repay." Which means we are not to take matters into our own hands, or hope that the Day of the Lord comes in its destruction, because then we would experience it as well. We are to - hate evil, love good and establish justice. That is what the church must pursue if it is to survive God's purifying fire.

In their book *This Precarious Moment,* James L. Garlow and David Barton indicate how far we as leaders in the church have fallen in America. America would never have become a great nation and a world leader for good in so many areas had it not been for the direct involvement of pastors and the church in the affairs of the nation. Their influence was directly felt through the sermons they preached, as well as the hands-on leadership they exercised in all areas of the culture, including in political and governmental areas.

By so doing, these earlier American pastors were merely following countless biblical examples of God's ministers addressing the pressing issues of the day and openly calling out bad public policies and leaders. Minsters such as:

- Elijah, who confronted King Ahab and Queen Jezebel over issues such as their unjust use of eminent domain and religious persecution (1 Kings 21:1-24; 1 Kings 18:18);
- Micaiah, who regularly challenged Ahab over wicked public policies (1 Kings 22:7-18);
- Isaiah, who came against King Hezekiah over national security failures and issues related to the treasury (2 Chronicles 32:27-31; 2 Kings 20:12-19);
- Eliezer and Jehu, who confronted King Jehoshaphat over his blunders in foreign relations and ill-advised foreign alliances (2 Chronicles 19:1-2; 2 Chronicles 20:35-37);
- John the Baptist, who called out King Herod over his divorce and marriage practices (Mark 6:18-19) and

condemned civil leaders for their hypocrisy (Matthew 3:7);

- Samuel, who confronted King Saul over not fulfilling his assigned responsibilities (1 Samuel 13:1-14; 1 Samuel 15);
- Daniel, who confronted Nebuchadnezzar over his pride and arrogance (Daniel 4:1-27) and Belshazzar over his moral debauchery (Daniel 5:17-28);
- And Azariah (along with eighty other priests), who opposed King Uzziah for usurping religious practices through an improper expansion of government powers (2 Chronicles 26:16-21).

There certainly is no biblical model where God had His ministers remain silent with civil leaders or about civil issues. Furthermore, His ministers frequently partnered with civil leaders in constructing good public policies and providing sound guidance on many issues.[lxv]

For example, in several New England colonies and states, it was common practice to open annual state legislative sessions with a sermon, and those sermons on legislative matters were often printed and sent throughout the state at government expense. Such sermons were preached in front of numerous Founding Fathers. Ministers had great impact on the thinking and worldview of that day.

In fact, John Adams specifically identified the Rev. Dr. Jonathan Mayhew as one of the individuals 'most conspicuous, the most ardent, and influential' in the 'awakening and revival of American principles and feelings' that led to American independence. Mayhew preached practical sermons, applying the Bible to issues in the news, including a famous sermon on the Biblically authorized use of civil disobedience that led to a motto of the American War for Independence: 'Rebellion to Tyrants is Obedience to God.'[lxvi]

We have lost the influence and ability to guide the nation spiritually because of our fear of man, our desire for earthly goods, and our moral failures. These thorns have crept into the church and pulpit of America to become the very briar and patch from which we now preach.

> Perhaps the Rev. Charles Finney (one of the most noteworthy ministers in the mid-1800's) best summarized the influence of the pulpit on America when he reminded ministers of his day: Brethren, our preaching will bear its legitimate fruits, [but] if immorality prevails in the land, the fault is ours in a large degree. If there is a decay of conscience, the pulpit is responsible for it. If the public press lacks moral discrimination, the pulpit is responsible for it. If the Church is degenerate and worldly, the pulpit is responsible for it. If the world loses its interest in religion, the pulpit is responsible for it. If the world loses its interest in religion, the pulpit is responsible for it. If Satan rules in our halls of legislation, the pulpit is responsible for it. If our politics become so corrupt that the very foundations of our government are ready to fall away, the pulpit is responsible for it. Let us not ignore this fact my dear brethren, but let us lay it to heart, be thoroughly awake to our responsibility in respect to the morals of this nation.[lxvii]

This is a very serious charge, but pastors, leaders, and others in the church need to carefully consider these words and repent of our part in the degradation of society. Instead of preaching and leading against cultural and political sin, we have become guilty of either being silent or even modeling it to a watching world. God help us all.

AMERICA'S HISTORY

"A nation which does not remember what it was yesterday, does not know what it is today, nor what it is trying to do. We are trying to do a futile thing if we don't know where we have come from, or what we have been about." – President Woodrow Wilson

There is a book by Cornell University professors Isaac Kramnick and Lawrence Moore called *The Godless Constitution*. This title is depictive of the contemporary view that our nation was not founded with Christian principles, but nothing could be further from the truth. It seems to be a tactic to test the theory that if you say something long enough and loud enough that people believe it, but the facts say something different. In fact, in less than a single generation, the relationship between Christianity and the Constitution was so obviously consented that it was concluded in major magazine publications like *Newsweek*. "Historians are discovering that the Bible, perhaps even more than the Constitution, is our Founding document" was one of the statements that was made.[lxviii]

Some of the statements by previous presidents indicate how prevalent the view is that Christianity is foundational to our Constitution:

- President Lyndon B. Johnson said, "For we can truly be said to have founded our country on the principles of this Book. The Holy Bible was the most important possession that our forebears placed aboard their ships as they embarked for the New World."
- President Teddy Roosevelt said, "The teachings of the Bible are so interwoven and entwined with our whole civic and social life that it would be literally—I do not

mean figuratively, I mean literally—impossible for us to figure to ourselves what that life would be if these teachings were removed."

- President Andrew Jackson said, "It [the Bible] is the rock on which our Republic rests."

Some of the written statements by some of the signers of the original founding documents sound more like notes from a pastor's sermon than from political figures.

- Benjamin Rush, signer of the Declaration of Independence, said, "My only hope of salvation is in the infinite transcendent love of God manifested to the world by the death of His son upon the cross. Nothing but His blood will wash away my sins (Acts 22:16). I rely exclusively upon it. Come, Lord Jesus! Come quickly (Revelation 22:20)!"
- Samuel Adams, signer of the Declaration of Independence, said "I...rely on the merits of Jesus Christ for a pardon of all my sins."
- John Witherspoon, signer of the Declaration of Independence, said, "Christ Jesus...is the only Savior of sinners...as He Himself says (John 14:6): 'I am the way, and the truth, and the life: no man cometh unto the Father but by Me.'...If you are not reconciled to God through Jesus Christ — if you are not clothed with the spotless robe of His righteousness — you must forever perish."
- Alexander Hamilton, signer of the Constitution, said, "I have a tender reliance on the mercy of the Almighty, through the merits of the Lord Jesus Christ."
- Roger Sherman, signer of the Declaration of Independence and the Constitution, said, "God commands all men everywhere to repent (Matthew 3:2; Mark 1:15). He also commands them to believe on the Lord Jesus Christ, and has assured us that all who do repent and believe shall be saved (Acts 3:19)."

"There are many more examples like these, which clearly

> are not consistent with so-called atheist, agnostic, and deist Founders. The overwhelming majority of Founders were strongly Christian, but today's tendency in education and academia is to make the exception into the rule —that is, to take Benjamin Franklin and Thomas Jefferson (who expressed beliefs in conflict with the basic Christian doctrines) and tell the nation all the other Founders believed like they did. But if historical truth were accurately taught, we would show how strongly Christian most Founders were and then point to Jefferson and Franklin as exceptions rather than vice versa."[lxix]

There is also significant evidence from state constitutions for the Christian influence in our founding as well. While the founders wisely did not make it a requirement to be a Christian to be a part of the nation or hold federal office, they initially saw no conflict with such allegiances at the state level. The same signers of the Declaration of Independence and the Constitution helped construct state constitutions that overtly required Christian adherence in order to serve.

> Delaware's Constitution from 1776 states, "Every person who shall be chosen a member of either house, or appointed to any office or place of trust...shall... make and subscribe the following declaration, to wit: "I, ______________, do profess faith in God the Father, and in Jesus Christ His only Son, and the Holy Ghost, one God — blessed forevermore; and I do acknowledge the Holy Scriptures of the Old and New Testament to be given by Divine inspiration."[lxx]

> Massachusetts' Constitution from 1780 states, "Any person chosen governor, lieutenant-governor, counselor, senator, or representative, and accepting the trust, shall — before he proceed to execute the duties of his place or office — make and subscribe the following declaration, viz. 'I, ________________, do declare, that I believe the Christian religion and have a firm persuasion of its truth.'"[lxxi]

To think that these signers who created these overtly Christian statements and requirements at the state level didn't believe the same things about the federal documents is either deeply delusional or a purposeful lie. You can argue about whether or not our nation is currently Christian, but to make the claim that it wasn't founded with Christian ideas, values, and principals is preposterous. Think about how prevalent Christianity must have been or esteemed by the populace in order to make it a law to that to hold public office at the state level one must be a Christian.

The courts and their justices also contain a plethora of information showing America's founding as a Christian nation. In fact, one of the early U.S. Supreme Court Justices, David Brewer, attempted to answer the very question of whether America was a Christian nation:

> "In what sense can it [America] be called a Christian nation? Not in the sense that Christianity is the established religion, or that the people are in any manner compelled to support it. On the contrary, the Constitution specifically provides that 'Congress shall make no law respecting an establishment of religion, or prohibiting the free exercise thereof.' Neither is it Christian in the sense that all its citizens are either in fact or name Christians. On the contrary, all religions have free scope within our borders. Numbers of our people profess other religions, and many reject all. Nor is it Christian in the sense that a profession of Christianity is a condition of holding [federal] office or otherwise engaging in public service, or essential to recognition either politically or socially. In fact, the government as a legal organization is independent of all religions. Nevertheless, we constantly speak of this republic as a Christian nation—in fact, as the leading Christian nation of the world...The calling of this republic a Christian nation is not a mere pretense, but a recognition of an historical, legal, and social truth."[lxxii]

As late as 1931, the U.S. Supreme Court ruled: "We are a Christian people...according to one another the equal right of religious freedom and acknowledging with reverence the duty of obedience to the will of God."[lxxiii]

There are also numerous state court rulings which reiterate the same understanding. Just one example from the Oklahoma Supreme Court in 1959 states: "It is well settled and understood that ours is a Christian Nation, holding the Almighty God in dutiful reverence. It is so noted in our Declaration of Independence and in the constitution of every state of the Union. Since George Washington's first presidential proclamation of Thanksgiving Day, each such annual proclamation reiterates the principles that we are such a Christian Nation...[W]e consider the language used in our Declaration of Independence, and in our national Constitution, and in our Constitution of Oklahoma, wherein those documents recognize the existence of God, and that we are a Christian Nation and a Christian State."[lxxiv]

Continuing with the judicial theme, there are also countless examples from those in the highest levels of the courts issuing opinions or statements, such as the following, which sound like a Gospel message more than a court ruling. This one was from U.S. Supreme Court Justice Joseph Story in 1812, as he responded to two defendants convicted of murder and piracy:

> [A]fter what has happened, how you can appear before that dread tribunal and that Omnipotent Judge Who searcheth the hearts and trieth the reins of all men [Psalms 7:9]. From His sentence there is no appeal, and before Him you must soon appear to render an account of all the deeds done in the body [2 Corinthians 5:10; Romans 2:3-8]...Let me entreat you—tenderly and earnestly entreat you, as dying sinners—to turn from your wicked thoughts, to ponder on the errors of your ways, and with penitence and humiliation to seek the altars of our holy religion. Let me entreat you to pray for mercy and forgiveness from that righteous God, Whom you have so justly offended.[lxxv]

To think that these judges had the faith to preach the Gospel confidently and publicly in such a manner and did not influence or typify the faith of our country at its founding and beginning is a ridiculous revisionist attempt to forcefully assert that which is untrue. So as to say it loud enough and long enough that it would be thought to be true, but you cannot argue with the historical documents which reveal the truth and motive of those who assert otherwise.

U.S. Supreme Court Justice Earl Warren (1953-1969) declared:

> I believe the entire Bill of Rights came into being because of the knowledge our forefathers had of the Bible and their belief in it: freedom of belief, of expression, of assembly, of petition, the dignity of the individual, the sanctity of the home, **equal** justice under law, and the reservation of powers to the people...I like to believe we are living today in the spirit of the Christian religion. I like also to believe that as long as we do so, no great harm can come to our country.[lxxvi]

> There was an interesting study conducted in the 1980's which looked at the influence of sources that were quoted or referred to in the founding documents of America. The original findings were described by Donald Lutz in the article "The Relative Influence of European Writers on Late Eighteenth Century American Political Thought." As he described, political scientists embarked on an ambitious 10-year project to analyze writings from the Founding Era (1760-1805) with the goal of isolating and identifying the specific political authorities quoted during that time...Selecting some 15,000 representative writings, the researchers isolated 3,154 direct quotations and then documented the original sources of those quotations. The research revealed the single most cited authority in the writings of the Founding Era was the Bible: 34 percent of the documented quotes were taken from the Bible (a percentage almost four times higher than the second most

quoted source)."[lxxvii]

Imagine that — a third of the quotes from the founding documents of this country came from the Bible. That is a telling statistic which is descriptive of Christianity's influence on this country. We are not talking about a few obligatory quotes to pacify Christian leaders. One third of the quotes came straight from the Holy Bible. That doesn't even count the ideas and inferences from the Bible, only specific quotes! If the Bible was by far the most quoted source for founding documents how could it or the Christian faith not be central to the country's formation?

11 AMERICA'S HISTORY OF MARRIAGE AND SEXUAL IDENTITY

In the article "The Historical & Christian Roots of Marriage" by David Theroux we see that marriage is a universal institution of civilization. We find no human society in which marriage has not existed in some form, and virtually all marriage ceremonies historically have involved religious elements. Yet, for many years now, natural ("traditional") marriage and the family have become the subjects of secular ridicule, with the family increasingly politicized and socialized by "progressive" government bureaucracies. As Charles Murray has shown in his books *Losing Ground* (1984), *In Our Hands* (2006), and *Coming Apart* (2012), the result has been an unprecedented decline of the family and civil society in America and the West, producing increasing rates of nonmarital births, divorce, juvenile crime, drug and alcohol abuse, and other pathologies. However, this unsustainable trend can and should be reversed, because the "progressive" narrative that supports it is deeply flawed and easily refuted.

In his book *The Rise of Christianity* (1996), sociologist Rodney Stark notes that in the Greco-Roman pagan world, legal marriage was reserved for citizens, and while a wife shared her husband's station as the mother of his children, she and the offspring were his. And whereas wives were prohibited from committing adultery, no obligation to sexual fidelity existed for husbands. Prepubescent girls were often forced to marry older men, and husbands could compel their pregnant wives to have abortions, almost always a death sentence for the young mothers as well. Moreover, infanticide was commonplace, with girl babies disproportionately abandoned, resulting in "131 males per 100 females in the city of Rome, and 140 males per 100 females in Italy, Asia Minor, and North Africa."

Stark shows that it was only with the arrival of Christianity that the status of women within marriage began to change, as obligations were placed on husbands. "Christians condemned promiscuity in men as well as in women and stressed the obligations of husbands toward wives as well as those of wives toward husbands.... The symmetry of the relationship Paul described was at total variance, not only with pagan culture, but with Jewish culture as well."

Stark further shows that Christianity began recognizing women as equal yet complementary to men, all being sacred in the eyes of God. Christian wives did not have abortions (neither did Jewish wives), and Christians opposed infanticide, polygamy, incest, divorce, and adultery, all prohibitions which improved the wellbeing of women. No longer serfs to men, women had dignity, could choose their own husbands, enjoyed better marriages, and served as leaders in the rapidly growing Christian communities. Christian women married at older ages than pagan women and into more secure families; if widowed, they were not forced to remarry; and if needy, they were given assistance.

In *Paul for Everyone: The Prison Letters* (2004), New Testament scholar N. T. Wright explains the unique and revolutionary complementarity of Christian marriage, in which *both* wife and husband are equally called to model their love for each other after the perfect sacrificial love of Jesus:

> The fascinating thing here is that Paul has a quite different way of going about addressing the problem of gender roles. He insists that the husband should take as his role model, not the typical bossy or bullying male of the modern, or indeed the ancient stereotype, but Jesus himself.... The church became the Messiah's bride, not by being dragged off unwillingly by force, but because he gave himself totally and utterly to her. There was nothing that love could do for the Messiah's people that he did not do. Although the crucifixion plays a central role in Paul's thought in almost every topic, nowhere else outside this passage is it so lyrically described as an act of complete, self-abandoning love.... Paul assumes, as do most cultures, that there are significant differences between men and women, differences that go far beyond mere biological and reproductive function. Their relations and roles must therefore be mutually complementary, rather than identical.... And, within marriage, the guideline is clear. The husband is to take the lead—though he is to do so fully mindful of the self-sacrificial model which the Messiah has provided. As soon as "taking the lead" becomes bullying or arrogant, the whole thing collapses.[lxxviii]

Ever since the sexual revolution of the 1960s, marriage and sexual morality have been falling downhill at breakneck speeds. It was not until 1969 that no-fault divorce was signed into law for the first time, and it wasn't until 2004 that same-sex marriage was recognized as allowable in the U.S. For nearly the first 200 years of this country's existence, marriage was highly esteemed, valued, and protected, but in the last 50 years we have seen no-fault divorce, cohabitation, and homosexuality become accepted norms. Can we not see the error in our ways and the deterioration of the family and society, or is that we are comfortable with it and the ramifications? Regardless of why this has happened, it continues to exist and tear at the definition and standard of marriage. We must realize how far we have fallen away from our history and moral standards that existed in our country for so long and repent.

In his book *The Theft Of America's Soul*, Phil Robertson from the Duck Dynasty franchise shares:

> Today many point to the Time article (Is God Dead? In April 1966) as the first time the elephant in the room—the question of whether God was still hanging around—was addressed in the broader market. Some of those same folks point to that article as the culmination of 1960s enlightenment. I know the truth about the sixties, because I lived them. The truth is, the sixties were anything but enlightened. They were very dark. In the sixties a deep sleep-ism settled over our country. Atheism, agnosticism, humanism, moral relativism, naturalism, personalism, rationalism, materialism—all the isms washed over us. These isms led America deeper into sexual immorality, greed, and the wholesale slaughter of the unborn. The isms led us into debauchery. I know this because, to my embarrassment, those isms washed over me.[lxxix]

Marriage in America is not just falling apart, it is being redefined. It is one thing to break the rules, but it is something else entirely to take the rules and say, "We don't like those, we're going to make new ones." It is the epitome of pride and independence to look at the institution of marriage and to redefine it. Sin is sin, but we must also recognize that there are characteristics of sin and degrees of sin that affect our relationship with God and with our neighbor. Even God says that there are certain sins that He hates and there is certainly a sharp degree of difference to our neighbor whether we commit adultery in our heart or in person. This is what is happening with the definition of marriage in America. It is no longer just in the heart of man to rebel or to be inclined to do what is forbidden. There is a conscious effort that is unafraid of the consequences of redefining the establishment of marriage. There is a difference between falling into sin through a series of bad decisions and coming to recognition and repentance when it is revealed, and purposefully thumbing your nose at God and saying, "I don't care what you say, I'm doing it my way." This is where America is at with regard to sexual sin and the definition of marriage. It is a blatant disregard of God's intention and design and scoffs at the Creator in such a way that suggests that we somehow believe we know better than God or don't care what He thinks. God have mercy on us all.

12 AMERICA'S HISTORY OF EDUCATION

Did you know that when America was founded the Bible was used for public education? In fact, in the first few years of its existence after the Revolutionary War, Congress approved and authorized the printing of a Bible for use in public schools. There was a man in Philadelphia by the name of Robert Aitken, who in 1781 had undertaken the task of reproducing one of the first Bibles in the new free America. He requested that the project be endorsed by the Congress and his intention was that they be printed for the public schools. This was Congress' response after review of the Bible:

> Whereupon, Resolved, That the United States in Congress assembled, highly approve the pious and laudable undertaking of Mr. Aitken, as subservient to the interest of religion as well as an instance of the progress of arts in this country, and being satisfied from the above report, of his care and accuracy in the execution of the work, they recommend this edition of the Bible to the inhabitants of the United States, and hereby authorize him to publish this recommendation in the manner he shall think proper.[lxxx]

This inscription of endorsement was printed in the very front of the Bible that Congress "highly approved" this work and authorized the publication and use for public schools as Aitken intended. I understand the argument for not wanting government or public leaders to be required to lead religious prayers, or publicly read Scripture, but what happened in effect was that all prayer and Bible reading was (and continues to be) banned, discouraged, or persecuted. The fact is, until the 1960s — for the first 200 years of our country's existence — prayer and the

Scriptures were an important and included part of public education. There are ways to allow and encourage prayer without endorsing a specific religion or, in effect, endorsing the dogma of atheism. This "School Prayer" article from All About History shows how prayer was removed from public education:

> School prayer was the focus of Madalyn Murray O'Hair, a militant, left-wing, atheist with close ties to the American Communist Party, who filed a lawsuit against the school board of Baltimore. The local court judge, J. Gilbert Pendergast, dismissed the petition, stating, "It is abundantly clear that petitioners' real objective is to drive every concept of religion out of the public school system." The case went to the Maryland Court of Appeals and the court ruled, "Neither the First nor the Fourteenth Amendment was intended to stifle all rapport between religion and government."
>
> The "School Prayer" case then made its way to the U.S. Supreme Court. Leonard Kerpelman addressed the court, saying prayer in the public schools had been tolerated for so long that it had become traditional, and that anything that is unconstitutional does not become constitutional through tradition. He went on to say the Constitution had erected a "wall of separation" between church and state, at which point Justice Potter Steward interrupted, asking where this wording appears. Kerpelman was stumped and an embarrassing silence followed. When he regained his composure, he stated that the text was not explicit on the point but that it had been interpreted to mean so.
>
> Remarkably, the National Council of Churches and several Jewish organizations favored Madalyn O'Hair's case! Not a single Christian organization filed a brief in support of school prayer. The Supreme Court ruled 8 to 1 in favor of abolishing school prayer and Bible reading in the public schools. Justice Tom Clark wrote, "Religious freedom, it

> has long been recognized that government must be neutral and, while protecting all, must prefer none and disparage none." The federal government considers atheism to be a religion, and this Supreme Court ruling favored atheism, at the expense of the Christian majority.[lxxxi]

The most disappointing part is that no Christian organizations even filed a brief to support school prayer in this case. There was no fight, no argument, only concession. And look where we are today. The primary argument shared by the opposition was that tradition does not constitute constitutionality. The ironic thing is that this is exactly what precedence is and what is often now used as an excuse by the courts to accomplish their liberal agenda when they choose the precedence of the last 40 years instead of the 200 years before that.

In the book *Faith in America* by Steve Green, he talks about Benjamin Rush, who was one of the youngest signers of the Declaration of Independence. Green notes that John Adams said Rush was one of the most influential signers of the Declaration of Independence, along with the likes of George Washington and Benjamin Franklin. When Adams became president, he appointed Rush to the position of Treasurer of the U.S. Mint. Rush was a man of great faith and deeply believed in the use of the Bible for educational instruction. In fact, he believed in it so much that Green included a portion of a letter that Rush wrote to defend the use of the Bible as a text book in school. There are other facts that also emphasize and note the importance of the Bible, the Gospel, and our Christian faith in the history and founding of our country. Some of the statistics that Green includes are that in 1890, over 90% of the universities surveyed had chapel services, 50% of the universities surveyed had compulsory chapel attendance, and 25% of the universities surveyed required church attendance in addition to chapel. These statistics are almost unbelievable in light of our education system today and show us exactly how prevalent faith was during our founding.[lxxxii]

There is also a section in Green's book on the Supreme Court's influence in abolishing prayer in public schools. In 1962, there was a case in New York where a school board agreed to allow a group of students to gather and pray at the beginning of the school day, as was their regular habit. There were objections to this practice, however, and the case eventually came before the Supreme Court. The Supreme Court ruled that the prayer group should not be allowed, and its influence, along with the O'Hair case effectively ended prayer in public school. Mind you, this was not a prayer meeting organized by the administration or sanctioned as mandatory for attendance or participation, but yet the freedom to pray was still stolen away. At least one Supreme Court Justice, Potter Stewart, dissented from the decision:

> "A local school board in New York has provided that those pupils who wish to do so may join in a brief prayer at the beginning of each school day, acknowledging their dependence upon God and asking His blessing upon them and upon their parents, their teachers, and their country. The court decides today that, in permitting this brief non-denominational prayer, the school board has violated the Constitution of the United States. I think this decision is wrong...At the opening of each day's Session of this Court, we stand, while one of our officials invokes the protection of God. Since the days of John Marshall, our Crier has said, 'God save the United States and this Honorable Court.' Both the Senate and the House of Representatives open their daily sessions with prayer. Each of the presidents from George Washington to John Kennedy has, upon assuming his Office, asked the protection and help of God. Countless similar examples could be listed, but there is no need to belabor the obvious. It was all summed up by this Court just ten years ago in a single sentence: 'We are a religious people whose institutions presuppose a Supreme Being.' I do not believe that this Court, or the Congress,

> or the President, has, by the actions and practices I have mentioned, established an 'official religion' in violation of the Constitution. And I do not believe the state of New York, has done so in this case. What each has done has been to recognize and to follow the deeply entrenched and highly cherished spiritual traditions of our nation—traditions which come down to us from those who almost two hundred years ago avowed their 'firm Reliance on the Protection of divine Providence' when they proclaimed the freedom and independence of this brave new world. I dissent."[lxxxiii]

So, we removed prayer from school, the Bible from school, and creation from school, and now look at where we are. There are multiple school shootings every year and everyone is asking why. The sad thing is that the rest of our institutions are destined to the same fate unless something changes. Most of the judgment that takes place is actually the natural consequence of our own sin. We shake our fist at God and say, "Why did that child have to die in that school?" when we were the very cause, as we stood idly by and allowed God to be removed from the school. The rest of society will be subject to the same judgment if something doesn't change as we remove the Ten Commandments from the courts and the monuments from our parks. How is it that we can't see the correlation between removing God and the natural consequences of our actions?

In this article from *Answers In Genesis* we see that early American writings show the public schools of today are quite different from the public schools of the past:

> It being one chief project of the old deluder, Satan, to keep men from the knowledge of the Scriptures ... it is therefore ordered ... [to] appoint one within their town to teach all such children as shall resort to him to write and read ... "

Imagine today's public schools in America having as their goal to teach children to read the Bible. Believe it or not, that quote is from the first public school law ever passed in America, the "Old Deluder Satan Act" of 1647. This was just the first of many early American writings that show how the public schools of today do not resemble the public schools of yesteryear.

Into the colonial and founding periods of American history (the early 1600s to the late 1700s), Christianity, the Bible, and creation were taught openly in public schools and incorporated throughout the various topics of education. For example, in a 1749 booklet on education, Benjamin Franklin said the teaching of history in schools should "afford frequent opportunities of showing the necessity of a public religion ... and the excellency of the Christian religion above all others."

When the use of the Bible was threatened to be diminished by an abundance of new textbooks available around 1800, prominent American educators spoke up to ensure the Bible's place as America's premier textbook. Fisher Ames, an educator and prominent statesman, said, "[I]f these [new] books ... must be retained, as they will be, should not the Bible regain the place it once held as a school book?" In a widely distributed pamphlet, Benjamin Rush (the "father of public schools under the Constitution" as well as a signer of America's Declaration of Independence) argued from reason and revelation for the continued use of the Bible as a schoolbook.

Even Thomas Jefferson was involved in religious aspects of education. While president, he made the Bible a primary reading text for Washington, D.C., schools. Noah Webster, one of America's greatest educators, wrote an appendix to his 1832 school history text reminding students of the importance of the Scriptures, and warning that "miseries

> and evils" will result from a lack of following the Bible. In 1844, the U.S. Supreme Court ruled that no college could exclude teachings from the Bible. In fact, it was lawyer and senator Daniel Webster, the famous "defender of the Constitution," who argued before the Supreme Court that Christianity is inseparable from education.
>
> The downhill trend in schools is already far progressed. In fact, practically every moral measurement for schools is on a downhill trend. Interestingly, these statistics worsen significantly in the mid-1960s, correlating with two significant events. First, the BSCS textbooks were released, reemphasizing evolution as a unifying concept in science. Second, the Supreme Court removed prayer and Bible reading from schools. Why should students be expected to behave well when they are taught that they are just animals and the absolutes of the Scripture are banished from the classroom?
>
> We must understand that the implication of evolution is that man is the highest product of evolution; therefore, man takes the place of God in deciding what's right and wrong. The implication of creation, on the other hand, is that God created everything and He decides what's right and wrong. It is obvious why we have a problem with morality from the products of public schools today — they are being taught that they can decide what's right and wrong for themselves.
>
> The fact is, America's public school system is a failing effort. Religion and morality — what George Washington termed the "essential pillars of society" — are generally not to be found in public schools. Rather what is being taught is leading to irreligion and immorality.[lxxxiv]

The conclusion from this article is that without a miracle, American public schools have no future hope. There needs to be widespread repentance and change. In addition, the university system provides no additional help, as the number of students committed to following Christ after leaving university in America is abysmally low. Think about how far we have fallen in an education system in which schools were initially established and founded for the teaching of the Scriptures to where now they are openly and defiantly attacked. While some fault must lie in the church and family for these youth and their lack of faith, how can we not evaluate the higher education system as a whole to realize what outcomes and worldviews they are producing? Universities can no longer be seen as apathetic or impartial to the Gospel, but must be seen as what they have become — antagonistic foundations where Christ is questioned, challenged, and attacked, implicitly and explicitly.

13 AMERICA'S HISTORY OF VALUING LIFE

In the article "The Moral Outcry," Cindy Collins talks about the travesty of abortion and its history. Global Coordinator for Operation Outcry, Collins talks about a dream she had in July of 2016:

> I was standing at my kitchen sink, I had something in my left hand, the water was running and I reached with my right hand to flip on the switch to my garbage disposal and ran my left hand under the water. I instantly knew I had just crushed an embryo. I began to weep deeply. I woke up weeping and heard the Lord say "I'm sorry, I don't know how else to show you how I feel about this. Whether a human life is so small that the human eye cannot see it or an 8 month gestational baby being torn from its mother's womb, I knew them both! I stood before them declaring their plans, purposes, and destinies. I grieve equally for both!"
>
> My husband and I are pro-life to the core. We have a ministry to awaken the church to adoption of the newborn as an answer to end abortion, we also educate on the origins of abortion biblically and historically. This dream awakened me in a fresh way. The Lord values life from the moment of conception. The question I began to ask Him was what was He trying to show me?
>
> It wasn't until that someone shared with us that Roe v Wade had never been successfully challenged, that we were thrust into prayer and fasting for strategy. On March 9, 2017 during my prayer time I kept envisioning William Wilberforce rolling out his petition before Parliament

bringing an end to the slave trade as he says...

"Never, never will we desist till we have wiped away this scandal from the Christian name, released ourselves from the load of guilt, under which we at present labor, and extinguished every trace of this bloody traffic, of which our posterity, looking back to the history of these enlightened times, will scarce believe that it has been suffered to exist so long a disgrace and dishonor to this country." House of Commons Speech April 18, 1791

The great, great grandson of the successful anti-slavery campaigner William Wilberforce, believes his ancestor who campaigned for the end of the slave trade in 1807, which led to the abolition of slavery throughout the British Empire in 1833, would consider abortion to be the contemporary slavery.

Over 60 million babies have lost their lives to abortion in our nation since 1973 when Roe v Wade authorized the withdrawing of legal protection by the government from this class of human beings, children in the womb, thus allowing them to be killed without fear of punishment. The United States Constitution, one of the oldest written constitutions in the world today, states that no person shall be deprived of life without due process of law, in both the Fifth and Fourteenth Amendments.

So we went to work and together Mr. Allan Parker and I wrote a petition to the Supreme Court of the United States to reverse, overturn, cancel and annul Roe v Wade, Doe v Bolton and Planned Parenthood v Casey, and restore the right to life as written in the United States Constitution to persons in the womb. Just as William Wilberforce petitioned Parliament to abolish the slave trade, the purpose of the petition is to provide an outlet for the people to show their government they do not accept its decisions on abortion and can never be accepted by a just society.

The petition also educates Americans to the fact that there is another mechanism that women can rely upon for birth control rather than abortion through the Safe Haven laws which are now available in all 50 states. A woman can transfer responsibility for her child to the state simply by dropping a child off at a state-approved location within a reasonable time after birth. See www.nationalsafehaven.org or by choosing an adoption plan for the child with the help of one of the estimated 3000 pregnancy resource and adoption agencies in the United States. There are 1 million estimated families waiting to adopt a newborn each year. This is a "change in law" since 1992, the last time the court evaluated Roe and Doe. Safe Haven laws were not present in 1992. The Supreme Court is justified in overturning precedent when facts, circumstances, and law have changed that make the original decision no longer just — if it ever was, which Roe and Doe were not.

Plessey v. Ferguson, which led to the "separate but equal doctrine" or the "law of the land," was a 58-year old precedent of the Supreme Court. This decision was a crime against humanity, just as Dred Scott (slavery) was another Supreme Court crime against humanity by withdrawing legal protection from African-Americans. Abortion is not only about a fundamental right, in fact it is a crime against humanity.

What is a crime against humanity? According to Wikipedia, "Crimes against humanity, as defined by the Rome Statute of the International Criminal Court Explanatory Memorandum, 'are particularly odious offenses in that they constitute a serious attack on human dignity or grave humiliation or a degradation of human beings. 1) They are not isolated or sporadic events, but are part either of a government policy (although the perpetrators need not identify themselves with this policy) or of a wide practice or atrocities tolerated or condoned by a government or de facto authority. Murder; extermination; torture; rape; political, racial, or religious persecution and other inhumane acts reach the threshold of crimes against humanity only if they are part of a widespread or systematic practice. Isolated inhuman acts of the nature may constitute grave infringements of human rights, or depending on the circumstances, war crimes, may fall short of falling into the category of crimes under discussion."

Note that murder is one of the most basic and obvious crimes against humanity. Why? Because the right to life is one of the most basic human rights of all and has been widely recognized in international documents. The International Declaration on the Rights of Man, which established the United Nations, declares that there is an international right to life as a basic human right. In order to be a crime against humanity, the crime must be widespread and supported by the government. Of course, in every nation where abortion is legal, it is the government that has made it so. In fact, in some countries, such as the United States of America, it has been judicial institutions rather than the will of the majority of Americans that has made abortion legal.

Obviously, the Supreme Court up to this point has failed to settle the controversy. Abortion is still one of the most controversial issues in American society today. Planned Parenthood v. Casey, which weakened but did not reverse Roe and Doe, has been called the worst constitutional decision of all time because it placed the reputation of the Supreme Court above the lives of innocent children.

We view this petition as a holy document. A Joel 2 call to the nation at www.themoraloutcry.com. No matter where we find ourselves in the storyline of the past 44 years, if we would repent on behalf of the innocent blood that has been shed, and simply believe the Word and what it says is true that God Himself forms each life in the womb

> of its mother, God will once again show mercy and we will see this atrocity of abortion abolished.
>
> Why petition the court? This is an unusual step, but ending a crime against humanity justifies an unusual action. The people of the United States did not vote for Roe v. Wade, instead the Supreme Court created the crime against humanity with Roe, Doe, and Planned Parenthood v. Casey. It is the Supreme Court which must be petitioned by the people to change its decision. It is also right and just to give the court the opportunity to correct their own error. There are significant reasons why the Supreme Court should do the right thing, as the Supreme Court did in Brown v. Board of Education, ending segregation and reversing the crime against humanity it had inadvertently created. In 1992, in Planned Parenthood v. Casey, the Supreme Court did not overrule Roe and Doe because the court stated that Americans had come to rely upon the cases and the Supreme Court was going to settle the abortion controversy for all time.[lxxxv]

Again, for 200 years abortion was illegal, which made it the precedent in the U.S. until 1973. So when precedent is an advantage to your opinion then you can use it, but when it states an opposition to your opinion then we call it unnecessary tradition? The injustice and inconsistencies of the highest court to accomplish their own agenda instead of the will of the people or the original intent of the founders is gross and obverse. The original intent of the founders for the Supreme Court was to be a check and balance system and to fairly interpret law, not invoke it. In effect, the Supreme Court has become its own legislative body by determining right and wrong for our nation and has miserably failed our founding fathers and their intentions and 200 years of precedence in support of creationism, prayer, and Bible in schools, while removing protections from the life of unborn children, the definition of marriage, and now sexual identity. There must be accountability and reform. Repent, for the kingdom of God is at hand.

The incorrect understanding about the concept of the separation of church and state is one of the biggest injustices our courts have attempted to establish, which has led to our faulty moral compass. By examining our founders' Christian heritage and intentions, it is clear that they instituted the view of separation so that no one denomination could be forcibly compelled upon the country. It was never their intention that religion would be removed from schools, courts, institutions, or businesses. It is a gross neglect and misrepresentation of the original intent of the Constitution to interpret otherwise. In the book *God's New Israel*, Conrad Cherry shares an article that demonstrates the original intent by our founders:

> "This was the original intent of our nation's founders when they framed the Constitution. Justice Joseph Story, who sat on the Supreme Court from 1811 until 1845 and taught law at Harvard University, stated unequivocally in his commentary of the Constitution: 'The real object of the [First] Amendment was ...to prevent any national ecclesiastical establishment which should give to a hierarchy the exclusive patronage of the national government.' The objective was not, in Story's word, to "prostrate" Christianity by excluding it from the public square, but to prohibit the elevation of one sect or denomination above the others. Church and state jurisprudence has gradually shifted in recent decades to a point that the framers of the First Amendment would not recognize it. They saw the state as the threat; today the courts see the church as the threat."[lxxxvi]

A San Francisco district judge ruled recently that the undercover journalists who exposed the aborted baby body parts practices of Planned Parenthood must pay the abortion giant over $1.5 million, plus all of its attorney fees. Judge William Orrick III of the U.S. District Court of the Northern District of California also prohibited Center for Medical Progress (CMP) project lead, David Daleiden, and his associates from ever entering Planned Parenthood conferences indicated in the ifapray.org article.[lxxxvii] Talk about the epitome of injustice! So the very ones who exposed this injustice are those being punished by law? That is how corrupt and perverted our justice system has become ... Lord have mercy on us all.

14 AMERICA'S HISTORY OF REBELLION AND PREJUDICE

For the other chapters on America's history, we have been examining ideologies of the country that were founded in righteousness and justice and through time and error have become problematic. But in this chapter, we are examining that which has been problematic in our country since its inception and still has not been eradicated. Both rebellion and prejudice have sadly marked our nation from its very beginning, and we are in great need of continued repentance in these areas. Even though there were great Christian men that founded our country, how minorities were largely treated and the existence of slavery — even while we fought for our own independence — shows just how problematic prejudice was and continues to be; it's an infection that must be eradicated.

The birth of our nation in rebellion against the English was argued by many at that time to be a necessary action to overcome injustice and provide opportunity for economic, religious, and political freedom. The problem is that being birthed in that rebellion has become a standard of action which is neither profitable nor desirable in most cases. God is very clear throughout His word that He is a God of order and not chaos and that He values obedience, not rebellion. We know that at times rebellion is necessary due to injustice and mistreatment (and even endorsed by God), but because of our history, we have jumped to the conclusion of rebellion far too often. We appreciate and value independence and freedom, but when it becomes an identity that does not honor authority or structure, then it becomes harmful and damaging. Instead of being the big brother, at times we have become the bully, and the bully is never an acceptable position. We see throughout Scripture that those with resources and power are expected to look out for and protect the weak and needy.

America's history of rebellion (beginning with the Revolutionary War) is a long and complicated narrative. Usually rebellion is used in a negative way, just like the term judgment, but neither term is necessarily negative. Rebellion means fighting and/or usurping authority. What makes it negative or not is dependent upon the authority that you are rebelling against or the reason that you are rebelling. That's what makes it complicated. Jesus' disciples were rebellious toward the religious leaders at the time who told them not to preach in the name of Jesus and answered that they must obey God rather than man. So often we see similar instances where rebellion has been courageous and just, in support of accomplishing a great good. More often we know it today as "civil disobedience," in which good men and women in history stood up to injustice and evil in their day to stand up for truth. We saw this with Martin Luther (even though it was not in America) when he said, "Here I stand, I can do no other." There are other instances from American history, like Rosa Parks or Martin Luther King, Jr. during the Civil Rights era. The very beginning of our country was born out of rebellion against Great Britain. These are examples in which serious injustices were taking place and necessary adjustments — including disobedience and rebellion — were required to accomplish justice.

The problem is that we have come to value disobedience and rebellion as a strength when really it is sin, except in unusual circumstances. The primary posture of God's people and the order of creation that God put in place was one of order and obedience. There are countless scriptural examples of God honoring obedience and disciplining or denouncing rebellion and disobedience. That was Satan's sin, Adam and Eve's downfall, etc. In America, we have inappropriately valued rebellion as a strength instead of seeing it for the sin that it is. Whether it is against political leaders of a different party, children against their parents, wives against their husbands, or employees against their employers, we don't even see it as a problem. This is a huge blind spot of sin in America and we must repent for it. We have not recognized the slippery slope of pride and rebellion that has led us to where we are as a nation with how we define marriage, how we treat those that we disagree with politically, relations between husbands and wives, and even in the church. God's commendation throughout Scripture is to endure suffering in unjust situations and that our normal modus operandi should be obedience. If we trust Him to take care of us and defend us, even in the midst of inappropriate and unjust treatment, instead of taking things into our own hands, He will deliver us in His timing. That is why Dr. Martin Luther King Jr. left such an incredible legacy, because he was able to be civilly disobedient in an appropriate, non-violent way, and yet still accomplished so much. We also know that there are times when God allows (and even encourages) civil unrest and war to defend basic freedoms but, again, these are the exceptions, not the rule. An example of this is when Israel fled from Egypt. But consider that even in that circumstance, the Israelites fled while God fought for them, causing the plagues, and bringing destruction upon the Egyptians. Our primary way of functioning with regard to authority should be like David, who would not kill the Lord's anointed even though he had the opportunity when King Saul was trying to chase him down and take his life.

Jesus was obedient in everything — to His parents, to the rightful human authorities. He obeyed in all things, even to the end, and even in private and in secret. This is not a tremendous value in our country; we value independence and we celebrate "Independence Day." I am all for celebrating our freedom and our nation — especially as it was founded and in line with the intentions of the founders — but we need to be very careful about the concept of celebrating independence because (in most cases) it is in opposition to God's will. He desires obedience and structure and created His divine order to have such structure. Christ is the head of man and man is head of the woman and children are to submit to their parents. There is a created order that God instituted, and He desires obedience to that created order. There is a difference between civil disobedience and rebellion and in America we have crossed the line with looting, vandalism, violence, and the destruction of property. Due to how we were founded and the very beginning of our nation, we are much too quick to rebel instead of obey. In effect, we are saying that we can be our own high priest: "I'll do it my way." But Jesus' way was obedience and our way should be obedience too, unless we are certain that God is calling us to another path when we are being asked to do something illegal or immoral. Otherwise, the Lord's commendation is mostly to suffer in the perfection of our obedience. It isn't fun, but it strips the sinful flesh. God tells us that rebellion is compared to witchcraft, so we should be careful not to engage in it. Obedience is important to God, and our inattentiveness to it and our disregard of it is an offense and stench to His nostrils.

The other topic that we need to tackle is America's history of prejudice. Whether it's with Native Americans, African Americans, women, or other specific ethnicities and groups, our country has had a painful and embarrassing history with regard to prejudice. This remains one of the prominent black eyes of our founding as a country, that the Christian men and leaders who fought for their own freedom failed to recognize the depravity of slavery. Thankfully, God has allowed us to make great strides in racial and gender equality, but we still have far to go. To think otherwise is foolish and naïve. The riots that have surrounded the murder of George Floyd demonstrate the frustration and anger of many, many Americans. We cannot accept the systemic racism that still infiltrates many of our government agencies and organizations and, ultimately, the hearts of our people. Earlier in this chapter, we talked about the inappropriate action of taking matters into our own hands. But it cannot be denied that the extent of prejudice still in this country that has been revealed of late is frightening and alarming. We must understand our standing before God as those who have been made in His image and that we are all one flesh in our common ancestry of Adam and Eve and Noah and his wife. We have not understood this as Americans. We have claimed to be united but in reality, have been divided, and it has to stop. A house divided cannot stand. The temptation is to hate anybody different than us. God has called us to love those that are different than ourselves and to treat them as we want to be treated. African American parents in this country have to have conversations with their children about how their behavior must be exemplary if they are approached by a police officer after being pulled over or if they are in an altercation, so that nothing bad happens. We can do better in America. We need to lead in the church with loving and embracing our brothers and sisters in Christ, regardless of race. Ultimately, we are not to love our creed or color — it's a Jewish man who gave us eternal life — we must repent of the idea that some lives have more value than others. We must truly begin to embrace the understanding that all lives matter, and until we do, it may be necessary to remind people when they are not being treated fairly that there are specific lives that need to be highlighted and protected, such as the lives of Black people and unborn children. It shouldn't be an offense to doctors that unborn lives matter, and it doesn't need to be an offense to police that Black lives matter. We need to see injustice and work especially in the church to come against it to bring about the desirable justice of equal standing and treatment for all. We must repent for our inappropriate actions and paradigms. The Baltimore Ravens in the NFL released this telling and profound statement after the shooting of Jacob Blake:

> With yet another example of racial discrimination with the shooting of Jacob Blake, and the unlawful abuse of

> peaceful protestors, we must unify as a society. It is imperative that all people – regardless of race, religion, creed, or belief – come together to say, "enough is enough!" This is bigger than sports. Racism is embedded in the fabric of our nation's foundation and is a blemish on our country's history. If we are to change course and make our world a better place, we must face this problem head on and act now to enact positive change. It is time to accept accountability and acknowledge the ramifications of slavery and racial injustice.[lxxxviii]

There must be change and there must be repentance, but how do we go about it. The ultimate reality is that all lives do matter, but we must examine further what that means. For instance, Black lives matter, but the organization Black Lives Matter has been exposed as being anti-Christian and anti-American. So as Christians, our allegiance must be with Christ and not organizations that don't honor Christ. Maybe we should say, "African Americans Matter" or "Black lives have meaning" instead. I don't know what the answer is, but I know the answer is not to dishonor God in our fight for justice. For instance, I would march with Dr. King because he endorsed justice in the right way, but I wouldn't align myself with radical groups that endorse violence and destruction. How we fight becomes just as important as the fact that we fight. The same is true for any other cause. The temptation is either to not fight and relegate injustice to other people while protecting ourselves or to fight inappropriately, taking matters into our own hands. We must recognize that in order to win back America, we must fight in the right way — on our knees in repentance, asking God to intervene. Yes, we must raise our voice, cast our vote, and proclaim our cause, but when those things don't work, then we must turn to the Lord and ask Him to fight on our behalf and realize that the battle is the Lord's. That's why it is so important to understand obedience and civil disobedience, so that we can fight in the right way about the right things. For instance, with regard to moral issues, we have been too quick to run from the national culture and create our own safety net as Christians, instead of fighting for justice, and now we are reeling. The condition of our public schools is one example of this, as well as the widespread acceptance of homosexual marriage. Even today we continue to be under siege as we learn to navigate transgender issues. We often justify this by rationalizing that if it doesn't immediately impact us or our situation then we don't have to fight it. The issue is, when we allow immorality to become a system in the public square, it will eventually infiltrate all of culture. We have too often had the perspective, "As long as it doesn't affect my school, my neighborhood, or my church then I don't need to be concerned about it." That is not true; once immorality becomes established, it tends to affect everything. I know that this is difficult and challenging to think about, but that is part of what we are doing in this book, taking a hard look at how we have failed, where we are at and why we are there. With regard to schools, please don't misunderstand me to think that I am against home schooling or even private schools. My family has participated in both and especially loved the private school environment, where our kids could learn about Christ and were taught to have a strong moral compass with excellent education. The issue that I would like to propose is that maybe we have been too eager to create our own utopia instead of fighting for justice in the public arena of education, or in any sphere of influence for that matter. If there had been no other options besides public schools, would we have stood for evolution being presented as the only viable option? What about the implementation of Common Core standards? I don't have all the answers, but I know that the condition of many of our public schools do not honor God. And not only do they not honor Him, their curriculums are diametrically opposed to Him and His order. The only redeeming quality is often the teachers and students themselves. The same can be said for homosexual marriage. Many Christians think, "As long as it doesn't happen in my church and it's at the courthouse or in that 'other' church,

I guess it's not that bad." Or when encountering transgender issues: "Let's just give them their own bathrooms and then they can do what they want." Do you see how our inattention and aloofness has allowed these systems to infiltrate our culture? Now we are responsible for where we are at today in a culture that is offensive and putrid before a Holy God who established this nation in righteousness and justice. Instead of acting, we continue to build our own kingdoms, building bigger houses and buying newer cars, giving only our leftovers to the church, and thinking we are good. If we care about America, things have to change. These unrighteous systems and patterns have to be addressed, or I am afraid of what the result will be.

15 AMERICA'S HISTORY OF INFLUENCE — FROM MISSIONARY OUTPOST TO BABYLON THE GREAT

Since its inception, America has been a missionary nation that has sought not only its own faith to propagate but also to neighboring countries and throughout the world. One of the gifts and callings that the Lord established in America was to be a missionary nation and tell others about His Son, Jesus. Initially this began primarily as an effort to proclaim and profess to those who immigrated to the U.S. from other countries as well as to the Native Americans that were already inhabiting the land. Today, over 100,000 missionaries every year that hail from America preach the Gospel of Jesus Christ in other nations. The only problem is that it is nothing compared to those that are propagating trafficking, drugs, pornography, horror films, and all other manners of evil. The good is far outweighed by the bad and it has become a stench to the nations. Even some Muslim countries have a disdain for America because of its inappropriate characterizations and moral shortcomings. The other problem is that even though we know inside the church that American culture is no longer Christian; it is still perceived as Christian around the world. When people from around the world hear our music, watch our movies, and see our TV shows, they perceive them as coming from a Christian nation. That means we as a nation are giving God a bad name. We started with such a rich tradition of a Christian heritage and now we mock the name of Christ and drag His name in mud around the world. If you look at the history of our missions and Christian influence around the world, we should be ashamed of where we are at today.

> Until 1865, the churches in North America tended, more instinctively than we do today, to seek an outpouring of revival from God to awaken His people from spiritual lethargy. After 1870, the churches seemed to look less for revival (as historically experienced) and move to organization, technique, personalities, and evangelistic campaigns. In fact, the period of 1880-1935 is sometimes called the Era of the Evangelists.
>
> Undoubtedly the most prominent evangelist at the close of the nineteenth century was Dwight L. Moody. A converted shoe salesman, Moody had a passion for seeing souls converted to Christ. Active in the 1859 prayer revival in Chicago, Moody helped establish Chicago's YMCA and became its first full-time employee. In his eagerness to bring souls to Christ, Moody began preaching on the streets of Chicago. He packed his Sunday School with poor children he found roaming the streets, and he shocked many by bringing even slum dwellers to church.
>
> George Williams, founder of the YMCA, lived in London, and Moody traveled there on business. In the spring of 1872, he was asked to substitute preach at a London pulpit. When 400 people responded to his closing invitation, it seemed God's direction to do more evangelistic work. In 1873 Moody returned to England with his singing partner, Ira Sankey. What was planned as a small tour became a major two-year preaching tour throughout England, Scotland, and Ireland. Thousands packed churches and halls to hear the evangelists from America. Moody and Sankey

returned home heroes and began a series of successful "preaching missions" in America.

As the 1800's turned into the 1900's, Americans became enamored with a revivalist whose name (really) was Billy Sunday. A former baseball player with the Chicago White-Stockings, Sunday had been converted at the Pacific Garden Mission in Chicago. When he became an evangelist, he organized his staff like a business, with advance men, secretaries, managers, building supervisors, choristers, and local volunteers. He required that money for all his expenses be raised before he began a meeting in any city. In 1909, Sunday was joined by Homer Rodeheaver, a great trombone player and song leader. People flocked to Sunday's meetings. He had a talent for the dramatic, and his antics and rapid-fire delivery promised a good show. It was the age of vaudeville, and Sunday brought the trappings and theatrics of the stage to the tent meeting revivals. He had sawdust put on the floors of the "tabernacles" built for his meetings to muffle the noise of feet, and the "sawdust trail" became an expression referring to revival meetings.[lxxxix]

To think about the original influence of the church and Christianity on our nation is almost inexplicable. The number of hospitals and universities that were founded specifically by the church, and even for the church at their onset, is comprehensive. As this article from *Answers in Genesis* shows their Christian influence was immeasurable:

Most of the colleges in the U.S. that started over 300 years ago were Bible-proclaiming schools originally. Harvard and Yale (originally Puritan) and Princeton (originally Presbyterian) once had rich Christian histories. Harvard was named after a Christian minister, Yale was started by clergymen, and Princeton's first class was taught by Reverend Jonathan Dickinson. Princeton's crest still says, "Dei sub numine viget," which is Latin for "Under God she flourishes."

The book *The Sacred and the Secular University* (2000) is an insightful study by Jon H. Roberts and James Turner, two secular historians who show no evidence of overt Christian bias. They discuss the change in American universities from the Christian worldview to a more naturalistic philosophy. They point out that universities across the board fell first in the area of science: "In the sciences, the critical departure from this hegemonic construct took place in the 1870s." They add that "'methodological naturalism' was the critical innovation."

Naturalism opposes God's Word in Genesis, the foundational book of the Bible. As Psalm 11:3 states, "When the foundation is destroyed, what can the righteous do?" Cracks in the foundation led to a collapse of the Christian worldview at these schools.

The cracks first appeared in the late 1700s and early 1800s, culminating with the influence of Charles Lyell's three volumes of *Principles of Geology* in the 1830s. Belief in an old-earth seriously wounded widespread acceptance of the Flood and the biblical chronology, and Lyell just "finished off the victim and nailed the coffin shut," as *Answers In Genesis* historian Dr. Terry Mortenson says.

This old-earth belief permeated universities by the mid-1800s, setting the stage for Darwin's evolutionary model in 1859 (*Origin of Species*) and his later work on human evolution *The Descent of Man* (1871), both of which required long ages. After Christian universities adopted these compromises, the slide from biblical Christianity to naturalism soon followed.

Roberts and Turner explain why Christians compromised

with naturalistic scientists:

> The determination of scientists to bring phenomena within the purview of naturalistic description evoked a mixed response from Christians outside the scientific community. ... Many clergymen and theologians—most commonly those who embrace a 'liberal' approach to Christian thought—sought to avoid that outcome by joining scientists in embracing an immanentist conception of God's relationship to the world [emphasis added].
>
> An immanent position holds that deity would be bound within the universe, which is what these naturalistic scientists were teaching. Undoubtedly, compromise with belief in an ancient earth and evolution contributed greatly to the spiritual downfall of these institutions. Once Christians began adopting a naturalistic view, including evolution or earth history over millions of years, it didn't take long for the rest of their faith to come crumbling down. They had given up the Bible as their starting point and had accepted naturalistic science instead.[xc]

This article by April Shenandoah aptly describes the ignorance of contemporary culture about our Christian foundation and the distance of America's fall from grace. She states:

> Bill Maher, of *Politically Incorrect*, said, "America has never been a Christian Nation." However, as we read about the founding of our universities and the first textbooks that were used in this country, we cannot dispute our Christian foundation. 106 of the first 108 colleges were started on the Christian faith. By the close of 1860 there were 246 colleges in America. Seventeen of these were state institutions; almost every other one was founded by Christian denominations or by individuals who avowed a religious purpose.
>
> Harvard College, 1636 - An Original Rule of Harvard College: "Let every student be plainly instructed and earnestly

pressed to consider well, the main end of his life and studies is, to know God and Jesus Christ which is eternal life, (John 17:3), and therefore to lay Christ in the bottom, as the only foundation of all sound knowledge and learning."

William and Mary, 1691 - The College of William and Mary was started mainly due to the efforts of Rev. James Blair in order, according to its charter of 1691, "that the Church of Virginia may be furnished with a seminary of ministers of the gospel, and that the youth may be piously educated in good letters and manners, and that the Christian religion may be propagated among the Western Indians to the glory of Almighty God."

Yale University, 1701 - Yale University was started by Congregational ministers, "for the liberal and religious education of suitable youth...to propagate in this wilderness, the blessed reformed Protestant religion..."

Princeton, 1746 - Associated with the Great Awakening, Princeton was founded by the Presbyterians. Rev. Jonathan Dickinson became its first president, declaring, "cursed be all that learning that is contrary to the cross of Christ."

University of Pennsylvania, 1751 - Ben Franklin had much to do with the beginning of the University of Pennsylvania. It was not started by a denomination, but its laws reflect its Christian character. Consider the first two Laws, relating to Moral Conduct (from 1801): "1. None of the students or scholars, belonging to this seminary, shall make use of any indecent or immoral language: whether it consist in immodest expressions; in cursing and swearing; or in exclamations which introduce the name of God, without reverence, and without necessity. "2. None of them shall, without a good and sufficient reason, be absent from school, or late in his attendance; more particularly at the time of prayers, and of the reading of the Holy Scriptures."

Some other colleges started before America's Independence include: Columbia founded in 1754 (called King's College up until 1784), Dartmouth, 1770; Brown started by the Baptists in 1764; Rutgers, 1766, by the Dutch Reformed Church; Washington and Lee, 1749; and Hampton-Sydney, 1776, by the Presbyterians. It may surprise many to know that the Bible was truly the first textbook. The New Haven Code of 1655 required that children be made "able duly to read the Scriptures... and in some competent measure to understand the main grounds and principles of Christian Religion necessary to salvation."

a. The Bible was the central text - John Adams reflected the view of the founders in regard to the place of the Bible in society when he wrote: "Suppose a nation in some distant region, should take the Bible for their only law-book, and every member should regulate his conduct by the precepts there exhibited!... What a Utopia; what a Paradise would this region be!" John Adams, Feb.22, 1756

b. Hornbooks - Hornbooks were brought to America, from Europe, by the colonists and were common from the 1500's - 1700's. A hornbook was a flat piece of wood with a handle, upon which a sheet of printed paper was attached and covered with transparent animal horn to protect it. A typical hornbook had the alphabet, the vowels, a list of syllables, the invocation of the Trinity, and the Lord's Prayer.

c. Catechisms - There were over 500 different catechisms used in early education. Later, the Westminster Catechism became the most prominent one.

d. The New England Primer - It was the most prominent schoolbook for about 100 years and was used through the 1800's. It sold over 3 million copies in 150 years.

e. Webster's Blue-Backed Speller - First published in 1783 it sold over 100 million copies. It was one of the most influential textbooks and was based on "God's Word."

f. The McGuffey Readers - Written by minister and university professor William Holmes McGuffey, the McGuffey Readers "represent the most significant force in the framing of our national morals and tastes" other than the Bible.

While there were many other textbooks (especially in the 1800's), the ones just mentioned were some of the most important.

Education in Religion was central to our Founders: Benjamin Rush signer of the Declaration of Independence wrote, "...the only foundation for a useful education in a republic is to be laid in religion. Without this, there can be no virtue, and without virtue there can be no liberty, and liberty is the object and life of all republican governments." The type of education that shaped our Founders character and ideas was thoroughly Christian. It imparted Christian character and produced honest, industrious, compassionate, respectful, and law-abiding men. It imparted a Biblical world-view and produced people who were principled thinkers.[xci]

With regard to hospitals and their Christian influence, Charles Rosenberg shows in his volume, *The Care of Strangers, The Rise of America's Hospital System*, "the modern hospital owes its origins to Judeo-Christian compassion. Evidence of the vast expansion of faith-based hospitals is seen in the legacy of their names: St. Vincent's, St. Luke's, Mt. Sinai, Presbyterian, Mercy, and Beth Israel. These were all charitable hospitals, some of which began as foundling hospitals to care for abandoned children. In 1800, with a population of only 5.3 million, most Americans would only have heard of a hospital. Philadelphia's Pennsylvania Hospital was founded in 1751, New York Hospital in 1771, and Boston General did not open until 1821. But by just after the mid-century mark, hospitals were being established in large numbers, and most of them were religious."[xcii]

We don't really need any proof of how far we have fallen off the wagon as America, because we know it intuitively, but check out these recent statistics about where we are at in the church today. Unfortunately, we can see the sad state of evangelism that has permeated our culture and churches today:

> Only 2 in 10 adults from the general population think that sharing their faith is their personal responsibility. Now this is the general population, so the respondents could belong to any religion. But when the researchers singled out Christians, they found that only one quarter of Christians "believe they are called to promote the gospel." But the Bible makes it clear we are to "go into all the world and proclaim the gospel to the whole creation" (Mark 16:15).
>
> And it's not just the lay population of Christians who aren't applying the Great Commission to themselves. More than one in four theologically conservative pastors don't believe they have a responsibility to share the gospel. No wonder many Christians aren't sharing the gospel—their pastors don't believe it's a priority or even their responsibility! The study also found that, if people are sharing their faith, they probably aren't sharing a biblical version of the good news.
>
> Among the concepts most likely to be shared by conservative believers are that people are basically good; that having some faith is more important than the substance of that faith; that God exists and is omnipotent and omniscient but that humankind has evolved from other life forms; He remains aware of what happens in the universe and is involved in our lives; there is absolute moral truth but it is located in various places; eternal security can be assured either through the sacrificial death and resurrection of Christ or by doing enough good deeds to earn God's favor; a person's life can be considered "successful" based upon the personal goals accomplished; the Bible is the reliable Word of God; Jesus understands our struggle because He sinned while on earth; and that sin is real but Satan and the Holy Spirit are not.

> Preaching a gospel other than the gospel revealed through Christ and the Scriptures is nothing short of a false gospel, and Scripture has severe warnings for those who do not present the truth of the gospel (Galatians 1:6–12).[xciii]

Consider too some of the financial statistics below about the church in America. As a pastor, I understand the struggle with money within the church and how intentions are often good but when you evaluate your church's balance statement does it look any different than the following? We can do better. We must do better. We have lost our way, yet, because everyone else is doing it too, we have decided that it is acceptable when it is not. It is the same for individuals, as we give minuscule percentages of our income to support the work of the church. God demands the first fruits and the best, and we have barely left the scraps for Him and His work.

Disturbing Statistics About the Church in the USA

- 85% of all funding goes towards internal operations.
- 50% to pay the salary of pastors and church staff.
- 22% to pay for upkeep and expansion of buildings.
- 13% for church expenses such as electricity and supplies.
- 13% to outreach, which includes 3% for local missions.
- 2% for overseas missions (both evangelistic and charitable).
- In the end, if you only give to your local church, odds are that only 2% of 2.58%, or 0.05% of your income is going towards "preaching the gospel to every nation" and helping the "poorest of the poor" combined. To put that in perspective, if you make $50,000 a year, that is only $25.80 per year.[xciv]

America used to be a missionary sending nation that was responsible for evangelizing the world and spreading the Gospel to the four corners of the earth. Now most missionaries from America are in already "Christianized" cultures, not working with previously unreached people groups. In conjunction with that, America is now responsible for spiritually influencing other nations in a negative manner. I remember coming to this stark and lasting impression of America's negative influence during the 2018 Olympics in South Korea. There is a song called "Imagine" by John Lennon of the Beatles that has a horrible message of imagining that there is no God and it was played as part of the opening ceremony. I listened to that song and saw the nations of the world joyously proclaiming it (whether they knew it or not) and realized at that moment that America had become a negative spiritual influence on other nations right under our nose. There are missionaries and agencies that are trying to combat this and proclaim the Good News of Jesus Christ, but the work that is being done pales in comparison to the amount of money and negative propaganda that comes from our nation infecting the countries of the world.

ISRAEL AND AMERICA

Will America Be Judged? By John Piper Desiring God 2/25/14:

> The Bible portrays God's relation to nations as tolerating sin up to a point, and then bringing calamity. God said to Abram that his descendants would spend four hundred years in a foreign land as slaves (Genesis 15:13). Then God would 'bring judgement on the nation that they serve' (Genesis 15:14). Why such a long delay before God gave the Promised Land to Israel? God answers, 'Because the iniquity of the Amorites is not yet complete.' (Genesis 15:16). In other words, there was a level of corruption that would be reached among the nations of the Promised Land that would justify God's judgement on them when Israel returned to Egypt. So God taught his people not to say, 'It is because of my righteousness that the Lord has brought me in to possess this land.' Rather, 'it is because of the wickedness of those nations that the Lord is bringing them out before you' (Deuteronomy 9:4).[xcv]

God's delay in judgment shows His mercy and kindness. Though it will not last forever, that is what prevents the Lord from judgment upon those that forsake His name, participate in wickedness, or corrupt His church. Those who don't experience the judgment perceive it as inattention or the fact that the Lord doesn't care, neither of which are true. It is simply that God is being merciful and allowing even the most corrupt among us the opportunity to turn from sin and seek Him. All the while, if those who abuse and corrupt and oppress do not repent, they are actually heaping more judgment upon themselves, as the merciful high priest patiently waits to intervene. So many people wonder why God allows evil in the world if He is a good God, but what they fail to see is that it is God's kindness even to the unjust and evil that allows injustices to occur.

As Piper points out above, there is a tipping point where the cries of the oppressed reach the ears of the Lord. You can see this in the stories of Sodom and Gomorrah, Israel in the land of Egypt, or even with the fall of Israel and Judah in the Promised Land. There were commandments. There were warnings. There were calls to repentance. But finally, God released His judgment. We saw that with Israel — God's own people, His dearly loved children, His sons and daughters. Will it be any different with America?

America is a great country, and I am so thankful to be an American. I am thankful for the freedoms, the prosperity, the free enterprise, the elected government, and a host of other things. But America is not an idol. God must be first. He has certainly blessed our nation and shed His grace on thee, but if Christians must choose between God and country, there should be no hesitation. This isn't *A Few Good Men*, where it is espoused that the military code is honor, corp, God, and country.

Isaiah 40:17-18

[17] All the nations are as nothing before Him;
they are considered by Him as nothingness and emptiness.

[18] Who will you compare God with?
What likeness will you compare Him to?

It doesn't matter what nation it is — America, Israel, or another — God is sovereign and king. The Israelites thought similarly that they couldn't be judged because they were God's holy city and maintained His divine temple. They were wrong. Don't make the same mistake, America. You are accountable to God and to His laws.

We know the faith of our spiritual fathers, but we do not know the faith of our founding fathers and because of that we have been fooled to believe that our prosperity and success as a nation has been accomplished by chance or ingenuity instead of by divine ordinance. Listen to this realization of someone who actually took the time to examine the truth and look at the source documents from the book *Original Intent* by David Barton:

> ...a notable ACLU attorney decided he would disprove our thesis that the Founding Fathers were largely Christian. He therefore took *Original Intent* and undertook a project to expose what he considered to be its falsehoods; he went back and checked our quotes against the original sources cited in the book. At the end of his research, he concluded that we had understated the faith of the Founders – that there was actually much more evidence to support their Christian faith than even what we had cited. This ACLU attorney was completely converted and went on to become an eminent court of appeals judge – all because he followed Paul's model of Acts 17:11 and checked the evidence for himself. We have numerous similar testimonials of the dramatic change that has occurred in individuals who investigated the original facts for themselves."[xcvi]

Hopefully by now you can see some of the parallels between ancient Israel and America, but even if you do not, please note that the founders did. There was a prevailing understanding and hope that God had divinely appointed America to be a special part of His kingdom on earth and that His blessing was upon her. In God's New Israel by Conrad Cherry he indicates this understanding in the new America:

> Although the Great Awakening brought about a renewal of the idea that the New World was the Promised Land, the birth of the republic lent special credence to the idea. The birth pangs of the revolutionary War both announced the coming of independence and awakened the colonists to a new errand into the wilderness. Victory was interpreted as both a hard-earned opportunity for American self-determination and a proof of God's blessing on Ameri-

> can tasks. The achievement of constitutional government was seen as the first step in a bold experiment that would assure basic human freedoms; it was also understood as a serious effort to erect an American model for the Old World. God's New Israel was transformed into a republic; a colonial destiny became a national destiny.[xcvii]

This was the pervasive understanding of America's early political, religious, and civil leaders. The great preacher Jonathon Edwards espoused this notion as well in a sermon entitled *The Latter-Day Glory Is Probably to Begin in America.* Conrad Cherry continues with this line of thinking:

> The belief that America has been elected by God for a special destiny on the world has been the focus of American sacred ceremonies, the inaugural addresses of our presidents, the sacred scriptures of the civil religion. It has been so pervasive a motif in the national life that the word 'belief' does not really capture the dynamic role that it has played for the American people, for it passed into 'the realm of motivational myths.' It became a myth in the sense that it provided a religious outlook on history and its purpose, and by finding a place in the feelings and choice as well as in the ideas of the people, it proved to be capable of moving them to action. When interpreters of the civil religion have appealed to this myth, therefore, they not only have struck a responsive chord in their auditors, for if they have dramatized their subject, they have been able to elicit a commitment.[xcviii]

Whether it is true that America was designed by God to be a picture of the new Israel or whether we still believe it today can be argued, but the fact that the people who founded our nation saw it as a prevalent theme throughout is evident. As we explore Israel and America's relationship and whether or not we are in danger of the judgment that Israel underwent, I would like to take time to talk about why God would allow or cause judgment. The first reality to remember is that the message of impending judgment is really a message of grace because if there is a clear and present danger then alerting someone of that danger is the most loving thing that you could do. Even if you have that mature understanding of the message of judgment, it can still be hard to endure the circumstances that are encompassed by it. In order to alleviate misunderstanding and bitterness let us explore the Biblical reasons for judgment.

The most classical understanding and definition of judgment is usually understood as the punishment of God for gross negligence and sin. This is the Biblical example of Sodom and Gomorrah when there were not enough righteous individuals in the entire region to stay God's hand. There are situations and times when things get so bad that God decides He needs to intervene and when He says, "enough is enough". Ultimately this type of judgment is understood as punishment for those who do not follow Christ and will result in eternal separation and torture without repentance. The second reason that God allows or causes judgment is to shake, awake, discipline, prune, and purify. When we suffer God tells us to evaluate it through the lens of discipline. This type of judgment feels incredibly painful, but it is part of God's eternal good and perfect plan for His people to awaken or prune them to purity. It is painful, but helpful. It is hard, but good. It is challenging, but rewarding. It does not feel good at the time, but in the end, it yields the peaceful fruit of righteousness. This is the type of judgment that Judah underwent in the Babylonian captivity. They had turned their backs on the Lord, and they were no longer following Him or His instructions. Therefore, God created an opportunity for discipline and judgment upon the nation to give them the chance to come back to Him. Through their captivity, they gained the understanding of their need and dependence on God and they returned to rebuild and experience redemption. The third reason that God allows or causes judgment is to set the captives free. Sometimes, there is a person, group, people, or even nation that are unduly oppressed and when they cry out for justice - God hears them and moves on their behalf. In this scenario, judgment is released upon the oppressors in order to get God's point across until the captives are free. The Biblical example for this is Israel being set free from Pharaoh and the Egyptians. God commanded the Egyptians to release the Israelites and He brought forth judgments until they complied. Sometimes God will allow or inflict judgment in order to defend and release His people. Considering the conditions in America I think you would agree that at least a couple of these reasons could be valid for judgment to occur. We need to understand that God is concerned about the long term condition of His followers who He wants to be with Him in heaven. If the best or only way to make that happen involves pain, suffering, and discipline then He is not ashamed of doing what is the greatest long term good for His people. We pray that judgment will not be necessary in America to wake us out of our stupor or to release those who are oppressed, but we shouldn't be offended if it happens.

16 ISRAEL AND AMERICA: HOW THEY BEGAN

If you are reading this book, you probably have a strong Biblical knowledge of the process of Israel becoming a great nation. You are probably very familiar with God calling Abraham, the continuation of the covenant through Isaac and Jacob, the gradual growth of the people in the land of Egypt, and their eventual freedom through the hand of Moses. But you may not be near as familiar with some of the stories of the individuals that helped found our nation in America. You may be familiar with their names, but you may not know their stories unless you have specifically studied them because these stories are not typically included in our history books (which is a travesty in and of itself).

George Washington started his military career with the English forces as they fought against the French and Indians in the French and Indian War about a decade before the American Revolution. This story shared in a famous sermon preached in Hanover County, Virginia, on August 17, 1755, by Samuel Davies, tells the story of one of Washington's early battles and the providence that guided his preservation:

> During the ill-fated Battle of the Monongahela (near present day Pittsburgh), Washington, who was recovering from illness, exhibited remarkable courage and leadership when British forces marched into an ambush and suffered a disastrous defeat. Washington's survival was miraculous. After the battle, he wrote his mother, saying, "I luckily escaped without a wound, though I had four bullets through my coat and two horses shot under me...I was not

> half recovered from a violent illness that had confined me to my bed and a wagon for above ten days." Washington believed God had providentially protected him, and it infused him with confidence in God's guarding, guiding hand. Writing to his brother, John, he said, "By the all-powerful dispensation of Providence I have been protected beyond all human probability or expectation; for I had four bullets through my coat and two horse shot under me yet escaped unhurt, although death was leveling my companions on every side." The Native Americans were equally perplexed at Washington's survival. One of the chiefs had repeatedly fired at him and ordered his young warriors to do the same, all of them being true marksmen. But their bullets were "turned aside by some invisible and inscrutable interposition." Chief Red Hawk claimed to have personally shot at Washington eleven times. Another chief, perplexed at Washington's survival, is said to have predicted, "He will become the chief of nations, and a people yet unborn will hail him as the father of a mighty empire." Washington's incredible survival created a sensation in the Colonies, and many felt God's hand was on him for a special purpose.[xcix]

An equally miraculous story shared by Robert Morgan details the survival of John Adams:

> In the 1740's, the American Colonies became a rope in the tug-of-war between Britain and France. One of the harshest periods of conflict, King George's War, raged from 1744 to 1748, some thirty years before the Declaration of Independence. In the midst of the conflict, in October 1746, Bostonians heard with alarm that the French admiral duc d'Anville was preparing to sail his fleet from Nova Scotia to Boston Harbor to attack the city and ravage New England. It was the largest naval armada to have threatened the American coastline. The governor of the Massachusetts colony had no adequate way to protect Boston, the jewel of American cities, or its fifteen thousand inhabitants. The

French were coming to burn the city to the ground. Sunday, October 16, 1746, was appointed a citywide day of prayer and fasting. Panicked citizens gathered into the city's churches, with hundreds of them crowding into the historic Old South Meeting House. The only thing pleasant that day was the weather, which was peaceful and calm. Not a breeze ruffled the waters in the bay, and not threatening clouds drifted through the skies. The pastor of Old South Church was Rev. Thomas Prince, a powerful force in the Great Awakening, a friend of George Whitefield, and a man of prayer. Climbing into the high pulpit, Rev. Prince earnestly interceded on behalf of the Colonies. "Deliver us from our enemy," he reportedly prayed. "Send Thy tempest, Lord, upon the waters to the eastward! Raise Thy right hand. Scatter the ships of our tormentors and drive them thence." Suddenly a powerful gust of wind struck the church so hard the shutters banged, startling the congregation. Rev. Prince paused and looked up in surprise. Sunlight no longer streamed through the windows, and the room reflected the ominous darkness of the sky. Gathering his thoughts, Rev. Prince continued with greater earnestness, saying, "Sink their proud frigates beneath the power of Thy winds." Gusts of wind caused the church bell to chime "a wild and uneven sound...though no man was in the steeple." Raising his hands toward heaven, Rev. Prince bellowed, "We hear Thy voice, O Lord! We hear it! Thy breath is upon the waters to the eastward, even upon the deep. The bell toils for the death of our enemies!" Overcome by emotion, he paused as tears ran down his cheeks, then he ended his prayer saying, "Thine be the glory, Lord. Amen and amen!" That day a storm of hurricane force struck the French ships. The greater part of the fleet was wrecked, and the duc d'Anville either took his own life or died from a stroke. Only a few soldiers survived.

In his book *Anatomy of a Naval Disaster: The 1746 French*

> *Expedition to North America,* Professor James Pritchard wrote, "Not a single French military objective had been achieved. Thousands of soldiers and sailors were dead... No one knows how many men died during the expedition; some estimates range as high as 8,000. So great was the calamity that naval authorities hastened to wind up its affairs and bury quickly and effectively the memory of its existence." Back in Boston, the governor set aside a day of thanksgiving, and according to historian Catherin Drinker Bowen, "There was no end to the joyful quotation: If God be for us, who can be against us? Somehow that verse came to people's mind, reminding them that when God is our advocate, no enemy—not even an entire navy—can overcome us...Meanwhile in nearby Braintree on that never-to-be-forgotten day, a child named John Adams knelt with his family as his father thanked God 'for this most timely evidence of His favor.'"[c]

To think how God miraculously and providentially saved these two men years and even decades before their years of influence gives us pause to consider God's great care and plans for the country that would later become the United States of America. It is quite evident through these accounts and countless others, that God was intentionally and intricately involved in the founding of America. To deny that is to fail to recognize the significance of farmers and shop owners and apprentices taking on and defeating the greatest military force of their day. There is no natural or human explanation, military or otherwise, that could explain how the Americans won their independence. But with God all things are possible, and by His grace they came to be victorious in the outcome of the Revolutionary War. The stories are many and varied as to how God intervened to fight on behalf of the Americans through fog, weather patterns, illnesses, and the encouragement from pulpits and leaders to maintain the resolve necessary to endure and prevail. They were emboldened and empowered by their faith that God was fighting for them and that their cause for freedom was divinely inspired.

Another miraculous account details a British invasion upon New York Harbor that began before dawn on Thursday, August 22, 1776:

> Within days the Revolutionary Army was trapped in Brooklyn across the East River from Manhattan and facing annihilation, which would have ended the War less than two months after the signing of the Declaration of Independence. When British ships, carrying thirty-two thousand troops, sailed into New York, their masts tilting with the tides, they looked like a forest of trees swaying in the wind. One observer said, "I thought all London was afloat." It was "the largest, most powerful force ever sent forth from Britain or any nation." Washington didn't stand a chance.
>
> Late on the afternoon of August 29, Washington gave the order to retreat. The escape of nine thousand weary, rain-soaked troops across a mile-wide river was a desperate gamble. If the British caught on, the entire army would be decimated. Many of the men wrote their last wills and testaments on the spot. Just after nightfall the weakest warriors headed for the ferry landing as the retreat began.
>
> Immediately the weather became an ally. A strong northeast wind kept British ships from venturing into the area; yet at about 11:00pm the wind died down, allowing Washington's hastily assembled armada to cross the river without danger. Sympathetic New York sailors and fishermen mobilized, loading soldiers, horses, wagons, cannons, and all manner of equipment onto boats.
>
> Wagon wheels were wrapped in cloth to muffle their sounds on the cobblestones and not a word was spoken. The soldiers were told not to cough or make any sounds, and orders passed through the ranks by whispers. Camp-

fires were kept burning to deceive the enemy.

All night, boats silently ferried the army back and forth across the river, yet when the sun arose, a large portion of the army was still trapped. But a fog had rolled in during the night, thick as velvet, shielding the remaining evacuees, and it remained until the evacuation was completed. One soldier wrote:

> *In this fearful dilemma fervent prayers went up to Him who alone could deliver. As if in answer to those prayers, when the night deepened, a dense fog came rolling in, and settled on land and water...Under cover of this fog...Washington silently withdrew his entire army across to New York.*

Another eyewitness said:

> *It was one of the most anxious, busy nights that I ever recollect, and being the third in which hardly any of us had closed our eyes to sleep, we were all greatly fatigued. As the dawn of the next day approached, those of us who remained in the trenches became very anxious for our own safety, and when the dawn appeared there were several regiments still on duty...At this time a very dense fog began to rise off the river, and it seemed to settle in a peculiar manner over both encampments. I recollect this peculiar providential occurrence perfectly well, and so very dense was the atmosphere that I could scarcely discern a man at six yards distance...We tarried until the sun had risen, but the fog remained as dense as ever...In the history of warfare, I do not recollect a more fortunate retreat. After all, the providential appearance of the fog saved a part of our army from being captured, and certainly myself among others who formed the rear guard.*

When the fog lifted, the Americans were gone. Historian David McCullough wrote, "The immediate reaction of the British was utter astonishment. That the rebel army had

> silently vanished in the night under their very noses was almost inconceivable."
>
> The evacuation occurred near the current site of the Brooklyn Bridge and has been called the Colonial Dunkirk, referring to the similar, almost miraculous evacuation of the British Army from France during World War II. The "fervent prayers" of the army were answered. Thirteen years later, General Washington took the presidential oath of office at the old Federal Building in lower Manhattan, just a few moments' walk from the spot he had stepped ashore in 1776, divinely shielded by the fog of war.[ci]

David Avery, who was one of the Revolutionary Army's first chaplains, left his post as pastor straight from church after a stirring sermon garnering support for the cause of independence and about twenty men from the congregation joined him in enlisting for the cause:

> In the Battle of Bunker Hill, Avery stood on the hilltop watching the fighting unfold on Breed's Hill, and there in the open he lifted his arms like Moses and appealed for divine aid amid the bloodshed. These words went into his diary: "I stood on [Bunker Hill] with hands uplifted, supplicating the blessings of Heaven to crown our unworthy arms with success. To us infantile Americans, unused to the thunder, the carnage of battle, the flames of Charlestown before our eyes—the incessant play of cannon from their shipping-from Boston, and their wings in various cross directions, together with the fire of musketry from more than four times our number, all heightened the majestic terrors of the field, exhibiting a scene most awful and tremendous. But amid the perils of the dread encounter, the Lord was our rock and fortress." Avery was there in Boston when George Washington arrived to take control of the army. He stood in the ranks of Dorchester Heights on the morning the Americans took their brave stand; and when the British retreated, he exclaimed, "Give God the

praise, for He hath done it."[cii]

These and other miraculous stories and events led the American people to believe in a special destiny for the U.S. and to compare Washington to Moses. Again, this doesn't prove such a relationship exists, but it does prove that early Americans believed it to be true. Regardless, the hand of God was evident and strong in the lives and establishment of our great nation.

17 ISRAEL AND AMERICA: HOW THEY PROSPERED

America has done amazing things and had tremendous success. We have had our Constitution for over 200 years while other countries in Europe have had 15 different government documents in the same amount of time. Although we only have about 4% of the world's population, we produce, on average, between 25-30% of the world's GDP. That's not just because of natural resources either, because countries like South America and Africa have far more than we do. The United States also accounts for about 96% of the world's inventions. These statistics indicate the success and blessing of a great nation. When you look at how this nation was founded and how it began, it becomes very clear that it is because of the grace of God.

I think most people are familiar with the prosperity of Israel in the Old Testament, which included the expanse of David's kingdom and the splendor and glory of the temple and Solomon's palace. God had miraculously provided and blessed the people of Israel in such a way that they were the most prosperous and influential nation in the world. The U.S. has enjoyed a similar status since it started out-producing Great Britain in 1916. Yes, there have been depressions and recessions in the U.S., but as a whole, it has been one of the greatest nations in the world by many standards for the past 100 years. During the early 1900's, there was a conglomerate of nations that rose and fell due to issues around war, debt, and production. When the dust settled, the U.S had become one of the clear world superpowers, both economically and militarily. As the century continued, it became more and more clear that the U.S. had established itself as a perennial superpower. When Russia's iron curtain fell, the United States stood alone upon the pedestal of the world powers. It has been that way until recently, when China began to challenge the U.S. in economic prosperity. Those in older generations have never known a time when the U.S. was not among the world's superpowers, while younger generations have only known the United States to be the world's lone superpower. The problem is that our success has been disconnected from our story. Current generations have simply inherited the success of the system without recognizing the hard work and miraculous nature of such accomplishments, which would not be possible but by the grace of God. People today do not understand our history or founding as a Christian nation and they don't understand the significance and the struggle of where we are today. Because of that, our success is taken for granted and assumed to be the product of American ingenuity. We can quote founding father after founding father who credited the Lord of heaven and earth for their success and status at the beginning and forming of our county (even as a fledgling country that did not have the notion of becoming a superpower as a twinkle in its eyes) and yet, we are far more prosperous and successful today and give God far less credit, if any. Thomas Jefferson, who was notoriously one of the least religious of the founding fathers, even weighs in on this subject. Enshrined at the Jefferson Memorial in Washington, DC, is a letter from Jefferson where he states: "Can the liberties of a nation be thought secure when we have removed their only firm basis? A conviction in the minds of people that these liberties are of the gift of God—that they are not to be violated but with His wrath. Indeed, I tremble for my country when I reflect that God is just—that His justice cannot sleep forever."[ciii]

I think Jefferson is indeed trembling. Our founding fathers based our Declaration of Independence on five immutable principles, as described in David Barton's presentation on "Providential History."[civ] First, there is a divine creator, which means there is a power higher than government. Second, man's inalienable rights come from God; there is a list of those rights described in the Bible that are laid out in the Bill of Rights. Third, government exists to protect man's inalienable rights. Fourth, there is a fixed moral law, which is described in the laws of nature and by God's law. The final principle is that to be legitimate, any government must have the consent of the governed. These five immutable principles, upon which the Declaration of Independence is based, have provided the foundation and standard of rule for our nation and have allowed us to enjoy great success because ours is a government based on divine, immutable principles that do not change — unlike human laws. That is why we have had one Constitution over our 250-year history, whereas other nations (even in the second-most stable area in the world, Europe) have had multiple governments, Constitutions, and rewrites of the documents that govern their respective nation. Without a recognition that God has provided our grace and success and that these divinely established immutable laws that stem from God are what have allowed us to prosper, there is little to discuss. If we don't recognize God and His providence in our founding the only principle that we are left with is the consent of the governed. What detractors and doubters fail to see is that without the first four immutable principles involving God – the fifth one will never last or even be possible long term. There has to be a recognition and a turning from our current path. Without repentance for not recognizing the sovereign hand of God and His providence in establishing and preserving our nation, we are doomed to fall, as every other great nation has. I could give much more evidence of America's prosperity and success over the last 75 years, but I think that it is understood and is a given. It is widely recognized that we are a prosperous and blessed nation, we just take it for granted and fail to recognize the hand of God as the source and creator of that blessing. What is not understood and recognized is that we are hanging in the balance because the God who founded us and established us has been forgotten, offended, and rejected.

18 ISRAEL AND AMERICA: HOW THEY TURNED

America has shown great resiliency in the past, surviving other challenges, including numerous wars and even a bloody Civil War. Yet all great nations eventually came to an end, including the Assyrians, Aztec, Greeks, Romans, Persians, and many others. They came. They flourished. They rose to world status. They remained strong for generations. They assumed they would always be in power. They all fell.

The same fate may await the United States. America is in serious trouble today. Only the most naïve dare deny it. The same indicators that heralded the fall of other great nations are now present all around us. What are some of those indicators?

Moral Compass. Moral boundaries and sexual limits are rapidly disappearing. The sexual behaviors widely accepted and practiced in America today range from group sex to homosexuality, public sex to polygamy, nymphet sex to voyeurism, polyamory to incest, and much more. We are now in the condition the Bible describes as, "In those days...everyone did what was right in his own eyes" (Judges 17:6, 21:25, ESV).

A landmark study by Dr. J.D. Unwin, a noted professor at both Oxford and Cambridge, investigated more than eighty different civilizations and cultures across 5,000 years of recorded history. He found the degree of stability and longevity each experienced was directly proportional to the rigor of sexual morality it practiced. Whenever marriage became disrespected, divorce easy, and sex outside of marriage widely accepted, for 100 percent of those civilizations there was no 'example of a group retaining its culture after it has adopted less rigorous [sexual] customs.' The Bible is clear that rejecting Biblical standards of sexual morality bring judgment on a nation (cf. Deuteronomy 27:20-23, Leviticus 18:22-25, Colossians 3:5-6, etc.). God's blessings will not reside on any nation that rejects His moral standards, as America now openly does.

Innocent Blood. Sadly, murder abounds in America today, whether it is taking babies' lives in the womb, young men in gangs killing each other (and innocent bystanders), or extinguishing the elderly and handicapped through euthanasia. However, in earlier America when Biblical values still influenced the culture, murder of any kind was extremely rare. In fact, the state of New York experienced only eight murders over the span of sixteen years—a murder every two years. But today, New York has almost two murders a day—and there are some forty-seven murders daily across the United States. The Bible repeatedly condemns the shedding of innocent blood, and history demonstrates that God always removes His blessings from the land where it occurs. America is now such a land.

Education. America spends more on education than nearly any other nation in the world. Yet today, 19 percent of high-school graduates are illiterate—after twelve years of school, and average approaching $140,000 spent per student, one of five graduates can't read. And in international testing, American high school students regularly finish last, near the last, or in the bottom half of students in math and science testing. We are academically outperformed by what are considered third world nations such as Vietnam, Slovenia, and Latvia. American education is abysmal, but as Jeremiah 8:9, reminds us, "Since they have rejected the

> word of the Lord, what kind of wisdom do they have?"
>
> Debt. Each American pays an average of $15,202 per person in taxes each year. But the current federal debt of $20 trillion dollars is so great that if it were to be equally divided among citizens, every American would have to come up with an additional $61,539 per person in taxes in order to retire the current debt. But that does not include the additional financial obligations that federal law has made well into the future, which is called the debt liability. To retire this already committed debt, each person in America will have to pay an additional $260,300 beyond their annual taxes. So if America is to survive, it will have to find a way to retire its debt; yet to do so may drive American families and businesses into widespread bankruptcy and poverty. Significantly, when God blesses a nation, it lends rather than borrows (see Deuteronomy 15:6), but America is now just the opposite: it is a borrowing nation—big time."[cv]

Think about how much carnage and depravity has fallen upon us since this quote and resource were produced in 2018. The highlighted death of innocent African Americans at the hands of police. The financial stimulus package due to COVID-19 and the disease and death at the hands of the virus adding to our national debt. Injustice has escalated, hatred has grown, and sin has destroyed in increasing measures. Just recently, there was a "progressive" Christian author who had a daughter that came out as gay and the family made a big deal to publicly celebrate it. This is the epitome of the disparity in America. It is one thing to experience sin in our lives and families, but by the grace of God there go any of us. Be it divorce, alcohol, drugs, violence, homosexuality, or adultery, there is no shortage of problems in this life, or even in Christian families. The difference is living broken before the potter, continually asking for and depending upon Him and Him alone to put you back together, rather than maintaining that you're not broken. He says that when we confess our weakness and brokenness before Him, we will receive grace and mercy in our time of need. We are all clay pots subject to sin and brokenness in varying degrees in our lives. We will never escape the effects of sin entirely in this life, no matter how diligent we remain, so we must learn to recognize sin, repent of it, and do the best we can to live in the power of the Holy Spirit to overcome it. To think about taking sin — something that is an offense to God — and being proud of it is an affront to God and His character. Without repentance, the future is bleak for America.

It is no different than Israel, which came to power and prospered through David and Solomon to the ends of the earth. That prosperity brought pride and self-reliance, which in turn moved the country further away from God. They had periods of turning back to God based on their leadership, but they never recovered from the downward trends created by the pattern of their sin.

19 ISRAEL AND AMERICA: HOW THEY FELL

Isn't it interesting that the inclination of man is constantly bent toward rebellion? If you look at the people of Israel, time and time again they would rebel, experience discipline, turn toward the Lord, and then rebel again. It was the pattern during the Exodus, it was the pattern during Judges, and it is still the pattern today. In Psalm chapter 78, verses 33 and 34, it says, "So he ended their lives in failure, their years in terror. When God began killing them, they finally sought him. They repented and took God seriously" (NLT). Yes, that's really in the Bible. Why is it that the inclination of man is to wait until people start dying before turning to repentance? Is that the destiny of America, or will people take note and repent before it gets to that? That is not God's will. He does not delight in death and judgment. His heart is always to be the most effective in the least harmful way because He is full of loving kindness and compassion. But when there are no more options — all the warnings have been issued, the discipline has been measured, and the people have been told — He must preserve His people and defend His great name. He is completely merciful, but He is also completely just. Do not mistake God's kindness for weakness, or you will be sorely mistaken. He is not slow in keeping His promises because He desires that everyone be saved and come to the knowledge of the truth. If He were to tear the weeds out, the wheat would be damaged as well, because it is the weeds that give the wheat their testimony before the Lord. And yet, when the weeds are persistent and resistant to restraint, God's hand is forced and justice must be served, because the Lord reigns and His people will serve Him in everlasting righteousness. For those who do not take God seriously He would say, "Who are you, oh Israel, to question the Almighty? Where were you when the earth was being formed or when the waters covered the earth? If you think you understand justice, then tell me who will rule. What will come of your next breath, or tomorrow, or in the years from now? Who can see the past and the future of all who were and all who will be? Why do you question the justice of God? Shouldn't you question the nature and inclination of man to reject and disdain their creator and sustainer? Where can you go from my presence? Where will you hide your deepest secrets from me? Who knows your next move? Who knows your true intentions? My people will be free, and I will remove the yoke of bondage and the weight of oppression from their shoulders. You will know my name and you will bow in reverence at my sight for now and for eternity." In the resource *Multiply*, Francis Chan and Mark Beuving show that this repeated pattern of rebellion leads to less than desirable circumstances:

> God had promised this judgment if Israel disobeyed Him, and after generations of patiently waiting for His people to repent, God remained faithful to His promise. It's hard to read the Old Testament without being blown away by Israel's constant disobedience. As Moses led the Israelites through the wilderness, they continually complained. When Moses went onto Mount Sinai to receive the Law from God, they created a golden idol and worshipped it. When God placed them in the land of Canaan, they kept turning away from Him to worship idols. Idolatry shows up throughout Israel's history. Though there were times of reform, Israel seemed bent on rejecting God. God dealt with this idolatry patiently, but His justice would not be detained forever.[cvi]

In the pattern of Israel, we recognize ourselves and our own shortcomings. In the following article from "Truth or Tradition", the author shares how the consequences of Israel's behavior are a warning for us as well.

Although most cat owners are pretty accustomed to their pet's aloofness, dog owners generally expect a higher level of obedience, especially when you want them to "come." One morning I was confronted with some canine independence when I called my dog. As usual, he found the neighbor's activities a lot more intriguing than anything he thought I had to offer. Standing his ground firmly, almost as if his feet were welded in place, he looked at me over his shoulder. It was clear that he had no concern for my schedule or my need that he come, NOW!

It may seem far-fetched to some, but there was a spiritual lesson I gleaned from my pooch's self-centeredness. What struck me that morning was how God has been calling out to people in much the same way that I called to my dog, and just like my dog ignored me, for the most part people have ignored Him. One of the first stories in Scripture tells of God walking in the Garden, calling out to Adam, "Where are you?" (Gen. 3:8). God's repeated plea to people throughout human history has been, "Return to Me!" He has always sought those who will serve Him with more than mere words.

Therefore, tell the people: This is what the LORD Almighty says: '***Return to me,' declares the LORD Almighty***, 'and I will return to you,' says the LORD Almighty. Zechariah 1:3

"Even now," declares the LORD, "***return to me with all your heart***, with fasting and weeping and mourning." Joel 2:12

It is easy to see that most people go about their daily lives with little thought or concern for God or His ways. Sadly, few understand that God has told mankind that there are very clear and definite consequences for how people respond to God's call. There are great benefits for all those who obey God, so much so, that their obedience can actually affect their weather, the fruitfulness of the harvest, and the safety of their countries. God expresses this spiritual reality in a number of sections of Scripture, and the essence of this truth is captured in Leviticus.

"If you follow my decrees and are careful to obey my commands, I will send you rain in its season, and the ground will yield its crops and the trees of the field their fruit. Your threshing will continue until grape harvest and the grape harvest will continue until planting, and you will eat all the food you want and live in safety in your land. Leviticus 26:3-5

The lesson seems pretty clear: honor God and He will provide for and protect those who love and obey Him. But, just as obedience brings about God's benevolence, so too, disobedience can produce great disaster.

"'If you remain hostile toward me and refuse to listen to me, I will multiply your afflictions seven times over, as your sins deserve. This promise of reward or calamity applies to both individuals and nations as a whole. The following section is not just about God's chosen people, Israel. Some read it thinking it applies only to Israel, however it says, "... if a country..." meaning *any country*. Leviticus 26:21

"'Son of man, if a country sins against me by being unfaithful and I stretch out my hand against it to cut off its food supply and send famine upon it and kill its men and their animals even if these three men—Noah, Daniel and Job—were in it, they could save only themselves by their righteousness', declares the Sovereign LORD". Ezekiel 14:13-14

We cannot dismiss this section of Scripture as archaic or something that does not concern us today. I have heard some people say, "But that only applies to Israel because they had a covenant with God." But the record makes it clear that he is speaking unconditionally to *any country*. There are severe consequences for *any country* that turns its back on God. God's hope would have been that He got people's attention by naming the four judgments mentioned: famine, wild beasts, sword, and plague, since they were the four main causes of death among the ancient civilizations. We Christians want to live under the blessing of God, but far too frequently fail to see that many of His blessings in this life are conditioned upon our obedience to Him. Any nation that honors Him will be blessed, and "any" that does not will suffer for it.

Throughout time God has demonstrated His great love for people by His providence, that is, His provision and His protection. But sin always produces a separation between man and God, and because of His holiness and righteousness, it limits Him in His ability to come to our aid in the spiritual battle. It may help to think of God's favor by seeing it as a hand placed over us. Our sin causes Him to lift His hand, which allows the enemy to slip in under it and harm us. The lifting of God's hand, the withdrawing of His favor happens on both a personal and national scale. Although the following verse is specifically directed towards the people of Jerusalem, the principle seems clear: when people sin deliberately and grievously by rejecting God and His ways, He withdraws His favor.

Therefore as surely as I live, declares the Sovereign LORD, because you have defiled my sanctuary with all your vile images and detestable practices, I myself will withdraw my favor; I will not look on you with pity or spare you. Ezekiel 5:11

Many times, it is a dire state of events that helps people to see their need for God, and this, in turn, drives them right back into His arms. There is much to learn from the story of Israel's numerous rises and falls. The ups and downs are directly connected to how they waxed and waned in their service to God. He was clear with them when He called them as a nation. In essence He said, "Bless Me and I will bless you—ignore Me and you will suffer!"

"God bless America" is a very common maxim in this country, but in the spiritual battle, pithy platitudes are never enough. It is delusional to think we can have God's blessing when we live in a way that dishonors Him. It is arrogant to think that we as a nation can ban God from the schools, padlock Him from our public institutions, ignore Him in the justice system, and reject Him through our immoral behavior and then still think that He will "bless America." This is like waxing a rusted car fender, thinking that it will fix the problem. The issue is decay, and it cannot be fixed with cosmetics. It is prideful to think that a country can ignore God's directions and commands and not suffer for it.

Israel's arrogance testifies against him, but despite all this he does not return to the LORD his God or search for him. Hosea 7:10

"Their deeds do not permit them to return to their God. A spirit of prostitution is in their heart; they do not acknowledge the LORD. Israel's arrogance testifies against them; Hosea 5:4-5

How is the United States today any different from Israel in Hosea's day? America, as well as many other nations, are not honoring the Almighty, and at some point, our rejection of Him will result in calamity. I am not saying that there are no righteous, God-fearing and God-seeking people in our country. Many ask, "Are these the End Times?" Only time will tell, but one thing we do know for certain is that there has been a worldwide increase of geophysical disasters, wars, famines, religious upheaval, and economic implosion. These things will increase until people turn their hearts back to God.

I want God to bless America and I pray for that all the time, but what too few seem to remember is that in order for God to bless any nation, that nation must bless God. God would have to go against His very nature for this not to be the case. The spiritual rules God established tell us that "what one sows he reaps." When we sow unrighteousness, we will reap disaster. "Grace" is getting something we DON'T deserve, whereas "mercy" is not getting what we DO deserve. Grace never provides for toleration of sin. Not suffering the consequences of sin, that is, not getting what we deserve, happens when God extends His mercy. Thankfully, He renews His mercy every day because we certainly need it. God also says that He will have mercy on those to whom He wants to have mercy....it is always His prerogative and not something anyone is entitled to (Rom. 9:15). God has also told us that He will not be mocked. We should not think that we can reject God in our words and deeds and then not suffer for it. There may not be an immediate or even discernible consequence in our lives when we turn from God, but the nature of the spiritual battle is such that there are consequences for sin.

It is only natural for people to become downhearted and discouraged, and especially so when ungodly behavior and evil increases. God tells us that "when the wicked rise to power, people go into hiding" (Prov. 28:28). We can, and must, still pray for God to bless us and our nation, even if there is a lot of wickedness in it. It is good to remind ourselves that throughout human history, God has never been limited by a majority position. In the book of 1 Samuel, Saul's son Jonathan approached a Philistine outpost. He perfectly expressed his position of faith in what he said to his armor bearer:

Jonathan said to his young armor-bearer, "Come, let's go over to the outpost of those uncircumcised fellows. Perhaps the LORD will act in our behalf. Nothing can hinder the LORD from saving, whether by many or by few." 1 Samuel 14:6

No professional gambler would ever consider it wise to accept a bet where the odds were stacked against him a thousand to one. And yet, in God's spiritual economy, odds like that are irrelevant.

"The LORD has driven out before you great and powerful nations; to this day no one has been able to withstand you. One of you routs a thousand, because the LORD your God fights for you, just as he promised. Joshua 23:9-10

We must remind ourselves that our struggle against unrighteousness in our nation is never a matter of "flesh and blood," but against the "spiritual forces of evil in the heavenly realms." Our battle must be waged on a spiritual level. If one righteous person can set a thousand to flee then God is telling us that we have the ability to affect the outcome of the spiritual battle on an exponential scale, but only when people return to God with our whole hearts.

"Even now," declares the LORD, "return to me with all your heart, with fasting and weeping and mourning." Rend your

> heart and not your garments. Return to the LORD your God, for he is gracious and compassionate, slow to anger and abounding in love, and he relents from sending calamity. Joel 2:12-13
>
> God's heart to us is always saying, "Return to Me!" If we as a nation will humble our hearts and seek God, (2 Chron. 7:14), He will be faithful to His promise to hear from heaven and heal our land.[cvii]

As Christians, we understand the new covenant that God instituted through His Son, Jesus Christ and that ultimately, we will stand before our Lord as individuals on judgment day. But as Americans, we must also realize that there is a corporate responsibility before the Lord which we are responsible to help steward. That includes how we vote, govern, give, share, love, etc. We must be able to avoid getting stuck in despair or inactivity. I think that we can agree about the degradation of culture in America, but we mustn't give up in despair or quit trying to make a difference. We are to continue to use our talents the best that we can with the time that we've been given until the master returns. It isn't an option to just give up on America because we live here too! What happens to the rest of America will happen to us, unless God's people rise up to lead our nation in repentance. We will experience the fruit of our actions as a nation even though we live under the new covenant of individual judgment. Look at Jesus' own example and words:

Matthew 11:20-24

20 Then He proceeded to denounce the towns where most of His miracles were done, because they did not repent: **21** "Woe to you, Chorazin! Woe to you, Bethsaida! For if the miracles that were done in you had been done in Tyre and Sidon, they would have repented in sackcloth and ashes long ago! 22 But I tell you, it will be more tolerable for Tyre and Sidon on the day of judgment than for you. 23 And you, Capernaum, will you be exalted to heaven? You will go down to Hades. For if the miracles that were done in you had been done in Sodom, it would have remained until today. 24 But I tell you, it will be more tolerable for the land of Sodom on the day of judgment than for you."[cviii]

What we need to realize is that we actually have a greater accountability as a nation that has heard and knows God's word and yet has turned away. We have seen the miracles and signs and wonders. We have experienced His deliverance and His blessings. We have heard His prophets and evangelists and yet our condition is failing. We may not comprehend the entire understanding of the corporate nature of judgment and blessing upon cities and nations, but even Jesus testified that this will be an eternal reality not just something that happened under the old covenant.

20 ISRAEL AND AMERICA: HOW THEY ARE PRESERVED

In Walter Maier's book *America Turn To Christ*, which is a compilation of radio broadcasts from the *Lutheran Hour* radio show, he states:

> This commonwealth is great and glorious not because we Americans are a superior race, a morally perfect people, but because, despite our failings and shortcomings, God has chosen and exalted us. See how the Almighty directed America's course from the outset! He kept this continent undiscovered, preserving it for us. We might have come under Spanish rule, but He directed birds which led the ships of Columbus to the West Indies. We might have been brought under French rule, but God's wind destroyed a mighty armada of French ships which set sail from Nova Scotia to capture the New England colonies. We might have stayed under British rule, but He gave unusual strength to the ragged regimentals, pre-eminent wisdom to our leaders, and we became a free, vigorous people. We might have been split into two or three opposing nations, but the Lord kept us together. God also fixes the dates in our country's history. One of the highest governmental authorities on military preparation assured me that if the Pearl Harbor attack had come only one year before December 7, 1941, the United States, with its inadequate supplies of munitions and war materials, might have fared

badly. God likewise regulates the forces of nature to serve His purposes. As I recently surveyed the flooded portions of Central Illinois near Peoria, where tireless workers piled millions of sand bags to check the swollen streams, people told me: "God saved the city. For weeks the winds had been heavy. If they had continued during the flood crest, the water would have ruined us, but when the river rose, the Lord suddenly stopped the winds." Every page in our glorious history is emblazoned with marvels of divine providence so great that they fairly shout, "What wonders God has done for us!"

In past generations our country recognized the Lord's loving guidance. Go back to our early days, and as you read the name of Christ in the charters of our Colonies, in the regulations for their government, in the letters of these early settlers, and study their zeal in building churches, converting the Indians, training their young in Christian truth, you find the fundamental reason for America's greatness!

We have lost much of this devotion. We still keep the motto, "In God We Trust," on our coins, but have we preserved it in our hearts? Scripture warns us, 'Beware that thou forget not the Lord, thy God...and... say in thine heart my power and the might of mine hand hath gotten me this wealth!' Too often, in the spirit of power-mad Nebuchadnezar, people survey our country and declare, "This is the great America that we, our engineers, our industrial leaders, our farmers, our business men, our laborers, have built." Flushed by recent military successes, we are ready to give sole credit for those triumphs to our leaders, our superior tanks, our more powerful guns, our better supply and communication systems, our amazing production power; but we have little to say of Heaven's help...Have we

> begun to think that we do not need God? Such ingratitude and forgetfulness of the Almighty would be an insult to our dead, the most fatal error the country could make. Scripture declares and history agrees, "*The nation and kingdom that will not serve Thee shall perish.*"[cix]

The problem is what happened to Israel when they no longer acknowledged God as their king nor followed His statutes and commandments. God warned them over and over and sent prophet after prophet, but they would not return to the Lord. They had periods of returning and there were some kings that followed the Lord, but ultimately the first half of the kingdom fell in Israel and eventually Judah succumbed as well. Not because they were small or weak or unable to defend themselves but because they left their first love and refused to turn from their ways of wickedness and revelry. Is there anyone that truly believes that America will have a different fate? Unless America repents and returns to their first love their fate is set. No amount of national defense, nuclear weapons, walls, money, financial security, diplomacy, or military prowess can stop it or change it. The only hope is repentance and change so that God will have mercy and allow America to stand as a nation.

The Good News is that Nineveh repented and so can America. There is hope and there is a chance no matter how slim it may be that if America repents then God will relent. We serve a God who is slow to anger and full of loving kindness, who will relent if there is true repentance. America is on a course for destruction but that can change. God's arm is not too short to save nor is His ear to dull to hear, but time is up and the warnings are over. It is time to put up or shut up, repent or perish. The Lord is coming.

Revelations 19:11-15

[11]Then I saw heaven opened, and a white horse was standing there. Its rider was named Faithful and True, for he judges fairly and wages a righteous war. [12] His eyes were like flames of fire, and on his head were many crowns. A name was written on him that no one understood except himself. [13] He wore a robe dipped in blood, and his title was the Word of God. [14] The armies of heaven, dressed in the finest of pure white linen, followed him on white horses. [15] From his mouth came a sharp sword to strike down the nations. He will rule them with an iron rod. He will release the fierce wrath of God, the Almighty, like juice flowing from a winepress.[cx]

In Session 5 of "Life Changing Prayer" by Jim Cymbala, at the end of his presentation he says,

> That's where the battle is being fought in America. Will God's people arise? Because America will never change through any political party, any president, any policy – that's impossible. The only one that can change America is the one who can change an American heart and the only one who can do that is Almighty God through Jesus Christ. But to see that effectively done we need the church militant. We need the church on its knees or sitting or with their hands up in the air saying "Come God, you've invited us to do this and we're going to do it and now we're going to wait expectantly to see the great things you're going to do." God will do it![cxi]

Our nation's only hope is in turning to our Lord, Jesus Christ in repentance. Our hope is not in our political leaders, our hope is not in economic growth, and our hope cannot be in Supreme Court justices or in better laws. I pray that all these things will happen as a result of our repentance, but they cannot be our primary goal. Unless Christ and His kingdom are our first priority, America will be relegated to the fate of every other nation that has risen and fallen. All hope is not lost, but it is certainly hanging on by a thread, as we can see all around us. How will we respond? What will we do? Unless we return to the Lord in repentance and live out that repentance in faith by bringing forth justice, helping the poor and afflicted, releasing the oppressed, and living according to God's word, it is simply a matter of time until it collapses. You may not be able to do everything, but you can do something. What will you change? How will you help? What will you give up? How will you work at bringing justice? The clock is ticking.

JUDGMENT OR REPENTANCE

In Isaiah chapter 5, God describes the reason for His great disappointment with Israel. Given the parallels, I can only imagine He has similar feelings toward America at this point. Have you ever put a considerable amount of time into something that came to nothing? Maybe you poured your sweat and tears into a garden, caring for it like a child and making sure that it had everything that it needed. Or maybe it *was* a child that you raised, taught, and loved in an exceedingly sacrificial way, giving them special attention and extra time, sacrificing the things that you wanted to do for their benefit. But when it came time for your effort and sacrifice to bear fruit, it did not. You did everything you could and worked diligently to make sure that your garden or your child — or whatever example you can think of — had everything it needed, but it turned on you. That is God's description of Israel in Isaiah 5:1-4. He shows how He worked so hard to establish them as a nation, how He worked to defend them and keep them from harm and how He gave them the best of everything and therefore expected a good harvest in return. What He found instead was disturbing and disappointing, and the rest of the chapter goes into detail about the consequences for the people of Israel because of their disobedience in spite of God's extra care and concern. We know from history that this did happen and that Israel and Judah both fell, despite their relationship with God, despite their great prosperity, and despite the grace that was shed for them. Will America be any different? I pray that it will, but the only way that it can be different is if there is widespread repentance and reform in which people return to their first love and live according to the commands that God has given to His people.

There are so many issues that we are in need of repentance for as we consider God's judgment: economic disparity, abortion, oppression of the weak, racism, divorce, the definition of marriage, evolution, judicial activism, and gender identity, just to name a few. If there is not widespread repentance, if there is no change, if America continues in this direction, then it will be no different than Israel. We may not be able to pinpoint when it will happen or what will happen, but based on the history of Israel we can know for certain that it *will* happen. With regard to judgment, we know that it is not God's desire. He created the world and the Garden of Eden without sin, and then, because of the choices that mankind made to rebel from His rule, Adam and Eve were removed from the Garden and the curse of the land was the result. This was not God's creation or intention, but because of man's action, God responded in the most loving and appropriate way possible to curtail sin and give people the opportunity for eternal salvation. Judgment was not the hope or the plan, but it was a required response to rebellion. That is still the pattern and heart of God to this very day. Any discipline or judgment that is implemented is done with the most grace and love possible and with the least amount of suffering to get His point across. God is gracious, compassionate, and filled with loving kindness. Even with the nation of Egypt, which was oppressing the people of Israel, it took God 400 years before He took action and judged Egypt and delivered Israel. When bad things happen in the world like war and disease and poverty the first assumption is always that it is because of sin. And we need to remember that there is a difference between God's causative will and His permissive will. Most judgments on the earth are a result of sinful human nature in which God does not prevent. That is why not receiving the protection of God is tantamount to His judgment. The following selection shows how far we have fallen from the republic that was originally founded and why we as a society are now guilty before the Lord:

> This hostility [that the courts and America show toward religion] contrasts sharply with the early republic, when religion was synonymous with patriotism, and Christianity became equated with republican virtue. In the famous 1811 blasphemy decision of *The People of New York v. Ruggles*, Federalist jurist Chancellor James Kent ruled that although the Constitution forbade an established church and New York had no specific statute banning blasphemy, for any citizen to denigrate Christianity was "to strike at the roots of moral obligation and weaken the security of social ties." Kent was not himself a committed Christian. But he agreed that religion was, in the words of Leverett Saltonstall of Massachusetts, "the great bond of civil society." This same conviction caused a New York judge in 1831 to disallow the testimony of a witness who declared himself an atheist. The judge ruled that faith in God "constituted the sanction of all testimony in a court of justice" and that no one could be "permitted to testify without such belief." No one is suggesting that we return to the days when the testimony of nonbelievers is excluded from courts of law. But if the pendulum then swayed too far in the direction of religion, can anyone deny that today it has swung too far in the opposite direction? When prosecutors are reprimanded because they quote from the Bible, when attorneys are told to remove ashes from their forehead on Ash Wednesday, and when a Rabbi's simple prayer is ruled unconstitutional, our zeal for separation of church and state has curdled into a sour distaste for religious expression. Today it is the religious person whose testimony or political activism may be called into question based

solely on their belief in God."[cxii]

As the nation experiences COVID-19, it is impossible to interpret the disease as judgment without revelation from the Lord. That is why we should be very careful to assign suffering or tragedy as judgment from God. When Jesus spoke about those who died when the tower of Siloam fell on them, He did not assign the cause as judgment. It may very well be judgment, but without clarity from God, our assumption and the picture that we see of God is that He is loving and kind and compassionate and we seek His protection and deliverance. We may not be able to understand it, but our first response should always be that it is the enemy, or it is a result of sin. Is the COVID-19 pandemic the judgment of God? We know that God has both a causative will and a permissive will, so without hearing from God Himself, we cannot know which is responsible for our current suffering. Our assumption should always be in the goodness and grace of God, but we also know that it certainly feels like judgment and looks like judgment. So, was the pandemic the consequence of our fallen world, which cries out for redemption, an attack by the enemy, or is it the hand of God? Whatever the cause, be sure that God knows about it, God is in control over it, and God is working good through it.

The problem is that most of the time we are asking the wrong question. We shouldn't necessarily be asking "Was it judgment?" and we shouldn't be asking "Why?" which usually leads to groaning and complaining. We should be asking two very important questions instead. I remember my seminary professor sharing with our class one day that any time we are going through difficulty, trials, or shaking, it is a good reminder to look at the example of Saul on the way to Damascus. When he was struck with blinding light and heard a thunderous voice from the heavens, he asked two questions. "Who are you Lord?" And, "What do you want me to do?" Those were the questions he asked when confronted with the living God in the most troubling of times and those should be our questions today. "Who are you Lord? What do you want me to do?"

That being said, we must also understand the justice of God and that He is a jealous God. He is not content with "playing church," compromised agendas, meaningless traditions, or diverted affections. God desires loyalty, love, and allegiance. When He does not receive it, there are usually consequences for those who have pledged it to Him. In looking at 2 Chronicles 7:14, we understand that there is a distinction between prayer and obedience. President Trump just declared a National Day of Prayer in response to COVID-19. What a great thing to declare a day devoted to prayer to God, but if you examine 2 Chronicles 7:14, will that alone turn the heart of God? Most people are familiar with the fact that the verse says, "if MY people who are called by my name..." God is not asking the culture to be responsible or holding them to the same standards as His people. We also notice right away that this is a conditional statement in which God uses if/then and we are quick to realize that God requires us to humble ourselves and pray and seek His ways, which all seem possible within the auspices of prayer. But if we are serious about this conditional promise in which God says He will hear our prayers, forgive our sins, and heal our land, then we must also recognize that God asks His people to turn from their wicked ways. "Then if My people who are called by my name will humble themselves and pray and seek my face and turn from their wicked ways, I will hear from heaven and will forgive their sins and restore their land." If there is an expectation for God to hear us, forgive us, and heal our land, then we must also take seriously His command to turn from our wicked ways in repentance. This is not, "I'm sorry I got caught" or "I know things aren't going well, so I apologize." This is turning from sin and making a concerted effort to go in the other direction. A literal changing of mind and turning the other way. In mathematical terms, two plus two does not equal six; three plus three does. Prayer is needed, desired, and crucial to turning to God, but without repenting and turning from our wicked ways and actually changing how we do things, we cannot expect God to uphold His end of the statement when we have failed to understand ours.

In her prayer for the National Day of Prayer that was declared by President Trump in response to the coronavirus, Anne Graham Lotz included a large majority of her petition about the topic of repentance. That is the focus we need in America. National days of prayer are a tremendous blessing, but if we don't follow them up with repentant hearts and changed lives, then what are our words doing? It's like the abusive husband or the addict who apologizes for the hundredth time and promises to change but goes right back on doing what they had always done before. We in the church have learned the right things to say and the right way to say them, but if we want God to move on our behalf, it will be because of repentance and turning from our wicked ways, not just through prayer. It is great to pray. It is a blessing to worship. It is tremendous to give. It is essential to serve. Yet, if we don't repent and don't change, then the rest of it may be for naught. God desires obedience and not sacrifice.

One of the areas in which we need understanding is in knowing the difference between confession and repentance. Confession is a list, while repentance is real; confession is from the mouth, while repentance is from the heart; confession shows others, while repentance shows God; confession is a realization, while repentance is a response; and confession is a recognition that you got it wrong, while repentance is an attempt to make it right. I don't want to downplay or degrade the Biblical process of confession and God's command for us to confess our sins, but that is not the end. The idea of confession without repentance is similar to the idea of faith without works — it is dead. Confession is a great thing when it leads to repentance, but if you confess it and then just go out and do the same thing again, or confess with the full knowledge that you're going to do it again and not try and stop it, then your confession is not leading to repentance, it is just an act of religion. Confession is meant to lead to repentance, to a changed life, to salvation, to being born again, to being a new creature. We won't ever be perfect, but our confession should be a commitment to our earnest desire to avoid sin in the future. Zacchaeus is one of the best examples of what true repentance looks like in the Bible. When Jesus came to his house, Zacchaeus said that he would return what he had stolen and pay back four times as much to those he had stolen from. That is true repentance. Confession would have been Zacchaeus standing up and saying, "I stole," while repentance led him to the heart and behavioral change. When we repent, there is an inherent desire and attempt to make things right and a commitment to not repeat that action again in the future. It's easy to pretend to humble ourselves before God by prostrating ourselves, and it's fairly easy for us to pray to God with many words and much speaking, but it is the hard work of repentance — coming clean, making it right, and forsaking it in the future — that God requires. That was John the Baptist's call. That was Jesus' call. "Repent for the kingdom of God is at hand." It was also the message of the early church: "Repent therefore and be converted, that your sins may be blotted out, so that times of refreshing may come from the presence of the Lord" (Acts 3:19).

Repentance is turning away from sin and turning toward God. I remember realizing near the beginning of the COVID-19 pandemic that we needed to do more than pray. Prayer is necessary and vital, but it is not the only step. It's like skipping the final step of the directions in a complicated process and thereby sabotaging the whole effort. If we don't have the right relationship with the proper perspective, then our prayers are hindered and often ineffective. God will hear us, that's for sure, He just won't listen. One of the messages that the church needs to take from the COVID-19 outbreak and from the heart of the Lord is not just to pray, but to repent. The virus was just a warning shot, and I don't care to see the real thing. God's judgment is coming unless...

21 GOD'S JUDGMENTS ON ADULTERY AND HOMOSEXUALITY

There is a clear distinction between lost people who commit sin and the public acceptance of sin through law. Once sin becomes law, it is proof that such an act is deemed acceptable or valued by enough people or a culture to make it legal. This is a great offense before the Lord. When the sin of the land becomes accepted, agreed upon, and prevalent, beware of God's judgment. This is the difference between something just happening and you authorizing something to happen. You might be thinking, "I didn't authorize it personally," but America did, and your acceptance was implied. Ezekiel described this authorization as persistent unfaithfulness.

Ezekiel 14:13-14

[13] "Son of man, when a land sins against Me by persistent unfaithfulness, I will stretch out My hand against it; I will cut off its supply of bread, send famine on it, and cut off man and beast from it. [14] Even *if* these three men, Noah, Daniel, and Job, were in it, they would deliver *only* themselves by their righteousness," says the Lord God.[cxiii]

There comes a point when it is too late to repent, and I fear that America is coming to that point. We have received a great national warning with COVID-19, and I fear that God will not warn us again.

God says in Jeremiah 7:9-10 that adultery is detestable in His sight: "Do you steal, murder, commit adultery, swear falsely, burn incense to Baal, and follow other gods that you have not known? Then do you come and stand before me in this house that bears my name and say, 'We are rescued, so we can continue doing all these detestable acts'?"

In the Old Testament, adultery was punishable by death:

Leviticus 20:10 — The man who commits adultery with another man's wife, he who commits adultery with his neighbor's wife, the adulterer and the adulteress, shall surely be put to death."

Deuteronomy 22:22 — If a man is found lying with a woman married to a husband, then both of them shall die—the man that lay with the woman, and the woman; so you shall put away the evil from Israel.

Obviously, adultery was serious offense to God and something that He was intent on handling emphatically.

The reason for this is partly revealed for us in the New Testament as Paul teaches about marriage:

1 Corinthians 6:15-19

15 Surely you know that your bodies are parts of Christ himself. So I must never take the parts of Christ and join them to a prostitute! 16 It is written in the Scriptures, "The two will become one body." So you should know that anyone who joins with a prostitute becomes one body with the prostitute. 17 But the one who joins with the Lord is one spirit with the Lord. 18 So run away from sexual sin. Every other sin people do is outside their bodies, but those who sin sexually sin against their own bodies. 19 You should know that your body is a temple for the Holy Spirit who is in you. You have received the Holy Spirit from God. So you do not belong to yourselves.[cxiv]

Because our human bodies contain a soul, there is something spiritual about sex as well as physical; therefore, when someone commits adultery, it affects them both physically and spiritually. Imagine taking a golden idol into the Old Testament temple and placing it behind the curtain in the Holy of Holies. That is what it is like to commit adultery and place an idol in the temple of your body.

How can you say that you love God or your spouse if you commit adultery? Scripture is completely clear and definitive about adultery and its consequences. Even if you ignore the Old Testament command to not commit adultery and live only under the command to love God and love your neighbor as Jesus commanded, would it be possible to still do that while committing adultery? Of course not. Just as the Bible is clear that you do not love God if you don't keep the commandments, you do not love your spouse if you commit adultery. You might need them, have feelings for them, or even lust after them, but you certainly can't claim to love that which you flippantly hurt and offend. To say otherwise would be inconsistent with your actions. That is why the writers tell us so often in Scripture that if we love God we will keep His commandments — not because we love Him by keeping them, but that when we love Him we demonstrate that love by keeping them. In other words, the keeping of commandments is an effect of the relationship, not the cause of it. The same is true for committing adultery against your spouse. Just because you don't commit adultery doesn't mean you love your spouse, but committing adultery certainly indicates that you don't.

As Paul writes in 1 Corinthians, adultery must be judged within the church:

1 Corinthians 5:9-13

[9] When I wrote to you before, I told you not to associate with people who indulge in sexual sin. [10] But I wasn't talking about unbelievers who indulge in sexual sin, or are greedy, or cheat people, or worship idols. You would have to leave this world to avoid people like that. [11] I meant that you are not to associate with anyone who claims to be a believer[a] yet indulges in sexual sin, or is greedy, or worships idols, or is abusive, or is a drunk-

ard, or cheats people. Don't even eat with such people. [12] It isn't my responsibility to judge outsiders, but it certainly is your responsibility to judge those inside the church who are sinning. [13] God will judge those on the outside; but as the Scriptures say, "You must remove the evil person from among you."[cxv]

We need to acknowledge this inside the church and exercise discipline more frequently and severely with regard to adultery. Not that it can't be forgiven or repented, but it should be confronted and dealt with instead of swept under the rug. And we should certainly explain and remind that without repentance that there is a great danger of rejecting the very grace of God.

Adultery is one of the most frequently and severely condemned sins in the Bible. Adultery is mentioned 52 times, including in the Ten Commandments, all four Gospels, and ten other books of the Bible. Only the sins of idolatry, self-righteousness and murder are mentioned more often. Let marriage be held in honor by all, and let the marriage bed be kept undefiled; for God will judge fornicators and adulterers (NRSV, Hebrews 13:4).[cxvi]

In an article entitled "Reasons the Almighty God Would Bring Judgment Upon a Nation" we see that both adultery and homosexuality are included, according to Leviticus.

> According to context in Leviticus 18, and also in Leviticus 20, Sexual Immorality (specifically, incestuous relationships, adultery, homosexuality, and bestiality), Infanticide, and Idolatry are what causes nations to be judged by God. Each one of these sins are defined in Leviticus 18 as an abomination to God (Lev 18:29). Some would argue that this is a passage from the Old Testament, and we are not under Law, but under Grace, so these prohibitions do not apply to us. But is that true?
>
> Think about it. Did God change His mind concerning those things He called "abominations" when Jesus died for the sins of the world? Contrary to what many false teachers

> who have crept into the Church would have you to believe, the New Testament reaffirms the fact that God's Standards for Holiness have not changed.[cxvii]

God did not change His standards for morality in the New Testament, only the means by which we obtain forgiveness. It is no longer through the blood of bulls and goats, but through the precious blood of the Lamb of God who takes away the sins of the world. There are definitely differences in the ceremonial and civil laws between the Old Testament and the New Testament, but nowhere do we see a lightening or relenting of the moral law. That is why Jesus' forgiveness of sins was so revolutionary, because of the severity of the issues He was dealing with—like the woman caught in adultery. Jesus didn't look the other way or wink at sin. He said, "Don't do it anymore." He also said, "You don't have to be condemned." The implication being that if you repent and turn from your sin you can be forgiven of the most offensive and damaging stains, even when you're caught red-handed.

Homosexuality is a difficult and controversial subject in our world and in the church. Entire denominations have split over the definition of marriage, purity, and the identity of being male and female. One of the problems is that compassionate and understanding people have failed to see the severity of the judgment upon homosexuality. Whether you look at the Old or New Testament the message is the same: the act of homosexuality is just as much a perversion as adultery. At some point along the way, society decided it was more loving to allow people to live according to how they feel rather than live according to God's laws, whether societal, religious, or natural. It's undoubtedly a tough conversation, but if you don't love someone enough to tell them the truth, you are not following God's command to speak the truth in love. In the past, the argument that helped the cause of homosexuality to become a cultural norm was the idea that it was biological, not emotional. But the real problem is that it became normalized instead of seen as sin. The same thing has happened with adultery, as most people no longer see this behavior as abnormal or offensive. Those psychologists which are proponents of the homosexual lifestyle will admit that it is a choice and an act of will just as much as traditional marriage would be. For so long, the statement was always "I can't help how I feel," but the reality is that you *have* to help how you feel. You cannot let your emotions rule your life or your decisions. You must make them either logically or morally. It cannot be if you feel like it, eat it, take it, kick it, or even kill it. Decision-making never has and never will appropriately be an act of emotion. There has to be a rule of norm that governs behavior and keeps emotions in check. There is a "humorous" encounter in the end of the first *Guardians of the Galaxy* movie by Marvel in which the Guardians' criminal slates have been wiped clean but they are warned that any future illegal action will be punishable. Rocket the Raccoon asks the "officer" if he wants something more than someone else and takes it, would that qualify as illegal, and the officer answers, "Yes, of course." Then Drax the Destroyer asks, "What if someone makes me angry and I pull out their spine?" The startled officer says, "Well, that's actually murder, one of the worst crimes of all, and yes, that would definitely qualify." The viewers laugh it off as part of the fantasy of movieland, but in truth that is what we are saying as a society with regard to homosexuality. We have taken something that was against the law and decided that since there are enough people who said they feel like they want to do that, it's now ok. We have to deal with the reality of moral standards and the fact that the God who established those moral standards has not changed. We may have changed, society may have changed, and public opinion may have changed, but God never changes – His standards nor His love ever change;

both are constant and firmly set.

Since this is such a controversial and difficult topic, I think it is important to remember some crucial factors in dealing with the sin of homosexuality. First, the church needs to repent for its treatment of homosexuals as outcasts and abandoned. The prejudice against homosexuals that used to be in the church is unfortunate and has led us to where we are today. When in fact, we often look the other way at adultery. We need to recognize our hypocrisy and our contribution to this problem. Another clarification that we need to make is that homosexual feelings are very different than homosexual acts. Similarly to adultery, if we dwell on inappropriate thoughts and accept them, they are sin, but that is a much different sin than acting on them. We all have passing sinful thoughts that we deal with as followers of Christ and that we are trying to put to death and bring into alignment with God's word. We should not view passing thoughts or temptations as condemning behaviors, but we must agree on how to deal with the behaviors. Finally, we must remember to always lead with love in circumstances where we are trying to communicate truth, just as Jesus did with the woman caught in adultery. He released her from condemnation and told her, "Go and sin no more." Part of the problem in the church is that we have failed to do the hard things of loving and truth. Instead, we have found it easier to be one or the other — truth at the exclusion of love or love at the exclusion of truth. It is time to do the hard work of both, just like Jesus did.

22 GOD'S JUDGMENTS ON THE GUILTY

Micah 3:9-12

[9] So listen to my message,
you rulers of Israel!
You hate justice
and twist the truth.
[10] You make cruelty and murder
a way of life in Jerusalem.
[11] You leaders accept bribes
for dishonest decisions.
You priests and prophets
teach and preach,
but only for money. Then you say,
"The Lord is on our side.
No harm will come to us."
[12] Therefore because of you,
Zion will be plowed like a field,
Jerusalem will become a heap of rubble,
the temple hill a mound overgrown with thickets.[cxviii]

The Hebrew word for complaint is used by God in Micah chapter 6, verse 2: "Hear, O you mountains, the Lord's complaint, and you strong foundations of the earth; for the Lord has a complaint against His people, and He will contend with Israel." "The prophets frequently used this word as a technical, legal term in contexts pertaining to the Lord's covenant relationship with Israel (Jer. 25:31; Hos.4:1; 12:2) In this chapter, Micah had informed Judah that God had registered a formal, legal complaint against

> His people. He was ordering them to stand trial for violating covenant stipulations forbidding idolatry and requiring social justice (6:2-16)."[cxix]

It is this formal, legal complaint that I would like to address against the guilty. It is my aim to show you today that you are without excuse with regard to your behavior. If God were the prosecuting attorney these may be some of His questions and comments for the guilty: "Have you acted justly? Have you loved mercy? Have you walked humbly with Me? Your defense will be, "But I go to church. I give money and I participate in worship." But I do not look at the outward appearance, I look at the heart; I know your intentions and your desires to make your brother fall instead of helping him up and your plan to leave your sister out instead of including her as she should be. Is it that you think that I can't see you or that I am not in charge? Maybe you think that you are in charge. Or maybe you think someone you know is in charge. But who oversees that person? Do you not remember that every knee will bow and every tongue will confess? You think, "If I could only try another way or have more time, then I could escape," but your time is up. Why do you act as if there are no consequences? I have warned you over and over again with no response and now you think I will just sweep it under the rug. Do you not know that I have appointed this day from the foundations of the earth? Is there anything that you can offer me that I need? Or give me that I want? I do not bargain as with a man to lessen the sentence. My justice will be swift and complete, and no one will be able to stand and ask why that happened. For I am the Lord and I do not have to explain my actions to those whom I created and do not understand my ways."

In contrast to the prosecuting attorney, we see the heart of the Father in the parable of the vineyard owner in Mark 12. His loving kindness endures forever and His faithfulness is from generation to generation. If you just looked at the end of the story where the owner came to destroy the tenants and replaced them with different tenants, then your view would be skewed. When we consider the entire parable, we see that it was the owner who set up the entire vineyard. He built the barn. He irrigated the fields. He put the fence up. He created the entire thing and found some stewards to care for it while he was gone. The only thing that he asked is that they would be good tenants and that when he came for a portion of the harvest, they would provide it. The only problem is, when the owner sent his representative to retrieve his portion of the harvest, the tenants refused to give him any of the harvest and sent the representative away empty-handed. "Again, he sent them another servant, and at him they threw stones, wounded him in the head, and sent him away shamefully treated. And again, he sent another, and him they killed; and many others, beating some and killing some" (Mark 12:4-5). Notice that the owner sent ***many*** others. If it was me, I would have headed to the vineyard to get my portion and removed the tenants the first time that they refused me my share and treated my servant inappropriately, but the heart of the Father is such that He would send many. He set up the entire system. He created the perfect environment for them to be prosperous. It's not like He was overly demanding, saying that they had to plant such and such crop or provide Him with an unrealistic amount by such and such date. He simply sent for his portion and the tenants turned his representatives away, time after time after time, until time was finally up for them and the owner came to bring justice.

Some people assume that the owner's inaction constitutes a nonchalance or despondent attitude, but the truth is, as see in Romans chapter 1, his reluctance to bring justice or judgment is actually his kindness in giving time for repentance. It is actually the opposite of being unaware. He is so aware and cognizant of every single act of rebellion and refusal that his inaction demonstrates patience and loving kindness, because if He had to come then He would deal with the situation accordingly.

When our nation was founded, one of the primary verses frequently quoted and used to describe the vision and direction of the new country was from Micah 6:8. "In his book, Reading the Bible with the Founding Fathers, Daniel L. Dreisbach observes that the leaders of the American Revolution repeatedly referred to Micah 6:8. 'The literature of the founding era has numerous references and allusions to this biblical text,' he wrote. John Winthrop referred to this passage in his "City on the Hill" sermon. John Adams quoted it frequently. George Washington alluded to it in his farewell letter when resigning as commander in chief of the Continental Army."[cxx] This verse, which calls for justice and which provided a Biblical framework for our country's beginning, has been lost and ignored. We do not act justly. We do not love mercy. And we certainly do not walk humbly with the Lord.

Because of this, there will be a new Scripture that will frame our future if we don't repent.

Obadiah 1-4

1 The Lord God gave Obadiah
a message[a] about Edom,
  and this is what we heard:
"I, the Lord, have sent
  a messenger
with orders for the nations
  to attack Edom."

2 The Lord said to Edom:
I will make you the weakest
  and most despised nation.
3 You live in a mountain fortress,[b]
  because your pride
makes you feel safe from attack,
  but you are mistaken.
4 I will still bring you down,
even if you fly higher
  than an eagle

or nest among the stars.
I, the Lord, have spoken![cxxi]

23 GOD'S JUDGMENTS QUESTIONED

In the book of Habakkuk, we get a good look at one of the prophets having a conversation with God about His judgment (or lack thereof). He basically asks two questions of God. Here is the first one:

Habakkuk 1:2-4

[2] How long, O Lord, must I call for help?
  But you do not listen!
"Violence is everywhere!" I cry,
  but you do not come to save.
[3] Must I forever see these evil deeds?
  Why must I watch all this misery?
Wherever I look,
  I see destruction and violence.
I am surrounded by people
  who love to argue and fight.
[4] The law has become paralyzed,
  and there is no justice in the courts.
The wicked far outnumber the righteous,
  so that justice has become perverted.[cxxii]

He sees the affliction of the righteous remnant that are surrounded by the rich and powerful that have control of the courts and promote injustice. He sees the word of God have little effect and it is paid no attention to. He sees the weak and marginalized taken advantage of and destroyed by those more powerful than them. He has been crying out for justice and he does not see any answer, so he cries out to the Lord to ask why.

The Lord then answers Habakkuk and tells him that He is going to bring justice through judgment, provided by the hands of the

Babylonians. Habakkuk's second question is basically why that way? Habakkuk is beside himself with that answer because his contention is that Babylon is even worse than Judah. It would be like asking God for justice in America and God answering that He was going to use the hand of the Jihadists to bring judgment. Habakkuk is like what? That's not really what I had in mind.

Habakkuk's questions sound fairly reasonable until you hear the Lord's response. The Lord shows exactly why His actions are necessary and why the situation is so bad from His perspective.

Habakkuk 2:4-16

4 "Look at the proud!
They trust in themselves,

and their lives are crooked. But the righteous will live by their faithfulness to God.[a]
5 Wealth[b] is treacherous,
and the arrogant are never at rest.
They open their mouths as wide as the grave,[c]
and like death, they are never satisfied.
In their greed they have gathered up many nations
and swallowed many peoples.

6 "But soon their captives will taunt them.
They will mock them, saying,
'What sorrow awaits you thieves!
Now you will get what you deserve!
You've become rich by extortion,
but how much longer can this go on?'
7 Suddenly, your debtors will take action.
They will turn on you and take all you have,
while you stand trembling and helpless.
8 Because you have plundered many nations,
now all the survivors will plunder you.
You committed murder throughout the countryside
and filled the towns with violence.

[9] "What sorrow awaits you who build big houses
with money gained dishonestly!
You believe your wealth will buy security,
putting your family's nest beyond the reach of danger.
[10] But by the murders you committed,
you have shamed your name and forfeited your lives.
[11] The very stones in the walls cry out against you,
and the beams in the ceilings echo the complaint.

[12] "What sorrow awaits you who build cities
with money gained through murder and corruption!
[13] Has not the Lord of Heaven's Armies promised
that the wealth of nations will turn to ashes?
They work so hard,
but all in vain!
[14] For as the waters fill the sea,
the earth will be filled with an awareness
of the glory of the Lord.

[15] "What sorrow awaits you who make your neighbors drunk!
You force your cup on them
so you can gloat over their shameful nakedness.
[16] But soon it will be your turn to be disgraced.
Come, drink and be exposed![d]
Drink from the cup of the Lord's judgment,
and all your glory will be turned to shame.[cxxiii]

This is a good place to talk about not being offended by the Lord's actions. We may not understand what He is doing or why He is doing it, but we can trust Him and His character. We know that He is working for good and that He is in control and accomplishing all that He needs. It may not be what we want or how we would like it done, but we should trust that God knows what He is doing. So just because you see judgment or suffering or the unrighteous flourishing, don't think for a second that God has left the building. He knows exactly what He's doing and when to do it. As followers of Christ, we do not have to fear or be concerned about the coming judgment. He is the Lord and He will do it when He deems fit.

As we examine God's answer to Habakkuk, it is also a good reminder that we often don't know what we are asking for. I am reminded of Paul's desire and prayers as detailed in his visit to the Roman church in Romans chapter 1.

Romans 1:9-12

[9] God is my witness, whom I serve with my spirit in telling the good news about his Son—that I constantly mention you, [10] always asking in my prayers that if it is somehow in God's will, I may now at last succeed in coming to you. [11] For I want very much to see you, so that I may impart to you some spiritual gift to strengthen you, [12] that is, to be mutually encouraged by each other's faith, both yours and mine.[cxxiv]

Basically, Paul was saying "I am praying really hard that God would allow me to come and visit you." What is ironic is that God does indeed honor that prayer of Paul to get him to Rome, but in order to get there, he is imprisoned, beaten, shipwrecked, and bitten by a snake (See Acts chapters 21-28). Would he have prayed to visit the Romans if he knew what that would entail? Would Habakkuk have cried out for justice if he knew God would use the Babylonians to destroy Judah? What will it take to bring revival to America? We pray for it and cry out to God for it, but are we ready for what must happen in order for it to transpire? God's ways are higher than our ways and His mind beyond our understanding. Our call is to continue to cry out for justice and to promote the cause of Christ faithfully. We must let God figure out the details of how He will accomplish His will. Whatever it takes let His will be done. Whatever it takes let His word run.

It is normal for us to have questions because we cannot comprehend or understand the plan of God completely. God knows that and He is faithful to wait and to answer His people as they continue to seek Him in all ways. I'm sure many of us have questioned God's ways without an understanding of His work and deliverance (or failed to appreciate it even after the fact). The people of Israel didn't like their circumstances after they were freed from bondage. Remember their comments in the desert? God had heard, planned, worked, and delivered them from bondage, yet they turned around and complained to Him about their circumstances. The Israelites cried, "If only we had died by the LORD's hand in Egypt! There we sat around pots of meat and ate all the food we wanted, but you have brought us out into this desert to starve this entire assembly to death" (Exodus 16:3). Too often we are like the Israelites, unable to comprehend God's deliverance and mercy and then complain that it is not good enough. Before you question God's actions consider your own and come before Him in repentance so that you are not offended and that you can understand His justice.

24 GOD'S JUDGMENTS OF COMPLETE DESTRUCTION

Isaiah had the unique responsibility of being a prophet for both the northern kingdom of Israel and the southern kingdom of Judah. Although his ministry was probably around 740 BC to 681 BC, he was given the task of warning Israel of their impending doom (which took place in 722 BC) and prophesied to the southern kingdom of Judah that they would fall as well if they did not heed the Lord's warnings. He warned them of the impending judgment and exile that the southern kingdom would experience in the land of Babylon in 586 BC. Isaiah made it clear that these judgments were not accidents or the result of God's inattentiveness, this was the hand of God upon those who had disobeyed Him. As Isaiah noted,

Isaiah 42:23-25

[23] Who among you will hear this?
Let him listen and obey in the future.
[24] Who gave Jacob to the robber,[a]
and Israel to the plunderers?
Was it not the Lord?
Have we not sinned against him?
They were not willing to walk in his ways,
and they would not listen to his instruction.
[25] So he poured out his furious anger
and the power of war on Jacob.
It surrounded him with fire, but he did not know it;
it burned him, but he didn't take it to heart.[cxxv]

Isaiah made it clear that this was the hand of God at work and was very clearly the consequence of Israel's unwillingness to keep the law.

Isaiah described six woes to the Israelites in chapters 28-35 as a warning to those who refused to follow the Lord's commandments and what the impending consequences of that would be. The first woe is listed in Isaiah 28, and goes something like this, "Woe to those who indulge in pleasures and ecstasies, those who drink all day and party all night, those who find highness in drugs instead of with the Most High, and those who move from high to high and pleasure to pleasure, for their end will be quick and complete for the beauty that fades has come upon her and her influence is no more."

The second woe comes from chapter 29 and can be summarized: "Woe to those who have defiled His father's house, which was supposed to be called a house of prayer. Even in His sacred house, where it was supposed to be Holy ground, they have defiled and destroyed. The Lord has promised to silence His accusers and will not reveal Himself anymore, but instead when they look for Him they will not find Him and when they search for Him, He will be nowhere to be found. Instead, fire will define your lot and the torch will be your shield. You will run from it, but it will find you; you will evade, but it will chase you like a wildfire that cannot be extinguished, changing direction in a moment so that it may destroy because you have corrupted My Holy Hill."

The third woe also comes from chapter 29 and sounds similar to this: "Woe to all those who try and hide their deceit from the Lord. Woe to those who think that they can hide their deceit and their secret counsel as if the Lord doesn't see, like He is a god like them who has no eyes to see or ears to hear. Can you hide from the one who created the eye and can you keep secret from the one who formed the ear? Your day has come to receive judgment because of all those you have troubled."

The fourth woe is in chapter 30, where Isaiah cried woes to the rebellious: "Woe to those who have heard but have not heeded, woe to those who have known but not followed, and woe to those who have followed and yet have fallen away. Because of your rebellion and your obstinacy to ignore God's commands and directives, your failure will be swift and final; they will come upon you in an instance when you least expect it. It will be at the time that you have prepared for victory, only it will be your defeat, for you thought that you could outsmart the Almighty and afflict His chosen ones. Because you thought that you could trust in your advisors and that you could find help from God's enemies, you will turn from one trap only to fall into another one."

The fifth woe is in chapter 31. Here Isaiah declared woes to those who trust in their strength and in the strength of their allies. It goes something like this: "Woe to those who think that the strength of their strong man can hold Me back as if I am a man. I will not be delayed and there will be no army or tank that will stand in My way, for I will accomplish My purpose and My deliverance will be quick and decisive for My chosen ones. Therefore, you will be broken to pieces with no one to pick you back up again, for you have afflicted My anointed ones and have not listened to My warnings. You will see that your help will not stand up and that your hope will be for naught.

The sixth and final woe is detailed in chapter 33 where Isaiah declared woes on those who take advantage of the oppressed. "Woe to those who oppress for no reason and who trouble with no cause; because of that, you yourselves will be troubled. I will not fail to help the oppressed or to hear their cry for justice. I will not delay in the day of My coming, and My judgment will be swift because you thought that I would never show up. But behold, I am coming now and My reward is with Me, for My people and My cup is full for the oppressor. You who take advantage of the weak and poor only to pad your bank account will find your bank account padded shut and the weak ones you have trampled will themselves trample."

Like Isaiah, Jeremiah was also given the assignment of declaring judgments of complete destruction to the nation of Judah and the impending destruction of Jerusalem. Jeremiah's ministry in the natural seemed to be very unsuccessful. He preached for years and years to the people of Judah about their need for repentance, giving them specific warnings and conducting prophetic signs that the Lord instructed him to perform, yet the people still did not listen or repent.

Jeremiah 9:8-9

[8] Their tongues are deadly arrows—
they speak deception.
With his mouth
one speaks peaceably with his friend,
but inwardly he sets up an ambush.
[9] Should I not punish them for these things?
This is the Lord's declaration.
Should I not avenge myself
on such a nation as this?[cxxvi]

Jeremiah was direct and to the point and left little room for discussion, only repentance.

Jeremiah 5:7-9

[7] "How can I pardon you?
For even your children have turned from me.
They have sworn by gods that are not gods at all!
I fed my people until they were full.
But they thanked me by committing adultery
and lining up at the brothels.
[8] They are well-fed, lusty stallions,
each neighing for his neighbor's wife.
[9] Should I not punish them for this?" says the Lord.

"Should I not avenge myself against such a nation?[cxxvii]

The Lord used Jeremiah's message to prove Judah's guilt. In a way it was a picture of how Israel and Judah had treated the Lord Himself. He was beckoning to them and calling them to return to Him, but they would not listen and even became antagonistic toward His messenger. They were not attacking Jeremiah though. In reality they were attacking God, and this was the proof that demonstrated their guilt. So in the natural it did not appear that Jeremiah had much success, but spiritually God had used him to accomplish exactly what was required. It was through Jeremiah's message that the Lord could point at the people and say, "I tried to warn you, but you wouldn't listen."

Jeremiah 11:6-8

[6] Then the Lord said, "Broadcast this message in the streets of Jerusalem. Go from town to town throughout the land and say, 'Remember the ancient covenant, and do everything it requires. [7] For I solemnly warned your ancestors when I brought them out of Egypt, "Obey me!" I have repeated this warning over and over to this day, [8] but your ancestors did not listen or even pay attention. Instead, they stubbornly followed their own evil desires. And because they refused to obey, I brought upon them all the curses described in this covenant.'"[cxxviii]

This example of Jeremiah's ministry was one of great faith, in which he demonstrated the faithfulness and loving kindness of God. The same man who was despised, persecuted, neglected, and imprisoned did nothing but declare God's truth to the people, and that was the reward he received. Yet he did not give up. He did not forsake. He did not quit, and the Lord prevailed. To Jeremiah's dismay, the people never listened or repented and they experienced full and complete exile and judgment, just as he prophesied. I often wonder how America will respond to the message of judgment. On one hand, I see the example of Jonah and Nineveh in which people heeded the word of the Lord, while on the other hand, prophets like Jeremiah were ignored and the result was disastrous. I pray that America heeds its warning.

The nation of Israel was not the only nation to receive judgment in Scripture, and many other nations fell as well. One such example is Babylon, which fell to the Medes and Persians as recounted in the following article:

> Someday, every one of us is going to be on this world for the last day of our life. Every day that we live should be a day that we live in reference to that fact, because whether we live until Jesus returns, or die first, there will come a day when our destiny is fixed for eternity and there will be nothing that we can do to change it.
>
> There is a story of a man facing judgment. It was Belshazzar's last day on this earth, and we are told that he was giving a party. "They drank wine, and praised the gods of gold and silver, bronze, and iron, wood and stone." Daniel 5:4. Have you ever read the text in the Bible that says, "The heart of the wise is in the house of mourning; but the heart of fools is in the house of mirth"? Ecclesiastes 7:4. "In the same hour the fingers of a man's hand appeared and wrote opposite the lampstand on the plaster of the wall of the king's palace; and the king saw the part of the hand that wrote. Then the king's countenance changed, and his thoughts troubled him, so that the joints of his hips were loosened and his knees knocked against each other." Daniel 5: 5-6. Commenting on this verse, Ellen White tells us that, "When God makes men fear, they cannot hide the intensity of their terror."
>
> So, Belshazzar called in all of the wise men, those that understand science and philosophy, that they might tell him the meaning of the writing; but they could not do so. "The king cried aloud to bring in the astrologers, the Chaldeans, and the soothsayers. And the king spoke, saying to

the wise men of Babylon, 'Whoever reads this writing, and tells me its interpretation, shall be clothed with purple and have a chain of gold around his neck; and he shall be the third ruler in the kingdom.'" Daniel 5:7. Philosophy and science have their proper place, but learning and education will not save you on your last day on earth unless you know the God of heaven.

The queen mother then came to Belshazzar and said, "There is a man in your kingdom in whom is the Spirit of the Holy God. And in the days of your father, light and understanding and wisdom, like the wisdom of the gods, were found in him; and King Nebuchadnezzar your father—your father the king—made him chief of the magicians, astrologers, Chaldeans, and soothsayers. Inasmuch as an excellent spirit, knowledge, understanding, interpreting dreams, solving riddles, and explaining enigmas were found in this Daniel, whom the king named Belteshazzar, now let Daniel be called, and he will give the interpretation." Verses 11, 12.

So Daniel came in and gave the interpretation of the handwriting that was on the wall. He began by reviewing with him the providence of God in the life of Nebuchadnezzar.

"But when his heart was lifted up, and his spirit was hardened in pride, he was deposed from his kingly throne, and they took his glory from him. Then he was driven from the sons of men, his heart was made like the beasts, and his dwelling was with the wild donkeys. They fed him with grass like oxen, and his body was wet with the dew of heaven, till he knew that the Most High God rules in the kingdom of men, and appoints over it whomever He chooses. But you his son, Belshazzar, have not humbled your heart, although you knew all this, And you have lifted yourself up against the Lord of heaven." Verses 20–23. By his actions, Belshazzar had despised the God of heaven.

"The fingers of the hand were sent from Him, and this writing was written. And this is the inscription that was written: MENE, MENE, TEKEL, UPHARSIN. This is the interpretation of each word. MENE; God has numbered your kingdom and finished it." Verses 24–26.

When, in the judgment, we are weighed in God's balances; every detail of our character will be examined. "God weighs every man in the balances of the sanctuary. In one scale is placed His perfect, unchangeable law, demanding perfect obedience. If in the other there are years of forgetfulness, of rebellion, of self-pleasing, with no repentance, no confession, no effort to do right, God says, "'Thou art weighed in the balances, and art found wanting.'"

None of us can weigh out unless someone takes away our guilt and in its place supplies us with the righteous fulfillment of the Law. That is what the gospel is all about. We are living in a time when people have become unconcerned about this judgment. They believe that they can live in any way that they please and that it is sufficient to just say, "Lord, I am confessing my sins," and their sins will be forgiven. But as we just read, if there has been no repentance and no effort to do right, God will say, "No, you are not going to weigh out."

"A decree went forth to slay the saints, which caused them to cry day and night for deliverance. This was the time of Jacob's trouble. Then all the saints cried out with anguish of spirit, and were delivered by the voice of God. The 144,000 triumphed. Their faces were lighted up with the glory of God. Then I was shown a company who were howling in agony."

What were they howling and in agony about? "On their garments [that is, their garments of character] was written in large characters, 'Thou art weighed in the balance, and found wanting.' I asked who this company were. The angel said, 'These are they who have once kept the Sabbath and have given it up.'"

Sin is the transgression of the Law. When your time comes to be weighed, the Law is going to be on the other side of the balances. The Law demands perfect obedience, and therefore, if you are going to weigh out, you must be diligent and say, "Lord, help me by Your grace to get all sin out of my life now." That is one of the great problems for a lot of people in our generation. You think this over, relative to some people that you know, and you will realize that many of them plan to get sin out of their lives at some future time; but not now. It has been estimated that there are three million Seventh-day Adventists in the United States. There are not, however, three million Seventh-day Adventists in church every Sabbath. Where are these people? They know our message, and they profess their belief in it; but they are not living it.

Let me share some statements with you. "Since Jesus has made such an infinite sacrifice for us, how cruel it is that we should remain indifferent. Individually, we have cost the life of the Son of God, and He desires us to walk out by living faith, believing in Him with all the heart. He would have you bring the truth of God into the inner sanctuary [that is, your mind], to soften and subdue the soul; for when Christ is dwelling in your heart by faith, you will love those for whom He died. Suppose that the trump of God should sound tonight, who is ready to respond with gladness? How many of you would cry, "Oh, stay the chariot wheels; I am not ready"? Of how many would it be written, as it was written of Belshazzar, "Thou art weighed in the balances and art found wanting"? To be wanting in that day is to be wanting forever; for when Christ shall come in the clouds of heaven with power and great glory, we must be all ready to be changed in a moment, in the twinkling of an eye, and to be caught up to meet the Lord in the air. Your only safety is in coming to Christ, and ceasing from sin this very moment."[cxxix]

25 GOD'S JUDGMENTS RELENTED

The hope of repentance and God's relenting judgment is the primary theme throughout the book of Jonah. First, it is with a group of sailors who have seen the worst sailing conditions of their lives and after throwing Jonah overboard (at his request) the sea immediately calms and the sailors turn to the Lord. Second, the prophet Jonah himself who runs from the Lord was swallowed by a fish after being thrown overboard. In the belly of the fish, Jonah repented of his disobedience, so God relented, and the fish vomited Jonah on the shore. And finally, the people of Nineveh (which was known to be a wicked and ruthless nation) were confronted with one of the most successful sermons in human history. Jonah goes through the city of Nineveh preaching 8 words "Forty more days and Nineveh will be destroyed." Although Nineveh was an exceedingly great city, for whatever reason they believed Jonah and declared repentance for the entire region. We are not told if it was because of Jonah's story, or his enthusiasm, or simply the Spirit of the Lord, but we are told that the entire city responded. The king made a decree that everyone was to repent and fast — even to the extent that the animals were included! God in His mercy saw their repentance and turned from the judgment that He was going to bring.

We see through Jonah the possibility of God's relenting from judgment in multiple instances. That is His heart. He does not desire to bring judgment; upon response to His warning, He is open to change. The hard part is that the picture of repentance we see is comprehensive. We see everyone involved — from the oldest to the youngest, the irreligious to the super religious — because they all took Jonah's warning seriously. If we want God to relent of the impending judgment, we need to take seriously the warning to repent as an entire people and nation before the Lord. But the good news is that God will relent upon repentance, as we see throughout the examples presented in Scripture.

Another place where God relents of judgment is in the book of Joel. There was a horrible disaster upon the land (a plague of locusts) which Joel then used as an opportunity to call people to repentance. He declared that without repentance there would be something much worse to follow, which he describes as the "Day of the Lord." He recommends calling the people to repentance before it is too late. This is typically where the term "solemn assembly" comes from and where Joel describes it for the people of God.

Joel 2:12-17

[12] "Even now," says the Lord,
"Turn *and* come to Me with all your heart [in genuine repentance],
With fasting and weeping and mourning [until every barrier is removed and the broken fellowship is restored];
[13] Rip your heart to pieces [in sorrow and contrition] and not your garments."
Now return [in repentance] to the Lord your God,
For He is gracious and compassionate,
Slow to anger, abounding in lovingkindness [faithful to His covenant with His people];
And He relents [His sentence of] evil [when His people genuinely repent].
[14] Who knows whether He will relent [and revoke your sentence],
And leave a blessing behind Him,
Even a grain offering and a drink offering [from the bounty He provides you]
For the Lord your God?
[15] Blow a trumpet in Zion [warning of impending judgment],

Dedicate a fast [as a day of restraint and humility], call a solemn assembly.
[16] Gather the people, sanctify the congregation,
Assemble the elders,
Gather the children and the nursing infants.
Let the bridegroom come out of his room
And the bride out of her bridal chamber. [No one is excused from the assembly.]
[17] Let the priests, the ministers of the Lord,
Weep between the porch and the altar,
And let them say, "Have compassion *and* spare Your people, O Lord,
And do not make Your inheritance (Israel) an object of ridicule,
Or a [humiliating] byword among the [Gentile] nations.
Why should they say among the peoples,
'Where is their God?'"[cxxx]

The good news is that the rest of the book turns and describes the results of that repentance. The land was refreshed, God's Spirit was poured out, God's enemies were judged, and God's people were blessed. The bad news is that it required the hard work of repentance and actually turning from evil on a large scale to make that happen. It is possible. It is difficult and hard and painful, but by God's grace, this could be the greatest period of our history if the Lord brings another Great Awakening. Oh please, listen to what the Father's got to say! It's a matter of life and death, so please listen to what the Father's got to say.

There is an interesting case of repentance during the ministry of Zephaniah when judgment was not entirely prevented, but it was significantly delayed. God had determined that He was going to bring judgment to Judah and that they would be destroyed, but when Josiah led repentance and reform after finding the book of the law and turning to the Lord in repentance — God delayed His judgment. [27] "'Because your heart was gentle *and* penitent and you humbled yourself before God when you heard His words against this place and its inhabitants, and humbled yourself before Me, and tore your clothes and wept before Me, I also have heard you,' declares the Lord. [28] 'Behold, I will gather you to your fathers [in death], and you shall be gathered to your grave in peace, and your eyes shall not see all the evil which I am going to bring on this place and on its inhabitants.' So they brought back word to the king" (2 Chronicles 34:27-28).[cxxxi]

This is a great reminder and example that our attitudes and our actions do matter and they can affect God's response. This is not always true, but we see it time and time again in Scripture where, in the face of true repentance and humility, God responds in a positive fashion.

Zephaniah follows a similar pattern to the book of Joel, where judgment was announced and described, followed by a call to repentance, and finally resulting in a picture of restoration and future blessings. As we explore God's judgment as God's people, we are always reminded of His faithfulness and the hope of the future for His remnant, no matter how difficult things become. Josiah's response shows the serious nature of repentance and what it takes to humble ourselves before the Lord. Repentance is a recognition of the truth that God is God and we are not. That He is holy, and we are not. Upon recognition of that truth, the response should be confession and turning from the attitudes and actions that have beheld that sin. Josiah sought the Lord in his early years as king, but further truth was revealed to him in the book of the law, showing that even though he had previously sought the Lord, he was still well short of the Lord's expectations for him and his people. Repentance is a recognition of our sin and a turning from it. We cannot turn from it if we don't recognize it, and we can't simply know it without turning. Repentance must involve both the recognition and the turning away, which is why Josiah's example shows us what true repentance looks like. [29] "Then the king sent *word* and gathered all the elders of Judah and Jerusalem. [30] And the king went up to the house of the Lord with all the men of Judah, the inhabitants of Jerusalem, the priests, the Levites, and all the people, from the greatest to the least; and he read aloud so they could hear all the words of the Book of the Covenant which was found in the house of the Lord. [31] Then the king stood in his place and made a covenant before the Lord—to walk after (obey) the Lord, and to keep His commandments, His testimonies, and His statutes with all his heart and with all his soul, to perform the words of the covenant written in this book" (2 Chronicles 34:29-31).[cxxxii]

The very next thing Josiah did was to lead the people in following the Lord's instructions about keeping the Passover. He also made the people follow the law as well. Josiah was not just saying words or performing before the people or the Lord to look good. He was intent on keeping the law of the Lord, no matter the cost. That is true repentance.

CONCLUSION

As we conclude our study of judgment and repentance one of the greatest assurances that we need as a foundation in our soul is the sovereignty of God. When we trust God, His motives, His intentions, and His actions, then, as we live our lives to the glory of God, we can take comfort and hope in whether we experience blessing or judgment. Our highest aim isn't to be blessed, it is to live for the glory of God and the cause of Christ. If we *are* blessed, then praise the Lord; if the road is long and hard, then praise the Lord. If we recognize that God is in control of all of human history, that there is nothing that escapes His notice and that He is always trying to work out the best scenario for eternity, then there's a lot we don't have to worry about.

There are a couple of questions from the *Heidelberg Catechism* that will help us understand this concept of God's sovereignty.

> Heidelberg Catechism question 28. What advantage is it to us to know that God has created, and by his providence does still uphold all things?
>
> Answer: That we may be patient in adversity; thankful in prosperity; and that in all things, which may hereafter befall us, we place our firm trust in our faithful God and Father, that nothing shall separate us from his love; since all creatures are so in his hand, that without his will they cannot so much as move.
>
> Heidelberg Catechism question 27. What dost thou mean by the providence of God?
>
> Answer: The almighty and everywhere present power of God; whereby, as it were by his hand, he upholds and governs heaven, earth, and all creatures; so that herbs and grass, rain and drought, fruitful and barren years, meat and

> drink, health and sickness, riches and poverty, yea, and all things come, not by chance, but by his fatherly hand.[cxxxiii]

To doubt God's sovereignty is to doubt His power. To doubt God's control is to doubt His concern. To doubt God's working is to doubt His goodness. What, then, shall we say about issues like the COVID-19 pandemic that have been so destructive and so painful? What about the plagues of Egypt? What about the plagues described in the book of Revelation? It is impossible for us to speak with authority on the intent and plan of God without His direct communication, but we can rest assured that He is in control, He is involved, and He is good. The problem is that humans as a whole blame God for their suffering and pain, yet give Him no credit for their joy and bountiful blessings, when the exact opposite is the truth. His kingdom is not of this world, and yet He intervenes in the kingdom of the world for the benefit of those who would be His heirs. It is with this assurance that we face any trouble or tribulation with confidence that God always seeks the highest ultimate good for His kingdom and His people. At times, we (like Jesus) may feel that we have been forsaken. Just as Jesus' death accomplished a great-yet-invisible victory over the spiritual forces of evil, we know that He is accomplishing that victory still. We may not see it or understand it, but we continue to believe, even in the most painful and devastating circumstances, that God is accomplishing good and overcoming the evil one.

Neither the people of the world nor the devil understood God's plan when Jesus went to the cross. Jesus' followers believed their hopes were dashed and the devil believed he had prevailed upon Christ's crucifixion, yet there had to be a death and a propitiation for the sin of man to provide the opportunity for salvation. And so it is, that in the most difficult circumstances of death and disease, we know that God's ways are higher than our ways and that He is fooling the devil and prevailing for His people, who may feel defeated.

The sovereignty of God is a complicated and complex doctrine which we will never understand completely. Look at just one chapter of Scripture for instance in Acts 21 when Paul was finishing his third missionary journey and wanted to head back to Jerusalem. There are multiple statements in this one portion of Scripture with conflicting information all directed by God. Looking at verse 4, disciples told Paul through the Spirit not to go to Jerusalem. If this was just the opinion of the disciples, then we might assume that it was just their flesh which was scared about what would happen to Paul, but the Scripture is clear that the disciples told him ***through the Spirit***. In verse 10, Paul travels to Caesarea and encounters the prophet Agabus, who then proceeds to take Paul's belt and bind his hands and feet, saying that the owner of the belt will be bound in Jerusalem. Then the people pleaded with Paul not to go to Jerusalem, but verse 13 shows him asking the people to stop, saying, "For I am ready not only to be bound, but also to die at Jerusalem for the name of the Lord Jesus." Paul knew the consequences and what was going to happen, as evidenced by the previous chapter, "except that the Holy Spirit testifies in every city, saying that chains and tribulations await me" (Acts 20:23). So he was insistent that he must go to Jerusalem and finally the followers in Caesarea responded, "So when he (Paul) would not be persuaded, we ceased by saying, 'The will of the Lord be done'" (Acts 21:14). What an interesting conversation and final phrase from the believers. There was a recognition that Paul's impending suffering and arrest would be the "will of the Lord." They knew they had heard about what would happen from the Lord, but they also trusted that the Lord had set Paul's heart to go to Jerusalem as well. From the surface, it appears like God was communicating to the disciples that Paul shouldn't go, but God was actually leading Paul to go to Jerusalem no matter what the cost. We can't possibly know the reason for the two different communications, but what we do know is that Jesus Himself came to visit Paul, as is detailed in Acts 23:11: "But the following night the Lord stood by him and said, 'Be of good cheer, Paul; for as you have testified for Me in Jerusalem, so you must also bear witness at Rome.'" We also know that not only did Paul then have the opportunity to witness to rulers and those who were in authority, but that because of his imprisonment, he was then able to write much of the New Testament — not to mention the fact that he was transported at the expense of the government to the center of the known world to continue his ministry of the Gospel of Jesus Christ.

The will of the Lord is complex and convoluted by human perceptions and notions. To realize that God can communicate a different message to two different people and both messages can be true and part of the divine plan should give us great pause and reverence for the providence and will of God. He is at work in ways that none of us can know or imagine, to accomplish what we can't comprehend or understand. That should not disappoint you, it should cause you to marvel in amazement at the mind and will of God.

The other issue that we need to address as we close is that God has the right and authority to exercise judgment. I know there will be people who will claim offense at a God who exercises judgment, and that is a condemnation on the church for not preaching the whole counsel of God and not emphasizing His holy and righteous nature. People that have issues with crediting God with acts of judgment by His causative will either do not understand God's nature or they do not understand their own. Those that have issues with God bringing judgment will find the following examples compelling.

One of the clearest illustrations that God does this is because He has said so in Scripture. Repeatedly, He has said that He will judge, He will condemn, and He will bring destruction. It is very clear that He has said He will do what He wants to do when He wants to do it, and He doesn't need to explain Himself. Unfortunately, "Christianity light" has taught us that God is only mercy and not truth, He is only kindness and not justice, and He is only humility and not the King of the universe. In effect, those who deny that God would judge either think that it's not in His character (which is not consistent with Scripture), or they don't believe that the God of the Old Testament is the same as the God of the New Testament, or they believe that He wouldn't ever do that because it's too extreme, which denies the severity of sin and rebellion. When, in fact, consistently in Scripture God has said otherwise:

Isaiah 45:7 — "I form the light and create darkness, I make peace and create calamity; I, the Lord, do all these things."

Isaiah 13:11 — "I will punish the world for its evil, and the wicked for their iniquity; I will halt the arrogance of the proud, and will lay low the haughtiness of the terrible."

Jeremiah 18:17 — "I will scatter them as with an east wind before the enemy; I will show them the back and not the face in the day of their calamity."

Notice that all of these verses feature the first person pronoun. God Himself has said that He is the one who is responsible, and He is doing it.

Some people look at the life and ministry of Jesus and argue that He did not come to judge the world, He came to save it, which means that God can't possibly judge. What they fail to see is that Jesus' statement was about timing, not ability or intention. At that *time*, He came to save it. There was a period of time in history when Jesus came to save the world, but there will also be a period of time in history when Jesus will come to judge the world. God is not schizophrenic. The messenger to introduce Jesus was John the Baptist, and his entire message was repentance. We don't even have to go to the Old Testament to understand that God endorses both messages and that His character displays both — He is judge and father, He is prosecutor and defender, He is avenger and creator. It is our humanness that makes us incapable of wrapping our minds around the fact that God is equally both. It is easier and less complex not to talk about the complete nature of God, but it is also erroneous and incomplete. Only once we agree that God demonstrates the mercy of Jesus and the justice of the Father equally can we even begin to have intelligible discussions about His motives and actions.

Some people presume to think they know what God would and wouldn't do. Again, it is not what we think or feel, it is what God has communicated in His word. God is God; who do you think you are to tell God what He can or can't do, like He has to check with you before He acts or moves? One of God's closest followers was Job, and God spent four solid chapters rebuking Job's lack of understanding regarding God's actions. Read it sometime, I dare you. In fact, I triple-dog dare you to read Job 38-41 and not be amazed at God's omnipotence and authority. Please don't pretend that you know what God should or should not be doing.

The last piece that I'm going to share about the reality of God's judgment has to do with the greatest act of judgment that ever transpired which afflicted His own Son Jesus. No one deserved judgment less and no one received it more. How is that fair? How can we begin to complain about judgment or suffering or trial when we, all like sheep, have gone astray, while there was yet one who never sinned? In the greatest irony of all time, the one who deserved it least got it most. That is the epitome of injustice, but yet, because it benefits you, you are fine with it and not fine with the kind that inconveniences and afflicts you. How can you accept good and not bad as if God owes you a certain standard of justice that His own Son did not receive?

As we consider the reality of the satisfaction of God's judgment at the cross upon His son, Jesus, consider the following Scripture verses which show Him bearing sin and judgment on the cross as the sinner's substitute.

Isaiah 53:4-6 – "Surely our griefs He Himself bore, And our sorrows He carried; Yet we ourselves esteemed Him stricken, Smitten of God, and afflicted. But He was pierced through for our transgressions, He was crushed for our iniquities; The chastening for our well-being fell upon Him, And by His scourging we are healed. All of us like sheep have gone astray, Each of us has turned to his own way; But the LORD has caused the iniquity of us all To fall on Him."

2 Corinthians 5:21 — "He made Him who knew no sin to be sin on our behalf, that we might become the righteousness of God in Him."

1 Peter 2:24 — "and He Himself bore our sins in His body on the cross, that we might die to sin and live to righteousness; for by His wounds you were healed."

Romans 3:24-26 — "being justified as a gift by His grace through the redemption which is in Christ Jesus; whom God displayed publicly as a propitiation in His blood through faith. This was to demonstrate His righteousness, because in the forbearance of God He passed over the sins previously committed; for the demonstration, I say, of His righteousness at the present time, that He might be just and the justifier of the one who has faith in Jesus."

Sin requires a penalty, the penalty of death as God's holy judgment on sin. Jesus Christ, the sinless and perfect Son of God, the only one who could qualify as our substitute, died to satisfy the demands of God's absolute holiness. Sin calls for judgment and the cross of Jesus Christ became that place of judgment. It was there Christ paid the penalty for the sin of the world (1 John 2:2).[cxxxiv]

As we seek to understand sovereignty and God's judgment, we should try not to be so naïve as to say that something could not be the hand of God or so proud to say that it was definitely God's judgment (and who it was against). We should continue to walk humbly with the Lord. The Lord Himself does not desire judgment or death and neither should we.

Ezekiel 18:23 — The Lord says, "Do I take any pleasure in the death of the wicked? Declares the Sovereign LORD. Rather, am I not pleased when they turn from their ways and live?"

Ezekiel 18: 32 — "For I take no pleasure in the death of anyone, declares the Sovereign LORD. Repent and live!"

This verse is yet another reminder that God doesn't like any of it. He's not waiting up in heaven, wringing His hands, and waiting for His chance at judgment. He wants all to be saved and to come to the knowledge of the truth. His desire is that none should perish, but that is dependent upon repentance.

Before I share some closing thoughts, I would like to examine a couple of important historical documents that have greatly influenced our country as a final reminder about how we were founded and how dependent upon God we began.

The song *America The Beautiful* was penned during the summer of 1893 by a teacher named Katherine Lee Bates who had encountered a sight she would never forget. In her own words:

"One day some of the other teachers and I decided to go on a trip to 14,000-foot Pikes Peak. We hired a prairie wagon. Near the top we had to leave the wagon and go the rest of the way on mules. I was very tired. But when I saw the view, I felt great joy. All the wonder of America seemed displayed there, with the sea-like expanse."

After that climb, Bates returned home to pen the poem that we know as "America The Beautiful," one of the most patriotic and well-known songs about our nation.

God has blessed America. God has indeed shed His grace on thee. God has crowned thy good with brotherhood. Now we have determined that what God has given us isn't good enough and that we no longer want Him or His laws to rule our nation. Can we return to our dependence upon God and His leadership and again ask Him to be at the head of our country? I hope so. Only time will tell, and only repentance will bring it about.

O beautiful for spacious skies,
For amber waves of grain,
For purple mountain majesties

Above the fruited plain!
America! America!
God shed his grace on thee
And crown thy good with brotherhood
From sea to shining sea!

O beautiful for pilgrim feet
Whose stern impassioned stress
A thoroughfare of freedom beat
Across the wilderness!
America! America!
God mend thine every flaw,
Confirm thy soul in self-control,
Thy liberty in law!

O beautiful for heroes proved
In liberating strife.
Who more than self their country loved
And mercy more than life!
America! America!
May God thy gold refine
Till all success be nobleness
And every gain divine!

O beautiful for patriot dream
That sees beyond the years
Thine alabaster cities gleam
Undimmed by human tears!
America! America!
God shed his grace on thee
And crown thy good with brotherhood
From sea to shining sea![cxxxv]

The next document comes from the Constitutional Convention of July 1797, as an elderly Benjamin Franklin rose to address the president and those who were gathered. His comments came at a crucial time when they were deeply needed, as America had supplanted its independence but could not agree on a constitution, with each state vying for influence. The delegates had spent weeks debating how the Constitution of their new nation should be framed, but had made little progress up until that point. Many were frustrated, and some probably wondered if it would even be possible to construct a unifying document to govern these United States. These were Franklin's words.

> In the beginning of the contest with Britain, when we were sensible of danger, we had daily prayers in this room for Divine protection. Our prayers, Sir, were heard and they were graciously answered. All of us who were engaged in the struggle must have observed frequent instances of a superintending Providence in our favor....
>
> **And have we now forgotten this powerful Friend? Or do we imagine we no longer need His assistance?**
>
> I have lived, Sir, a long time, and the longer I live, the more convincing proofs I see of this truth: "that God governs in the affairs of man." And if a sparrow cannot fall to the ground without His notice, is it probable that an empire can rise without His aid? We have been assured, Sir, in the Sacred Writings that except the Lord build the house, they labor in vain that build it. I firmly believe this.
>
> I also believe that, without His concurring aid, we shall suc-

> ceed in this political building no better than the builders of Babel; we shall be divided by our little partial local interest; our projects will be confounded; and we ourselves shall become a reproach and a byword down to future ages. And what is worse, mankind may hereafter, from this unfortunate instance, despair of establishing government by human wisdom and leave it to chance, war or conquest.
>
> I therefore beg leave to move that, henceforth, prayers imploring the assistance of Heaven and its blessing on our deliberation be held in this assembly every morning before we proceed to business, and that one or more of the Clergy of this City be requested to officiate in that service.[cxxxvi]

After delivering his speech, he requested a two-day adjournment to seek the Lord's guidance, which was granted. From then on, sessions began with prayer to seek the Lord's counsel and direction, and this speech served as a great turning point in the construction of our Constitution.

We are in troubling times to say the least, between COVID-19, racial tensions, weather anomalies, financial woes, and distressing Supreme Court rulings. To quote Franklin, I would ask, "Have we now forgotten this powerful Friend? Or do we imagine we no longer need His assistance?" God is America's only hope, and I fear the result if we do not turn to Him during these troubling times. Pray that we will see our need and that we will seek Him while He may be found. God have mercy on us all. Francis Chan reiterates the crux of the problem in the following passage:

> Over the past decade, it has been refreshing to see Christians have a greater awareness of people's thoughts and feelings. Rather than quickly judging and labeling people, they take time to listen to their stories and consider their hurts and desires. This is a good thing. In so doing, however, many have made a damning mistake: they have lost sight of God's thoughts and desires. In their compassion for people, they have ignored the holiness of God. They have forgotten that what God feels about an issue dwarfs what any human feels. Or every human. "Let God be true though everyone were a liar" (Romans 3:4). In an effort to be sensitive to others, we often lose sight of truth. When we do this, we no longer help people but damn them. True compassion takes into account far more than what a person feels today; it takes into account what he or she will feel on judgment day. What some do in the name of being open-minded and compassionate is actually done out of self-love and cowardice. We want to be accepted, so we listen and coddle but refuse to rebuke. If that is love, then the prophets, apostles, and Jesus were the most unloving people to ever walk the planet.[cxxxvii]

I just watched a message from Francis Chan in which he explains that God has broken our treadmill during the pandemic. He was sharing about the idea of this treadmill of success which people are put on as soon as they are born. All our lives, we are constantly trying to turn up the speed to make sure that our kids are walking first, talking first, and smarter and more capable than everyone around them. This has turned into a giant rat race competition, but God just threw a huge monkey wrench into the whole thing. The worst thing that we could do is beat on the treadmill and try and get that thing up and running as quickly as possible. We need to learn what we need to learn. We need to be still and know that He is God. We need to slow down and get our priorities straight. We need to seek first the kingdom of God and His righteousness, and if it isn't about that then it's not that important. I know that it is a lot to take in with regard to America and judgment and its comparison to Israel. At the very least, with the history and stories that were shared, you must now see how far we've fallen.

Those who are older can remember days when shops were closed on Sundays, it was popular to go to church, there were dry counties and limitations on alcohol purchases, divorce was embarrassing, there weren't things like school shootings, marriage was between a man and a woman, and it was illegal to kill an unborn baby. Not that the legislation of these external factors would solve all of our internal problems, but it certainly bears the fruit of our internal condition as a nation. We have fallen so far as a nation, both in this past generation and in general since the founding of our country. A warning that God issued to the Ephesian church in Revelation 2 seems relevant for us today: **2** "I know your works, your labor, your [a]patience, and that you cannot [b]bear those who are evil. And you have tested those who say they are apostles and are not, and have found them liars; **3** and you have persevered and have patience, and have labored for My name's sake and have not become weary. **4** Nevertheless I have *this* against you, that you have left your first love. **5** Remember therefore from where you have fallen; repent and do the first works, or else I will come to you quickly and remove your lampstand from its place—unless you repent (Revelation 2:2-5).[cxxxviii] It is my prayer that you will take these words to heart, America, because God's warnings are clear and His examples are pristine. He will come quickly to remove your lampstand unless... I hope and pray that this book has given you the grace to "remember therefore from where you have fallen" so that through repentance America can see healing and restoration.

James 4:7-10

7 Therefore submit to God. Resist the devil and he will

flee from you. [8] Draw near to God and He will draw near to you. Cleanse *your* hands, *you* sinners; and purify *your* hearts, *you* double-minded. [9] Lament and mourn and weep! Let your laughter be turned to mourning and *your* joy to gloom. [10] Humble yourselves in the sight of the Lord, and He will lift you up.[cxxxix]

When Warren Candler was a young man practicing law, he defended a man accused of murder. The young lawyer went all out in his effort to clear his client of the charge. There were some extenuating circumstances, and Candler made the most of them in his plea before the jury. The defendant's aged father and mother were also in the court, and the young lawyer moved on the sympathies and emotions of the jury by frequent references to the God-fearing parents. In due course, the jury reached a verdict: not guilty. The young lawyer, himself a Christian, had a serious talk with his cleared client. He warned him to steer clear of evil ways and to trust God's power to keep him straight.

Years passed. The defendant was once again brought into court to face yet another murder charge. Candler, the lawyer who had defended him at his first trial, was now the judge on the bench. At the conclusion of the trial, the jury rendered its verdict: guilty. Ordering the condemned man to stand for sentencing, Judge Candler said, "At your first trial I was your lawyer. Today I am your judge. The verdict of the jury makes it mandatory for me to sentence you to be hanged by the neck until you are dead." Jesus is your attorney while you are on earth, but when He returns, He will be your judge.

When preparing this book, I had the thought of being like a prosecuting attorney similar to how Micah presented his case against Israel and Judah. America is guilty, and no matter how much we enjoy being American, believe in her, pray for her, and desire for her to be well, that should not keep us from speaking these truths. Like a prosecuting attorney whose mother is brought before him and who knows her guilt, it would be dishonest and unjust not to proclaim the truth of the case, even in order to protect our own mother/country. We have unduly protected our country for too long. We have hidden the truth. We have neglected the truth. We have ignored the truth. We have even covered up the truth in some cases for her. But no longer. The truth must be told to bring repentance. For many years, the church preached hellfire and brimstone and scared people into the kingdom of heaven by touching the flames of hell. The problem is that the opposite is now true and large portions of what people call "the church" now even questions the existence of hell. We have flipped the pendulum and America is in dire need of a course correction before one is forced upon her.

In addition, churches began to see that if they didn't preach as much law and if they were more relevant that more people came, and they liked it better. Churches grew. Pastors became celebrities and it appeared that the church was finally engaging culture. No one stopped to think about the long-term consequences of a spoiled church that is never told "no" and can do no wrong. The church in America today has, for an entire generation, only heard about what it can do and what it can become, with no mention of what it cannot do. The fear of God, the revelation of sin, repentance, and the holiness of God, in large part have been ignored, misplaced, and forgotten. We have made compromises along the way. The problem is that if people do not know the parameters of the law, they see no need for the Gospel. We as the church have to teach truth just as much as we have to teach grace. Jesus came as the fulfillment of both grace and truth. He did not come to abolish the law. He came to fulfill it. The problem with the church used to be that they simply condemned the woman caught in adultery. Now the church has learned to love and accept that woman but has forgotten the rest of Jesus' message. He also said, "Go and sin no more." It is right for us to accept, love, and forgive those that are caught in sin, but we cannot pretend that it is not sin. That is the opposite of love. That is cowardice disguised as love. How can you claim to be loving if you don't give someone the truth about their condition? Would a doctor be loving to hide your terminal illness? Yet the church has largely decided that it is unloving to tell the truth.

If you're reading this, then most likely I am preaching to the choir, but what are we going to do about it? The point is not to read this book, gain some knowledge about the history of America, and then put it down and do nothing. My prayer is that the Lord will bring conviction and repentance even for the parts that we have played in where we are at. I know you're busy. I know you have a lot going on and money is tight. That is all part of the enemy's plan of keeping Christians from doing anything with their convictions. So if you're too busy to do anything, to change or regroup, or to put any effort into a call to bring America to repentance, I get it. They said the same thing in the generation that allowed Darwinism to creep into the schools. They said the same thing when abortion was legalized. They said the same thing and had the exact same excuses when divorce became prominent. It was the same reasons and the same excuses when the definition of marriage changed. More of the same, "I'm disgusted, but what can I do?" More of the same, "My job (or family or whatever) is too important, I can't exhaust any more time or money on something so big."

What if instead of making excuses, we took action? What if Christians and churches all over America called for repentance and held solemn assemblies? What if every Christian in America fasted one day a week for repentance in America for the rest of their lives? What if instead of one National Day of Prayer, we held a solemn assembly across our country for 21 days to weep, mourn, fast, and pray for change in our country? What if instead of going to Disneyland or Hawaii we gave to the cause of the Gospel and organizations that fight to make change in our country? What if we worked as hard at building the kingdom of God and raising spiritual children as we did building our own kingdoms and our own children? What if God's people actually turned from their evil ways and humbled themselves and prayed and fasted? What can you do? No, not what *can* you do, what WILL you do? Israel did nothing. How about America?

There will be some that think that this message is too negative. They might ask, "Where is the hope?" That is part of the point; repentance is our nation's only hope and this message is meant to drive us to the throne instead of being focused on man-made interventions and pithy ideas that distract from the real issues. We are broken. Our schools are broken. Our government is broken. Our courts are broken. Our businesses are broken and even some of our churches are broken. Our nation is broken. If we want hope for the future, we have to embrace the reality of the present. There will be some that declare "Peace, Peace" and that we don't have to worry about judgment. But even if God is not causing judgment, at the very least, He is allowing us to be shaken as a nation. Our response should be repentance instead of ignoring it. We are in desperate need of radical change and anything other than repentance will lead us down the wrong road. Beware of quick fixes or settling for a new normal that does not get to the root of the issue. We need real change and true repentance, or we take our chances and roll the dice. Based on the findings in this resource – I hope and pray it's repentance. But unless there is widespread change it will only be a matter of time. This should not drive us to despair or worry, because the God who spared a remnant in Israel is the same God who rules over America; therefore, we must work to lead our nation in repentance and achieve reform before it's too late.

As we conclude, let me leave you with one final reminder that as we absorb this information, it is not meant to be used to judge others, but instead to lead us in repentance in our own lives. Heed the words of 85-year-old Dr. Corinthia Ridgely Boone, a Christian woman who has fought to advance Christian unity among leaders of all races, nationalities, and generations in the D.C. area:

> We must ask God to show us any part we have played in the problem. We must ask God for eyes to see our own faults rather than the faults of others, shifting the focus from others to ourselves. Pray to see clearly "create in me a clean heart and restore a right spirit in me" (Ps 51:10). "Have mercy on me and blot out my transgressions" (Ps 51:1-3). David understood as we must-- we have ultimately sinned against God. "Against you, and you only, have I sinned and done what is evil in your sight." (Ps 51:4). David asked as we must, "Lord restore the joy of my salvation." It is evident many are tired of going through the motions and not experiencing the fullness and joy that comes from living upright with a clear conscience.[cxl]

Share your prayer of repentance
@ www.repentance.us

APPENDIX A - A GUIDE TO PERSONAL REPENTANCE

"The Road To Revival" by Dr. Alan Redpath 1956 shared by Erwin Lutzer & Moody Publishing

I suppose first and foremost, that a church fellowship has been called into being in order that, through every one of its members redeemed by the blood of Christ and indwelt by His Spirit, there might be made manifest through the church the glory of the Lord Jesus Christ, that whether you be in workshop or factory, home, business, hospital, wherever it may be, whenever others come in contact with you and me they should be conscious that they are in the presence of Christ who indwells us. Then surely, a church, a fellowship is called together in order that through every member there may be an impact made upon a district, and a community. The great responsibility and burden of Chicago weighs heavily upon the hearts of many of us.

Furthermore, a church is called together in order that life may be reproduced in the uttermost parts of the Earth: that there may be a reproduction of the life of the home base in the mission field of the world. I would think that that should be a sufficiently clear definition of the objective of any New Testament Christian fellowship, that we might reveal the Lord Jesus Christ, that we might evangelize in our day, in our particular neighborhood in which we live, and that our lives may be reproduced by the power of the Spirit in the mission field of the world. That is why everyone of us is saved and why God has redeemed us, and we are allowed to live today in order that through your life and mine personally the impact of the indwelling Christ might be felt by other people.

Needless to say, that when that objective is put into practice Satan is on the attack. Wherever there is a work of the Holy Spirit there is a work of the devil. Wherever God moves, Satan counterattacks. There is always conflict and warfare. Let nobody imagine that the ministry of a church or the life of an individual Christian will ever be free from battle, but praise the Lord there is victory available all the time in it....

Dr. A.W. Tozer, a great personal friend of mine and loved and respected by everyone in this congregation, said this last Sunday in his church, that he gives American fundamentalism one more decade to survive, and if we do not have a movement of the Holy Spirit, we have no answer. The fact of the matter is we have the message, but we have not the authority and the power to shake a city for God. We have the truth but the truth does not grip our hearts as it should do. We have the Bible, but to so many of us it is just a textbook and it has never really gripped our lives to become part of the warp and woof of our character.

We have these things potentially with us. We have all that we need in Christ, and yet somehow Chicago seems to be slipping on untouched and unmoved while the evangelical section of the Christian church battles with each other, contends over this bit of doctrine and that bit of doctrine, divides over this issue and that issue.

I have chosen for our subject the "Pathway to Revival," and I want to make it perfectly clear that you understand what revival is. It is quite fantastic to announce to anybody in the paper that one is going to hold a "revival" in a church. The revival that will take place in this church does not work like that. Revival is the sovereign act of God; it is not something that God sends down. Revival is not a mass movement. Revival is the movement of one individual along certain clearly defined tracks in the Word of God, which inevitably brings into that man and through him all the fullness of God the Holy Spirit. That is revival.

Of course, in a sense one man is followed by another and another and another. What begins with one can spread until a whole mighty movement of God sweeps through a city. That does happen; it has happened; it can happen again. But it does not begin with large talk and great propaganda, and much advertising and the expenditure of big sums of money.

It can begin in your heart right now if you are prepared to pay the price of it. There is no need for any of us to plead, "Lord, send a revival." It can begin and start at this moment as I minister to you in this pulpit in the lives of those who are prepared to face the terms and the conditions and take steps to walk in the path that leads to revival: That to me is the most thrilling background against which any preacher can preach.

May I therefore, from this 6th chapter of Isaiah, show to you perfectly clearly what are the steps to a revival, for this story in these eight verses is nothing more than that of a personal revival. It is the story of a preacher whose life and whole ministry were completely transformed. This man had been in the ministry for years. He had been preaching, talking to the people, proclaiming the Word of God, but this chapter tells us of something that happened in that man's life that completely revolutionized his ministry.

The place where revival has to begin is in our pulpits today and in our Christian leadership. It is time those of us to whom God has entrusted responsibility recognize that we are not here to put on a program; we are not here to lead the people; but we are here to be men of broken hearts, bleeding hearts and a wounded spirit and contrite heart; men upon whom God can trust the Holy Ghost for we are giving Him the glory.

Let me ask you please, therefore, to look with me as we watch how revival really struck Isaiah in his own life. I am going to do it in rather an unusual way, because I am going to do it backwards. I want to show you the outcome of revival in this man's life and then trace back that fact to the root and the source of it until we have found the very place and spot where it first began.

I notice that this story concludes with a man with a sense of vocation. In the 8th verse we hear him cry, "Lord, here am I; send me." In response to the call of Almighty God, "Whom shall I send, and who will go for us?" this prophet leaps to his feet. Every faculty that he possesses; every part of this man is absolutely ready to respond to the call of God. There is no lethargy, uncertainty, or indifference, or any kind of weariness about him. He is tingling with life, pulsating with energy and with power, and he is on his feet and says, "Lord, I am ready; send me." God has called and spoken to him; He called him not to do a successful thing or go into an easy ministry to see many conversions and crowds of people blessed, but to go and speak to the people and tell them that their hearts have been hardened and that judgment is coming.

He was to be sent out into a desperately tough job. With every sense of calling and divine energy within him, this man just leaped before God and said, "Lord, I am ready; I want to go; send me." That is where we want to be, and where moment by moment, day by day we wish we were. That is the condition in which I believe we long to live. We reach it perhaps at the end of a missionary meeting, but it gradually fades out over one-half hour over an ice cream or a cup of coffee. We have it for a short while in the thrill of an emotional message and for a few moments after church. We feel somehow that we would go anywhere and do anything for God. It only lasts for a few moments and then it is gone.

God has to say to us like He said to His people Israel, "Thy goodness is as the morning cloud; it just vanishes away." We have been stirred in the depths of emotion and intellect and so on, but somehow or other it has never been a permanent condition with many of us, and yet here is this man set free from all lethargy, weariness and all sense of inability, ready and eager to respond, leaping to the call, "Lord, here am I; send me." It is the call of a soul set free, and the sound of a man who deep down in his heart knows that by the grace of God at last he is ready. That is where he got, and that is where, by the grace of God, we want to get, but how did he get there?

In the 7th verse of this chapter we read, "Thine iniquity is taken away, and thy sin purged." God had touched his man's life again; a live coal from the altar had been taken and touched his lips and suddenly this prophet was conscious that something had happened within him, that had cleansed his heart.

I do not know whether many of you were listening to the broadcast service this afternoon from the studio in connection with Mid-America Keswick, but how my heart thrilled again to be reminded, as Mr. Wildish spoke, that sin needs and has a double cure. Every time we sing that lovely hymn "Rock of Ages, be of sin the double cure, cleanse me from its guilt and power," how many of us sit in church week by week, and we have been forgiven sinners but we have been powerless as children of God.

Isaiah leaped to his feet to respond because he knew that there was a moment in his life when God had spoken to him and touched him, and there was also a new sense of cleansing. He had a spiritual spring cleaning in his own soul, and he was conscious that the blood of Jesus Christ had cleansed from all sin. I am not concerned now at the moment about any people who may be seeking to detect heresy in what I am talking about, nor am I here to argue with you about a second work of grace, nor anything of that kind. I am concerned about an experience that you and I need to know, and it is offered by the blood of Jesus Christ, and it is the whole message of the Gospel.

I am not preaching sinless perfection, nor saying that any man will be ever completely free from sin as long as he lives in a body yet to be redeemed, but I am saying that the blood of Jesus Christ and the power of God, the Holy Ghost can get into your life, if you are willing, and can clean you up and give you a spiritual spring cleaning, and that is what the church of Christ needs.

Don't get angry or cross with me and say that this is not the sort of thing that we teach. We don't stand for that. Don't you? Well, I do, and the Word of God stands for that, and some of us have never pressed in to possess the cleansing, the effectual permanent cleansing of heart that God the Spirit can give. Listen to the language of this great hymn written some years ago by [Charles] Wesley:

"Oh, that in me the sacred fire
Might now begin to flow;
Burn up the dross of base desire
And make the mountains flow.
Refining fire, go through my heart,
Illuminate my soul;
Scatter thy life through every part,
And sanctify the whole."

Do you believe that to be possible? Is that mere talk, mere sentimental language, or is it the cry of a man of God for cleansing? Do you mean to tell me, beloved, that the Gospel of Christ, the death, resurrection, ascension, the downcoming of the Holy Ghost, all that has taken place to leave you and me still hankering after worldly things and sinful things, still sinful in habit, in thought, and desire? Has all that happened simply to enable you and me to say, "Of course, my sins have been forgiven and I am on my way to heaven, and I believe this, that and the other thing"? Oh no, surely the blood of Jesus Christ has been shed to deal with the guilt and power of indwelling sin that by the power of an indwelling Spirit the flesh might be kept in subjection.

Isaiah leaped to a sense of calling and vocation because God had touched him, and is it not just the very lack of such an experience that makes us so lethargic in Christian work? Isn't it the lack of a real experience of inward cleansing that makes us so indifferent and careless and slipshod and hesitant in our Christian testimony and work?

There are moments when we are all on top, but the next moment we are right down in the depths. Why is it that I did not witness to that man to whom I had the opportunity to speak; to that person who is along side of us? God was telling us to do it. Why? Because deep down in our hearts there was a lurking sense that we are only hypocrites and that we are not real; that we can use the language and talk about it, but deep down in our hearts there has been no real deep cleansing because the soul has never been set free and the heart has never really been delivered and there has not been that inward coming of the Spirit in power to cleanse—we are hesitant in our testimony and afraid in our speech. We are reluctant in our witness and our lips are silent because it is out of the heart that a man speaketh and the heart has not been cleansed.

Ah, but here is a man who leaped in the sense of vocation because God has set him free. I am here to suggest to you that some of us need God's second touch. We desperately need the double cure. Yes, we have the pardon and forgiveness, but, O God, have we got the power? Have we really claimed it by the virtue of the blood, that by the power of our risen Lord we have claimed that second touch of deliverance from the power of sin that we might be made clean?

A new sense of cleansing—go back a step further. How did the man get a new sense of cleansing? Because he had *a new sense of sin.* What a paradox! Verse 5, "Woe is me!" says Isaiah, "for I am undone; because I am a man of unclean lips." You see there had come in this man's life a moment when he saw himself as God saw him. For years he had been preaching and talking, but he had never seen himself. There was a moment when suddenly his whole life was exposed to God, when as it were, he stood in the presence of a holy God and he saw God's holiness and his own sinfulness. He saw sin as God saw it, and because he saw that he recognized the desperate need in his life for cleansing and revival.

Let me speak this to you lovingly and earnestly, have you ever seen yourself like that? God grant that you and I may see ourselves as God sees us. Beneath the mask of evangelical fervor and language, beneath a mask and curtain, the cloak of the language and the orthodoxy of the teaching that we give out, there can be lurking passion, hidden deceit and pride, and self-ambition and self-righteousness—all sorts of wretched, devilish things that go on inside behind the curtain that we draw over it, all that we might present to people the impression of fervor and honesty and earnestness and keenness for God. Oh that God by His Spirit might just draw aside the veil that you and I might find ourselves exposed utterly, a soul naked before God.

That is the condition of fullness of blessing and the condition of cleansing. Are you prepared to come out from your darkness and out from your corner and get out into the light and stand before God? That is the condition. Honesty, sheer naked honesty with the Lord; absolutely ruthless honesty with sin and with self—a determination to turn from the whole business and to get right out into the very presence of a holy God—dare you do that?

A new sense of cleansing because there was a new sense of sin. Have you ever known what it is to have an interview with the Lord like that? Perhaps at a service, more often in some quiet corner in your own home, when you have felt His holy gaze looking you through and through as He gazed upon Peter, as He looked time and time again into the souls of men and have seen yourself exposed before God? Nobody experiences the power of God until there is a moment when they have stood in the light honestly before God exposed to sin. Are you prepared for that?

At the root of it all—a new sense of God. Verse 5, "Mine eyes have seen the King, the Lord of hosts." Here is the thing that got him on the pathway to revival and to blessing. What did he see? He had seen the Lord seated upon a throne, but that would not surprise Isaiah; that is what he would expect to see. He had seen Him high and lifted up, but Isaiah would expect that; that is the kind of God he had always worshipped. Oh, but there was something that that man saw that day that caused his heart to stand still and shook him to the very core, and made him altogether different through all the days of his life.

What was it? "I saw the Lord sitting upon a throne, high and lifted up, and his train filled the temple." He had never seen God like that before. What does that mean? Isaiah had always been accustomed to a temple with varying degrees of the consciousness of God. There was the outer court of traffic and busyness and service; there was the holy place of ministry in which, as it were, the presence of God was more felt and more real; but deepest of all there was the holiest of all into which only the priest could go once a year for there was the Shekinah glory.

This man had been brought up in the idea that God's holiness was gradually dwindling down. There was the outer place, the court, the holiest of all, and there was the increasing sense of God' presence and God's power—the quenchless flame of the very presence of God in the holiest of all. But now, after this man had been in the ministry for years, he was struck by the fact that God's train filled the temple, every section of it and every corner of it. The posts, we read, of the threshold move not merely the veil over the holy place, but the posts of the threshold; the house was filled with smoke; the whole place was covered and filled with the glory of God.

This man discovered that the presence of this holy God, His presence and power swept right over the temple, over an area which Isaiah had never thought was so near to the heart of God. There was not one inch of that temple that was exempt or excluded from the glory of the Shekinah.

Ah, that is the discovery that has burned its way into my own life and heart again and again recently. How do I interpret that for you and for me? There is no such thing as the division between what you call spiritual and secular. I cannot preach in a pulpit and pay homage to God in a church on Sunday and then go and have a vacation from a spiritual life for the rest of the week. I cannot imagine that simply within the walls of this building God is here in His power and in His holiness. He is also in my home, in my apartment, business, street—His train fills the temple.

The presence and the power and glory of God cover every area of my life and experience. You cannot escape it. That vision tells me that there is no division of my personality into different degrees of sanctity. You and I are made up of spirit, soul, and body, and says the Apostle, "Know ye not that your body is the temple of the Holy Ghost?" and Jesus fills that temple. If you belong to Him and you are His child, He has a right to every bit of your body, of yourself; it is His. What are you doing with it? How are you treating the body that is His temple? What have you done with it this week?

Your habits and thoughts, actions, movements, and the things you have looked at, read, heard, and the people you have spoken to and what you have spoken about, it has all been in the wonderful, all glorious presence of the Lord Jesus Christ. Well might that temple shake with the glory of His presence! Well might you and I tremble and fall upon our faces and cry out to God for mercy as we realize His presence in every part of our life. Do you see this—a new sense of God everywhere, a new sense of the presence of Christ controlling every part of my life, my body, soul, spirit all His? A new sense of that brought this man down upon his face in a new sense of sin.

That is what I need. That is what you need—just to recognize the greatness, the omnipotence and power of this living Lord Jesus and to fall at His feet like that. For out from that vision of God there came that vision of self; and out from that vision of sin in God's faithfulness, there came the vision of cleansing and the experience of deliverance, and then there was the cry, "Lord, here am I; send me."

Very well, my friend, that is the path to revival. Are you going to step on it? Are you going to begin walking on it? Have you the consciousness of the presence of the Lord filling the temple of your body? Come humbly before Him with a sense of the sin that brings you to trust Him for cleansing and to say to Him, "Lord, here am I; send me."

APPENDIX B - ABRAHAM LINCOLN'S CALL FOR REPENTANCE MARCH 1863

"Whereas, the Senate of the United States, devoutly recognizing the Supreme Authority and just Government of Almighty God, in all the affairs of men and of nations, has, by a resolution, requested the President to designate and set apart a day for National prayer and humiliation.

And whereas it is the duty of nations as well as of men, to own their dependence upon the overruling power of God, to confess their sins and transgressions, in humble sorrow, yet with assured hope that genuine repentance will lead to mercy and pardon; and to recognize the sublime truth, announced in the Holy Scriptures and proven by all history, that those nations only are blessed whose God is the Lord.

And, insomuch as we know that, by His divine law, nations like individuals are subjected to punishments and chastisements in this world, may we not justly fear that the awful calamity of civil war, which now desolates the land, may be but a punishment, inflicted upon us, for our presumptuous sins, to the needful end of our national reformation as a whole People? We have been the recipients of the choicest bounties of Heaven. We have been preserved, these many years, in peace and prosperity. We have grown in numbers, wealth and power, as no other nation has ever grown. But we have forgotten God. We have forgotten the gracious hand which preserved us in peace, and multiplied and enriched and strengthened us; and we have vainly imagined, in the deceitfulness of our hearts, that all these blessings were produced by some superior wisdom and virtue of our own. Intoxicated with unbroken success, we have become too self-sufficient to feel the necessity of redeeming and preserving grace, too proud to pray to the God that made us!

It behooves us then, to humble ourselves before the offended Power, to confess our national sins, and to pray for clemency and forgiveness.

Now, therefore, in compliance with the request, and fully concurring in the views of the Senate, I do, by this my proclamation, designate and set apart Thursday, the 30th day of April, 1863, as a day of national humiliation, fasting and prayer. And I do hereby request all the People to abstain, on that day, from their ordinary secular pursuits, and to unite, at their several places of public worship and their respective homes, in keeping the day holy to the Lord, and devoted to the humble discharge of the religious duties proper to that solemn occasion.

All this being done, in sincerity and truth, let us then rest humbly in the hope authorized by the Divine teachings, that the united cry of the Nation will be heard on high, and answered with blessings, no less than the pardon of our national sins, and the restoration of our now divided and suffering Country, to its former happy condition of unity and peace.

In witness whereof, I have hereunto set my hand and caused the seal of the United States to be affixed.

By the President: Abraham Lincoln"

APPENDIX C - MASSACHUSETTS THANKSGIVING PROCLAMATION BY JOHN HANCOCK

By His EXCELLENCY

John Hancock, Esq.

GOVERNOR of the COMMONWEALTH

of Massachusetts.

A PROCLAMATION,

For a Day of Public Thanksgiving.

proclamation-thanksgiving-day-1791-massachusetts

In consideration of the many undeserved Blessings conferred upon us by GOD, the Father of all Mercies; it becomes us no only in our private and usual devotion, to express our obligations to Him, as well as our dependence upon Him; but also specially to set a part a Day to be employed for this great and important Purpose:

I HAVE therefore thought fit to appoint, and by the advice and consent of the Council, do hereby accordingly appoint, THURSDAY, the seventeenth of November next, to be observed as a Day of Public THANKSGIVING and PRAISE, throughout this Commonwealth:—Hereby calling upon Ministers and People of every denomination, to assemble on the said Day—and in the name of the Great Mediator, devoutly and sincerely offer to Almighty God, the gratitude of our Hearts, for all his goodness towards us; more especially in that HE has been pleased to continue to us so a great a measure of Health—to cause the Earth plentifully to yield her increase, so that we are supplied with the Necessaries, and the Comforts of Life—to prosper our Merchandise and Fishery—And above all, not only to continue to us the enjoyment of our civil Rights and Liberties; but the great and most important Blessing, the Gospel of Jesus Christ: And together with our cordial acknowledgments, I do earnestly recommend, that we may join the penitent confession of our Sins, and implore the further continuance of the Divine Protection, and Blessings of Heaven upon this People; especially that He would be graciously pleased to direct, and prosper the Administration of the Federal Government, and of this, and the other States in the Union—to afford Him further Smiles on our Agriculture and Fisheries, Commerce and Manufactures—To prosper our University and all Seminaries of Learning—To bless the virtuously struggling for the Rights of Men—so that universal Happiness may be Allies of the United States, and to afford his Almighty Aid to all People, who are established in the World; that all may bow to the Scepter of our LORD JESUS CHRIST, and the whole Earth be filled with his Glory.

And I do also earnestly recommend to the good People of this Commonwealth, to abstain from all servile Labor and Recreation, inconsistent with the solemnity of the said day.

Given at the Council-Chamber, in Boston, the fifth Day of October, in the Year of our Lord, One Thousand Seven Hundred and Ninety-One, and in the sixteenth Year of the Independence of the United States of America.

https://wallbuilders.com/proclamation-thanksgiving-day-1791-massachusetts/

APPENDIX D – VIRGINIA THANKSGIVING PROCLAMATION BY THOMAS JEFFERSON

Proclamation – Thanksgiving – 1779, Virginia

Thomas Jefferson (1743-1826) was involved in many professions throughout his life. He was a lawyer, a member of the Virginia House of Burgesses (1769-1775), served in the Continental Congress (1775-1776) where he drafted the Declaration of Independence, was governor of Virginia (1779-1781), and the U.S. minister to France (1785-178). Jefferson also served as the first Secretary of State under George Washington, was Vice President under John Adams, and was the nation's third President. During his time as governor of Virginia, Jefferson issued the following proclamation on November 11, 1779 calling for a statewide day of thanksgiving and prayer on December 9, 1779. The text of this proclamation can be found in The Papers of Thomas Jefferson, Julia P. Boyd, editor (Princeton: Princeton University Press, 1951), Vol. 3, pp. 177-179.

Whereas the Honourable the General Congress, impressed with a grateful sense of the goodness of Almighty God, in blessing the greater part of this extensive continent with plentiful harvests, crowning our arms with repeated successes, conducting us hitherto safely through the perils with which we have been encompassed and manifesting in multiplied instances his divine care of these infant states, hath thought proper by their act of the 20th day of October last, to recommend to the several states that Thursday the 9th of December next be appointed a day of publick and solemn thanksgiving and prayer, which act is in these words, to wit.

"Whereas it becomes us humbly to approach the throne of Almighty God, with gratitude and praise, for the wonders which His goodness has wrought in conducting our forefathers to this western world; for His protection to them and to their posterity, amidst difficulties and dangers; for raising us their children from deep distress, to be numbered among the nations of the earth; and for arming the hands of just and mighty Princes in our deliverance; and especially for that He hath been pleased to grant us the enjoyment of health and so to order the revolving seasons, that the earth hath produced her increase in abundance, blessing the labours of the husbandman, and spreading plenty through the land; that He hath prospered our arms and those of our ally, been a shield to our troops in the hour of danger, pointed their swords to victory, and led them in triumph over the bulwarks of the foe; that He hath gone with those who went out into the wilderness against the savage tribes; that He hath stayed the hand of the spoiler, and turned back his meditated destruction; that He hath prospered our commerce, and given success to those who sought the enemy on the face of the deep; and above all, that he Hath diffused the glorious light of the Gospel, whereby, through the merits of our gracious Redeemer, we may become the heirs of His eternal glory. Therefore,

George Washington, Patrick Henry, and members of the First Continental Congress join with Rev. Jacob Duché in prayer.

Resolved, that it be recommended to the several states to appoint THURSDAY the 9th of December next, to be a day of publick and solemn THANKSGIVING to Almighty God, for his mercies, and of PRAYER, for the continuance of His favour and protection to these United States; to beseech Him that he would be graciously pleased to influence our publick Councils, and bless them with wisdom from on high, with unanimity, firmness and success; that He would go forth with our hosts and crown our arms with victory; that He would grant to His church, the plentiful effusions of divine grace, and pour out His Holy Spirit on all Ministers of the Gospel; that He would bless and prosper the means of education, and spread the light of Christian knowledge through the remotest corners of the earth; that He would smile upon the labours of His people, and cause the earth to bring forth her fruits in abundance, that we may with gratitude and gladness enjoy them;

that He would take into His holy protection, our illustrious ally, give him victory over his enemies, and render him finally great, as the father of his people, and the protector of the rights of mankind; that He would graciously be pleased to turn the hearts of our enemies, and to dispence the blessings of peace to contending nations.

That he would in mercy look down upon us, pardon all our sins, and receive us into his favour; and finally, that he would establish the independence of these United States upon the basis of religion and virtue, and support and protect them in the enjoyment of peace, liberty and safety."

I do therefore by authority from the General Assembly issue this my proclamation, hereby appointing Thursday the 9th day of December next, a day of publick and solemn thanksgiving and prayer to Almighty God, earnestly recommending to all the good people of this commonwealth, to set apart the said day for those purposes, and to the several Ministers of religion to meet their respective societies thereon, to assist them in their prayers, edify them with their discourses, and generally to perform the sacred duties of their function, proper for the occasion. Given under my hand and the seal of the commonwealth, at Williamsburg, this 11th day of November, in the year of our Lord, 1779, and in the fourth of the commonwealth.

THOMAS JEFFERSON

https://wallbuilders.com/proclamation-thanksgiving-1779-virginia/

APPENDIX E- CONNECTICUT DAY OF FASTING, HUMILIATION, & PRAYER BY SAMUEL HUNTINGTON

BY HIS EXCELLENCY

SAMUEL HUNTINGTON, ESQUIRE (1789, Governor of Connecticut & Signer of the Declaration)

Governor and Commander in Chief of the State of

CONNECTICUT

A PROCLAMATION.

Considering the indispensable duty of a people, to acknowledge the overruling hand of divine providence, and their constant dependence upon the supreme being, for all the favor and blessings they may enjoy, or hope to receive; and that notwithstanding the many mercies and signal instances of divine favor conferred upon the inhabitants of this land, yet the prevalence of vice and wickedness give us just reason to fear the divine displeasure and chastisement for our many offenses, unless prevented by speedy repentance and reformation.

I have therefore thought fit by and with the advice of council, to appoint, and do, hereby appoint WEDNESDAY the Twenty-Second Day of April next, to be observed as a Day of FASTING, HUMILIATION, and PRAYER, throughout this state; earnestly exhorting ministers and people of all denominations to assemble for divine worship; that we may with becoming humility, and united hearts, confess and bewail our manifold sins and transgressions, and by repentance and reformation obtain pardon and forgiveness of all our offenses, through the merits and mediation of Jesus Christ our only savior. Also, to offer up fervent supplications to almighty God the father of mercies, that he may bless the United States of America, gives wisdom and integrity to our national council, direct their proceedings at this important crisis, in such manner as shall best promote the union, prosperity and happiness of the nation: – That it may graciously pleas him to smile upon and bless the people of this state, inspire our civil rulers with wisdom and integrity becoming their station: bless his sacred ambassadors, and cause pure and undefiled religion to flourish, grant us health and plenty; prosper us in all our lawful employments, and crown the year with his goodness; succeed the means of education, extend the peaceful influence of the redeemer's kingdom, and dispose all nations to live as brethren in peace and amity, and fill the world with the knowledge and glory of God.

And all servile labor is forbidden on said day.

Given at Norwich, the 28th day of March, in the thirteenth year of the independence of the United States of America,

Annoque Domini 1789.

SAMUEL HUNTINGTON

By His Excellency's Command,

George Wyllys, Sec'ry

https://wallbuilders.com/proclamation-fasting-humiliation-prayer-1789-connecticut/

ENDNOTES

[i] The Proper Distinction Between Law & Gospel by C.F.W. Walther (p.6) Concordia Publishing House

[ii] The Harbinger by Jonathan Cahn (p.19ff) Charisma House Book Group

[iii] Holy Bible, New Living Translation, copyright 1996, 2004, 2015 by Tyndale House Foundation

[iv] Holy Bible, New Living Translation, copyright 1996, 2004, 2015 by Tyndale House Foundation

[v] http://www.sgnscoops.com/who-is-the-carter-robertson-band/

[vi] New York Daily News December 3, 2015 https://t.co/eKUg5f03ec

[vii] The Trellis And The Vine by Colin Marshall and Tony Payne (p.30-33) Matthias Media

[viii]viii https://www.vox.com/2018/6/25/17502170/pastor-robert-jeffress-america-christian-nation-trump-dallas-baptist

[ix] Holy Bible, New Living Translation, copyright 1996, 2004, 2015 by Tyndale House Foundation

[x] Holy Bible, New Living Translation, copyright 1996, 2004, 2015 by Tyndale House Foundation

[xi] https://www.magzter.com/article/News/Time/My-Generation-Was-Supposed-To-Level-Americas-Playing-Field-Instead-We-Rigged-It-For-Ourselves

[xii] https://www.magzter.com/article/News/Time/My-Generation-Was-Supposed-To-Level-Americas-Playing-Field-Instead-We-Rigged-It-For-Ourselves

[xiii] https://store.northpoint.org/products/god-country-audio-download

[xiv] **The Message (MSG)** Copyright © 1993, 2002, 2018 by Eugene H. Peterson

[xv] **Contemporary English Version (CEV)** Copyright © 1995 by American Bible Society

[xvi] **The Message (MSG)** Copyright © 1993, 2002, 2018 by Eugene H. Peterson

[xvii] **New International Version (NIV)** Copyright © 1973, 1978, 1984, 2011 by Biblica

[xviii] https://www.moodymedia.org/sermons/church-babylon/

[xix] https://ifapray.org/blog/valley-forge-crucible-of-freedom/ MAY 29, 2019 | FROM THE PROVIDENCE FOUNDATION

[xx] https://video.search.yahoo.com/search/video?fr=mcafee&p=david+barton+presentations+youtube#id=12&vid=cd089e4f5f4e840e9f2a279d8507cd1a&action=view

[xxi] https://www.thegospelcoalition.org/blogs/evangelical-history/many-founding-fathers-went-seminary/

[xxii] God's New Israel by Conrad Cherry p.65 © 1998 The University of North Carolina Press

[xxiii] https://theimaginativeconservative.org/2016/04/first-inaugural-address-george-washington.html

[xxiv] http://free2pray.info/5-SchoolShootings.html

[xxv] https://www.snopes.com/fact-check/darrell-scott-testimony/

[xxvi] **New King James Version (NKJV)** Copyright © 1982 by Thomas Nelson Luke 13:4

[xxvii] **New King James Version (NKJV)** Copyright © 1982 by Thomas Nelson Luke 13:5

[xxviii] The Living Bible copyright © 1971 by Tyndale House Foundation

[xxix] Concordia Self Study Bible p.852 for commentary on Psalm 66:10 Concordia Publishing House

[xxx] **King James Version (KJV)**

[xxxi] **King James Version (KJV)**

[xxxii] Butler, Trent C. Editor. Entry for 'Remnant'. Holman Bible Dictionary. https://www.studylight.org/dictionaries/hbd/r/remnant.html. 1991.

[xxxiii] https://ssnet.org/about-us/fundamental-beliefs-seventh-day-adventists/remnant-and-its-mission-fundamental-belief-13/#comments

[xxxiv] **Amplified Bible (AMP)** Copyright © 2015 by The Lockman Foundation, La Habra, CA 90631

[xxxv] **New King James Version (NKJV)** Copyright © 1982 by Thomas Nelson

[xxxvi] **Good News Translation (GNT)** Copyright © 1992 by American Bible Society

[xxxvii] **Amplified Bible (AMP)** Copyright © 2015 by The Lockman Foundation, La Habra, CA 90631

[xxxviii] **English Standard Version (ESV)** Copyright © 2001 by Crossway Bibles

[xxxix] https://genius.com/Switch-band-symphony-lyrics

[xl] **English Standard Version (ESV) Copyright** © 2001 by Crossway Bibles

[xli] **Living Bible (TLB)** copyright © 1971 by Tyndale House Foundation

[xlii] **Living Bible (TLB)** copyright © 1971 by Tyndale House Foundation

[xliii] **The Message (MSG)** Copyright © 1993, 2002, 2018 by Eugene H. Peterson

[xliv] New American Standard Bible (NASB) Copyright © 1960, 1962, 1963, 1968, 1971, 1972, 1973, 1975, 1977,
1995 by The Lockman Foundation

[xlv] New American Standard Bible (NASB) Copyright © 1960, 1962, 1963, 1968, 1971, 1972, 1973, 1975, 1977,
1995 by The Lockman Foundation

[xlvi] **Amplified Bible (AMP)** Copyright © 2015 by The Lockman Foundation, La Habra, CA 90631.

[xlvii] **The Message (MSG)** Copyright © 1993, 2002, 2018 by Eugene H. Peterson

[xlviii] **New International Version (NIV)** Copyright © 1973, 1978, 1984, 2011 by Biblica

[xlix] **New International Version (NIV)** Copyright © 1973, 1978, 1984, 2011 by Biblica

[l] https://www.gotquestions.org/judgment-begins-house-God.html

[li] This Precarious Moment p.215-216 Copyright © 2018 by James L. Garlow and David Barton Regnery
Publishing

[lii] This Precarious Moment p.219 Copyright © 2018 by James L. Garlow and David Barton Regnery Publishing

[liii] https://radical.net/sermon/the-gospel-demands-radical-sacrifice/

[liv] **New International Version (NIV)** Copyright © 1973, 1978,

1984, 2011 by Biblica

[lv] **New Living Translation (NLT)** *Holy Bible* © 1996, 2004, 2015 by Tyndale House Foundation

[lvi] **New Living Translation (NLT)** *Holy Bible* © 1996, 2004, 2015 by Tyndale House Foundation

[lvii] **New Living Translation (NLT)** *Holy Bible* © 1996, 2004, 2015 by Tyndale House Foundation

[lviii] **New Living Translation (NLT)** *Holy Bible* © 1996, 2004, 2015 by Tyndale House Foundation

[lix] LifeWay Press © 2019 David Platt, Radical Inc. p.35 Something Needs To Change

[lx] This Precarious Moment p.212 Copyright © 2018 by James L. Garlow and David Barton Regnery Publishing

[lxi] Radical p.15-16 © 2010 by David Platt

[lxii] https://churchpop.com/2016/03/31/mother-angelical-liberal-church/

[lxiii] https://capmin.org/theological-liberalism-in-america/ by RALPH DROLLINGER

[lxiv] **New Living Translation (NLT)** *Holy Bible* © 1996, 2004, 2015 by Tyndale House Foundation

[lxv] This Precarious Moment p.235-236 Copyright © 2018 by James L. Garlow and David Barton

[lxvi] This Precarious Moment p.236 Copyright © 2018 by James L. Garlow and David Barton

[lxvii] This Precarious Moment p.237-238 Copyright © 2018 by James L. Garlow and David Barton

[lxviii] https://christinprophecy.org/articles/americas-christian-heritage/ Kenneth Woodward and David Gates

(1982), "How the Bible Made America," *Newsweek*, December 27, page 44

[lxix] This Precarious Moment p.185 Copyright © 2018 by James L. Garlow and David Barton Regnery Publishing

[lxx] This Precarious Moment p.186 Copyright © 2018 by James L. Garlow and David Barton Regnery Publishing

[lxxi] This Precarious Moment p.187 Copyright © 2018 by James L. Garlow and David Barton Regnery Publishing

[lxxii] This Precarious Moment p.189 Copyright © 2018 by James L.

Garlow and David Barton Regnery Publishing

[lxxiii] This Precarious Moment p.190 Copyright © 2018 by James L. Garlow and David Barton Regnery Publishing

[lxxiv] This Precarious Moment p.190 Copyright © 2018 by James L. Garlow and David Barton Regnery Publishing

[lxxv] This Precarious Moment p.191 Copyright © 2018 by James L. Garlow and David Barton Regnery Publishing

[lxxvi] This Precarious Moment p.207 Copyright © 2018 by James L. Garlow and David Barton Regnery Publishing

[lxxvii] This Precarious Moment p.204 Copyright © 2018 by James L. Garlow and David Barton Regnery Publishing

[lxxviii] https://theimaginativeconservative.org/2016/04/the-historical-and-christian-roots-of-marriage.html by David J. Theroux

[lxxix] The Theft Of America's Soul p.xiii © 2019 by Phil Robertson Harper Collins Christian Publishing, Inc.

[lxxx] Journals of Congress p.574 on September 12, 1782

[lxxxi] https://www.allabouthistory.org/school-prayer.htm

[lxxxii] Faith In America p.130-131 Copyright © by Steve Green Looking Glass Books Inc.

[lxxxiii] Faith In America p.134-136 Copyright © by Steve Green Looking Glass Books Inc.

[lxxxiv] https://answersingenesis.org/public-school/evolution-in-us-education-and-demise-of-its-public-school-system/ by Lael Weinberger on January 31, 2005

[lxxxv] https://themoraloutcry.com/

[lxxxvi] God's New Israel by Conrad Cherry p.378 © 1998 The University of North Carolina Press

[lxxxvii] https://ifapray.org/blog/jury-rules-against-undercover-journalist-in-federal-planned-parenthood-case/

[lxxxviii] https://www.insider.com/baltimore-ravens-statement-jacob-blake-mitch-mcconnel-2020-8

[lxxxix] https://www.christianity.com/church/church-history/timeline/1801-1900/era-of-the-evangelist-11630566.html

[xc] https://answersingenesis.org/christianity/harvard-yale-princeton-oxford-once-christian/ by Bodie Hodge on

June 27, 2007

[xci] https://www.aprilshenandoah.com/history-of-education-pt-3

[xcii] https://biblemesh.com/blog/the-christian-origins-of-hospitals/

[xciii] https://answersingenesis.org/blogs/ken-ham/2017/04/27/study-state-evangelism-america-and-its-not-good/ by Ken Ham on April 27, 2017

[xciv] https://messagemissions.com/mission-statistics/

[xcv] https://www.desiringgod.org/articles/will-america-be-judged by John Piper on February 25, 2014

[xcvi] https://wallbuilders.com/john-adams-really-enemy-christians-addressing-modern-academic-shallownes/ by David Barton

[xcvii] God's New Israel by Conrad Cherry p.61 © 1998 The University of North Carolina Press

[xcviii] God's New Israel by Conrad Cherry p.19 © 1998 The University of North Carolina Press

[xcix] 100 Bible Verses That Made America p.53-54 © 2020 by Robert J. Morgan W Publishing Group

[c] 100 Bible Verses That Made America p.40-42 © 2020 by Robert J. Morgan W Publishing Group

[ci] 100 Bible Verses That Made America p.86-88 © 2020 by Robert J. Morgan W Publishing Group

[cii] 100 Bible Verses That Made America p.72-73 © 2020 by Robert J. Morgan W Publishing Group

[ciii] https://www.youtube.com/watch?v=a5JNh5nBJCI&t=11s Presentation by David Barton

[civ] https://www.youtube.com/watch?v=a5JNh5nBJCI&t=11s Presentation by David Barton

[cv] This Precarious Moment p.213-215 Copyright © 2018 by James L. Garlow and David Barton Regnery Publishing

[cvi] Multiply p.237-238 © 2012 Francis Chan, Mark Beuving David C Cook

[cvii] https://www.truthortradition.com/articles/return-to-me-god

[cviii] **Holman Christian Standard Bible (HCSB)** Copyright © 1999, 2000, 2002, 2003, 2009 by Holman Bible Publishers, Nashville Tennessee.

[cix] America Turn To Christ p.91-92 by Walter Maier © 1944 Concordia Publishing House

[cx] New Living Translation (NLT) *Holy Bible*, New Living Translation, copyright © 1996, 2004, 2015 by Tyndale House Foundation.

[cxi] Life-Changing Prayer Session 5 © 2018 by Jim Cymbala Zondervan

[cxii] God's New Israel by Conrad Cherry p.379 © 1998 The University of North Carolina Press

[cxiii] **New King James Version (NKJV)** Copyright © 1982 by Thomas Nelson

[cxiv] **New Century Version (NCV)** The Holy Bible, New Century Version Copyright © 2005 by Thomas Nelson, Inc.

[cxv] New Living Translation (NLT) *Holy Bible*, New Living Translation, copyright © 1996, 2004, 2015 by Tyndale House Foundation

[cxvi] https://www.christianbiblereference.org/faq_adultery.htm

[cxvii] http://crosscountry4jesus.com/index126.html

[cxviii] **Contemporary English Version (CEV)** Copyright © 1995 by American Bible Society

[cxix] The Nelson Study Bible NKJV (word focus) p. 1509 © 1997 by Thomas Nelson, Inc.

[cxx] 100 Bible Verses That Made America p.110 © 2020 by Robert J. Morgan

[cxxi] **Contemporary English Version (CEV)** Copyright © 1995 by American Bible Society

[cxxii] New Living Translation (NLT) *Holy Bible*, New Living Translation, copyright © 1996, 2004, 2015 by Tyndale House Foundation

[cxxiii] New Living Translation (NLT) *Holy Bible*, New Living Translation, copyright © 1996, 2004, 2015 by Tyndale House Foundation

[cxxiv] **Christian Standard Bible (CSB)** The Christian Standard Bible. Copyright © 2017 by Holman Bible Publishers

[cxxv] **Christian Standard Bible (CSB)** The Christian Standard Bible.

Copyright © 2017 by Holman Bible Publishers

[cxxvi] **Christian Standard Bible (CSB)** The Christian Standard Bible. Copyright © 2017 by Holman Bible Publishers

[cxxvii] New Living Translation (NLT) *Holy Bible*, New Living Translation, copyright © 1996, 2004, 2015 by Tyndale House Foundation

[cxxviii] New Living Translation (NLT) *Holy Bible*, New Living Translation, copyright © 1996, 2004, 2015 by Tyndale House Foundation

[cxxix] https://www.stepstolife.org/article/weighed-balance-found-wanting/ Copyright © 2020 Steps to Life

[cxxx] **Amplified Bible (AMP)** Copyright © 2015 by The Lockman Foundation

[cxxxi] **Amplified Bible (AMP)** Copyright © 2015 by The Lockman Foundation

[cxxxii] **Amplified Bible (AMP)** Copyright © 2015 by The Lockman Foundation

[cxxxiii] https://www.puritanboard.com/threads/heidelberg-catechism-question-27-28.40145/

[cxxxiv] https://bible.org/article/judgments-past-present-and-future

[cxxxv] http://www.americathebeautiful.com/lyrics.htm

[cxxxvi] https://www.americanrhetoric.com/speeches/benfranklin.htm

[cxxxvii] Letters To The Church p.136-137 by Francis Chan © 2018 Crazy Love Ministries

[cxxxviii] **New King James Version (NKJV)** Copyright © 1982 by Thomas Nelson

[cxxxix] **New King James Version (NKJV)** Copyright © 1982 by Thomas Nelson

[cxl] http://www.capitalregionndp.org/menu/IchcOverview.asp Family Research Council Prayer Team

Made in USA - North Chelmsford, MA
1165628_9780578727127
09.15.2020 1619